MORE PRAISE FOR *INSURGENT VISIONS*

"*Insurgent Visions* as a living record of Chandra Talpade Mohanty's scholarly activism is a gift to all of us fighting for justice and freedom in times of escalating violence. That Mohanty's wisdom derives from a deep and sustained engagement with community is everywhere evident in this powerful collection. Mohanty teaches us that we can only create different kinds of subjects, relationships, and worlds by insurgency, rising in revolt against imperialism, racial capitalism, and heteropatriarchy. Mohanty both calls for an insurgent feminism and gives us many inspired glimpses of that feminism at work. A vital and visionary contribution."—SARA AHMED

"*Insurgent Visions* is an invitation to imagine new horizons of freedom and dignity, but also an invocation to refusal. Chandra Talpade Mohanty urges us to refuse the normalization of patriarchal violence in settler colonialism, neoliberal dispossession, and racialized genocide. Taking us from the university's spaces to the US-Mexico border and the occupied territories of Palestine and Kashmir, Mohanty documents in an inspiring manner the struggles and hopes of marginalized communities."—R. AÍDA HERNÁNDEZ CASTILLO

Insurgent Visions

A John Hope Franklin Center Book

Insurgent Visions

Chandra Talpade Mohanty

FEMINISM,
JUSTICE,
SOLIDARITY

Duke University Press   *Durham and London*   2025

Printed in the United States of America on acid-free paper ∞
Project Editor: Liz Smith
Designed by Courtney Leigh Richardson
Typeset in Merlo and Real Head Pro
by Westchester Publishing Services

Library of Congress Cataloging-in-Publication Data
Names: Mohanty, Chandra Talpade, [date] author.
Title: Insurgent visions : feminism, justice, solidarity / Chandra
Talpade Mohanty.
Description: Durham : Duke University Press, 2025. | "John Hope
Franklin Center book." | Includes bibliographical references
and index.
Identifiers: LCCN 2024055541 (print)
LCCN 2024055542 (ebook)
ISBN 9781478032229 (paperback)
ISBN 9781478028956 (hardcover)
ISBN 9781478061175 (ebook)
Subjects: LCSH: Feminism—Political aspects. | Feminism—Economic
aspects. | Capitalism—Social aspects. | Decolonization—So-
cial aspects. | Racism. | Authoritarianism. | Feminist theory. |
Marginality, Social. | White supremacy (Social structure)
Classification: LCC HQ1236 .M62 2025 (print) | LCC HQ1236 (ebook) |
DDC 305.42—dc23/eng/20250210
LC record available at https://lccn.loc.gov/2024055541
LC ebook record available at https://lccn.loc.gov/2024055542

Cover art: *Dancing with the Moon*, 2022. Collage with linoleum
block elements on cotton rag paper, 22.375 × 14.875 in. © Favianna
Rodriguez. Courtesy the artist.

For Peoples and communities

building insurgent feminist worlds

Contents

PART II. **Neoliberal Academic Landscapes, Transnational Feminisms, Cross-Border Solidarity**

Acknowledgments

I think, learn, and create in dialogue, collaboration, and community. Over these many decades, I have been privileged to be part of many radical social justice scholar-activist communities. I begin, then, by acknowledging these radical collectives that have sustained, challenged, and inspired me to do the work I do. As a graduate student at the University of Illinois Urbana-Champaign in the early 1980s, I worked with an incredible group of anti-imperialist, antiracist feminist comrades to organize the Common Differences: Third World Women and Feminist Perspectives conference (1983) that set me on my intellectual and political path as a feminist scholar-activist committed to the theory and praxis of decolonization. The conference was also my entry into radical global South and feminists of color communities that have given me the courage to name and analyze the injustices in systems, ideologies, and narratives of power and work to create counterhegemonic narratives and praxis—to dream and work toward a different world.

The two most important collectives I have participated in since the turn of the century include the Future of Minority Studies Research Project at Cornell University (FMS, 2002–12) and the Democratizing Knowledge: Developing Literacies, Building Communities, Seeding Change Project at Syracuse University (DKP, 2009–25). Each of these projects was founded in principles of antiracist, feminist, decolonizing scholarship and practice in the US academy; each gathered and sustained communities of radical scholars; and each led to many research and pedagogical gatherings in universities and colleges across the United States. Each project generated multiple publications that foregrounded minority (defined not numerically but in relation to power), feminist, and antiracist praxis, subjectivities, identities, and communities. I owe an enormous debt to my comrades and colleagues in both FMS and DKP; they have provided an environment of intellectual challenge, political vision, and a community of care that has been fundamental to my work in *Insurgent Visions*. In each of these overlapping communities, there are too many comrades and colleagues to name individually, but some have been and remain key intellectual interlocutors for me: Satya Mohanty, Linda Martín Alcoff, Beverly Guy-Sheftall, Jacqui Alexander, Minnie Bruce Pratt, Leslie Feinberg, Linda Carty, Angela Davis, Gail Lewis, Avtar Brah, Zillah Eisenstein, Aida Hernandez-Castillo, Sandy Grande, and Margo Okazawa-Rey. My debt to each and every one of these amazing intellectuals and activists is profound—they have made me the scholar, teacher, and activist doing the "work that I do every day" (à la Audre Lorde). I have written, taught, struggled, and organized with each of them in different contexts and at different times, and in each instance they have made me a better thinker, organizer, and teacher. A mere thank-you is insufficient; I do believe deeply that we learn through dialogue and relationships across differences of all kinds, and my work in *Insurgent Visions* would not be possible without these comrades.

Early on and for many years I co-taught feminist faculty workshops with Beverly Guy-Sheftall, and since then we have remained fellow travelers and friends. My work and friendship with Jacqui Alexander have led to significant knowledge and growth in terms of an intellectual and political vision for radical transnational feminist praxis. Collaborations with Angela Davis, Aida Hernandez-Castillo, and Margo Okazawa-Rey have strengthened and deepened this vision. Linda Carty, my comrade and sister feminist freedom warrior (http://feministfreedomwarriors.org) has been and continues to be a coconspirator and accomplice in social justice work and in challenging and transforming academic spaces. Our work together at Syracuse University has taught me how to be a "thorn in the side" of the university or, as Linda would say, an "eyelash in the eyeball" of the academy. Zillah Eisenstein, my friend and comrade in Ithaca for many decades, continues to be an intellectual and political sounding board and fashionista par excellence! Exchanging earrings with her has brought beauty and lightness in times of darkness and crisis.

In 2011, I was fortunate to be a part of the Indigenous and Women of Color Solidarity Delegation to Occupied Palestine. This was a transformative experience in terms of my politics, my intellectual project, and my commitment to freedom and justice as a scholar-activist. My sister-comrades on this journey have remained treasured friends and sisters in feminist and Palestine justice work over many decades. Deep gratitude to Barbara Ransby, Rabab Abdulhadi, Angela Davis, Beverly Guy-Sheftall, Premilla Nadasen, Gina Dent, and Anna Romina Guevara.

From my former student and comrade/friend Donna Nevel, I have learned an incredible amount about political education, community organizing, and the importance of always speaking out in the face of injustice, even if it means standing against "our own people." I remain indebted to her thoughtful and insightful work on Palestine justice and anti-Semitism from a collective liberation perspective. I have been privileged to have taught students who grew into friends and comrades: Kimi Takasue, Carol Moeller, Michelle Tellez, Carolina Arrango, Keish Kim, Sarah Miraglia, and Taveeshi Singh. My FMS sister-comrades Elora Chowdhury, Sylvanna Falcon, Azza Basarudin, Khanum Sheikh, Sharmila Lodhia, Rachel Afi Quinn, H. L. T. Quan, and Crystal Griffith have traveled this feminist journey alongside me in friendship, love, and brilliant scholarship. I am grateful to each of them for their presence in my life and the lessons they continue to teach me.

My colleagues and comrades in Women's and Gender Studies at Syracuse University continue to be valued interlocutors—especially around feminist pedagogy and activism. For being on this journey with me, I thank my dear friend and fearless leader Himika Bhattacharya, my sister-comrade and coeditor Dana Olwan, and kick-ass colleagues Gwen Pough, PJ DiPietro, Eunjung Kim, Danika Medak-Saltzman, Vivian May, and Robin Riley. Each has taught me to analyze, understand, negotiate with, and stand against the increasingly privatized and carceral space of higher education in the United States.

Thanks are inadequate in relation to my immediate family. My partner and spouse, Satya, continues to teach, provoke, and inspire me to new heights in my scholarship and our everyday life. Our decades-long relationship has been key to my growth as a person and an intellectual—he remains my most careful and challenging interlocutor and critic through all our journeys together as friends, parents, teachers, and participants in multiple political and social justice communities. My daughter, Uma, inspires me with her deeply incisive questions about life, love, identity, and spirituality. Her emotional intelligence, her courage and kindness, her passionate politics, and her ability to face challenges head-on are amazing. I am so grateful for our friendship and the young woman she has grown into. My writing, my pedagogy, and my politics carry the imprint of these two remarkable people.

This manuscript would not have been completed without the smart, precise, and careful feedback and labor of Taveeshi Singh—graduate assistant par excellence! Finishing the book while Taveeshi finished her dissertation at the same time has been truly gratifying. I remain grateful for Taveeshi's work and for our growing friendship. Thanks also to Shiila Seok Wun Au Yong, an invaluable reader of the page proofs and a wonderful colleague in the feministfreedomwarriors.org video archive.

Finally, I owe deep gratitude to Ken Wissoker, my editor (and friend) at Duke University Press. His unwavering belief in my work, precise editorial feedback, and boundless patience are unparalleled. Many thanks, Ken—you have been a fabulous editorial birth doula! Needless to say, any inaccuracies or gaps in these pages are mine alone.

Introduction: Insurgent Feminisms
GENEALOGIES, STRUGGLES, FUTURES

Having lived as a feminist scholar-activist, confronting multiple systemic inequities in different geopolitical contexts, and being involved in many communities dreaming about and organizing for freedom, I see this book as an evolving record, a document of my work on many fronts over the past two decades. I have focused in particular on the challenge of insurgent praxis and anticapitalist feminist futures. Insurgencies are about resistance, about militant challenges to the status quo, about the radical transformation of everyday life; what I call "insurgent feminism" incorporates all these practices. Insurgent feminism seeks to explicitly contest and replace the imperialist, heteronormative, and racialized practice of violence grounded in gender relations. It seeks to unsettle existing power structures in order to imagine and enact new relationships, forging new subjectivities, epistemologies, and communities. It is precisely this kind of insurgent feminist praxis from which I draw inspiration and which I hope to support in my scholarly work.

Growing up in urban India, teaching high school in Lagos, Nigeria, and living for over four decades in the United States as an immigrant woman of color from the global South have all shaped my intellectual vision. While decolonization and antiracist, anti-imperialist feminist thought and the politics of common differences have always been key to my feminist praxis, what has preoccupied me in recent years are the implications of militarism, neoliberalism, settler colonialism, racial and religious supremacies, and the carceral state.[1] I believe some of the economic and political challenges for new generations of radical scholar-activists are continuous with late twentieth-century struggles against colonization, heteropatriarchy, and racial capitalism. But they also demand new ways of understanding the hegemony of the global right, the rise of authoritarian cultures, white supremacy and religious fundamentalisms, and the consolidation of carceral regimes both within and outside the borders of the nation-state.

I still remember the excitement of encountering the Combahee River Collective (CRC) statement as a graduate student in the late 1970s.[2] At that time, I was a young socialist-feminist reading everything I could lay my hands on, but it wasn't until 1979, when I read the CRC statement, that I understood that feminist praxis could speak to me—a (at that time) third world, postcolonial socialist-feminist teaching herself the landscape of race and capitalism in the United States. The CRC traces its formation to the mid-1970s on the East Coast. A few years earlier, in 1970, the Third World Women's Alliance (TWWA) emerged on the West Coast. The TWWA grew out of the Student Nonviolent Coordinating Committee (SNCC) in the late 1960s. Frances Beal started the Black Women's Liberation Committee within SNCC, which then split from SNCC and became the Black Women's Alliance (BWA). Between 1969 and 1970, the BWA added questions of capitalism and imperialism to its analysis of racism; it became the TWWA in 1970, out of a debate around whether to admit members from the Puerto Rican Independence Movement and the Puerto Rican Socialist Party. Using this US-grounded, third worldist framework, the TWWA eventually transformed into the Alliance Against Women's Oppression and subsequently into the Women of Color Resource Center in Oakland, California.[3]

I wanted to trace this parallel genealogy of the feminist politics of the TWWA and the CRC because how feminist theory and politics are articulated in the present moment depends on how we understand and learn from the genealogies of feminist praxis. So, instead of describing US feminist history in the conventional terms of first, second, third, and fourth waves, I believe we need to understand feminism in the present as inspired more fundamentally by this activist genealogy. My work is based on a fundamental theoretical claim, one that asserts the importance of the knowledge that emerges from the experiences of the marginalized groups that are engaged actively in struggles for justice. Key to our current conceptions of insurgent feminist practice, I propose, is our understanding of why and how critical knowledge about oppression, exploitation, and justice *emerged from* the lived experience and reflections of the most marginalized communities. This claim about the importance of the experiences of socially marginalized groups is not essentialist, and it is not based on a narrow identity politics. It should be seen, instead, as a radical materialist analysis of power and injustice that is key to imagining feminist insurgencies and futures. Let me explain.

I draw here on the materialist theorization of the nature of (social and cultural) identity and of the "epistemic privilege" of oppressed groups by postpositivist realist thinkers like Satya Mohanty, Linda Alcoff, Paula Moya, and Michael Hames-Garcia (among others).[4] In this "realist" formulation, identity is not essentialist, understood as some unchanging "essence" that is the property of particular groups of people (like people of color). Rather, it is based on the claim that theories about social and cultural identities refer not to inner essences of social groups but instead to the social world; they provide explanations of social reality from the location of oppressed groups engaged in struggles for freedom, and these explanations need to be evaluated just as other social explanations are. Knowledge derived from lived experience is not automatic; it grows out of sustained reflection, involving the kind of analysis that accompanies grassroots-level political organizing. Postpositivist realist thinkers draw attention to this materialist dimension of the growth of political consciousness, referring to the ongoing work that political organizing involves on every level.

Thus, the salience of identity in this context is theoretical: "People of color" is an analytical or explanatory category rather than a descriptive one. The category "people of color" is insignificant outside a social system whose defining features include racially organized exploitation and domination. This specific understanding of identity is then the basis for arguments regarding the epistemic privilege of the oppressed. Understood in this way, feminist praxis anchored in the everyday experiences and knowledges produced by the most marginalized (Black, queer, migrant, poor) women, as it is foregrounded by the CRC and the TWWA (and, in the case of India, by Dalit feminists), offers an analysis of power and a vision of justice based in a political engagement with the world that cannot be replicated from the point of view of dominant communities. Rather than an essentialist claim about automatically generated knowledge, this theorization of the epistemic privilege of the oppressed suggests that it is the reflection on social and economic inequities, often inherent in the collective praxis of marginalized communities, that provides the most comprehensive and compelling framework for the analysis of power and injustice. I argue this in more detail in my analysis of the emergence and success of Black Lives Matter (BLM) and the Movement for Black Lives (MBL), as well as in my discussion of Dalit feminist praxis, suggesting that it is the analysis of state violence from the epistemological point of view of the most marginalized Black and Dalit communities that allows for a vision of justice and a capacious and inclusive grassroots politics. And it is this particular understanding of the knowledges and strategies generated through the epistemic privilege and activism of the most marginalized communities that undergirds my scholarship and connects the analytic sites and examples I explore below: Palestinian feminist struggles, abolitionist feminism in the United States, and Dalit feminist thought. In each of these cases it is the experience of settler colonialism, occupation, and genocide (Palestine/Gaza); the prison-industrial complex, carceral state practice, and criminalization and disposability of Black, brown, migrant, bodies (abolition feminism in the United States); and Brahmanical supremacy and the politics of sexual violence based on caste and Islamophobia (Hindutva and Dalit feminism in India) that forms the theoretical basis for insurgent feminist, anticapitalist frameworks and organizing. I argue that it is in fact the theorization of epistemic privilege anchored in the everyday lives and collective organizing of Palestinians; Black, migrant, and poor women of color; and Dalit feminists that connects these geopolitical contexts and suggests new freedom horizons.

Over the years I have been privileged to work in friendship and solidarity with a number of feminists of color from the United States, Europe, and the global South. My work owes an immense debt to the pioneering work of Black and anticapitalist, anti-imperialist feminists globally; it is also a challenge and provocation for us to imagine and work toward insurgent feminist solidarities at a time when neoliberal, militarized, racist, and protofascist regimes are on the rise. I believe imagining radical/insurgent futures means to always hold two (often contradictory) ideas/perspectives in our organizing and scholarly work. Let me point to just two instances: (1) We must focus on the sociopolitical and socioeconomic challenges of the present *and* on the insurgent feminist practices and movements evident around the globe, and (2) we must understand the epistemologies of violence created by colonial legacies, racial capitalism, heteronormative patriarchies, and supremacist nation-states *and* focus simultaneously on epistemologies of dreaming—of imagining new horizons for relationships, communities, and ecologies.

In early 2023 I was interviewed by two Canadian middle schoolers (Clara and Kaya) about my views on antiracist feminist praxis and gender justice. I thought their questions were smart, instructive, and a good place to begin mapping what it means to imagine insurgent feminist futures for generations of girls, women, and gender nonconforming communities. After all, these are the young folks who will inherit both our achievements and our shortcomings![5] As Sara Ahmed teaches us, "feminism is a building project," and knowledge-building projects require careful research, strategic analysis of systemic power relations, and collaborative envisioning of structures of everyday life that sustain and grow our visions of gender justice.[6] Feminism has been a lifelong building project for me, and while inevitably there have been mistakes and misstarts along the way, it is this collaborative praxis of building feminist futures that inspires me. I believe my answers to Clara and Kaya's questions are a good place to begin mapping the urgencies of feminism as a building project at this historical moment.

Kaya and Clara asked me questions they were curious about, ranging from my understanding of "white feminism and its dangers" to the application of critical race theory and intersectional feminism in the classroom. They asked what I consider the most pressing and/or controversial issues in gender studies at the present moment. Given the public culture of the normalization of white supremacy and the rollback of policies affirming women's reproductive rights, affirmative action, and the intellectual and social achievements of feminist, antiracist, and queer movements in the United States, Clara and Kaya's queries focused on the current and future challenges their generation confronts. How were they/we to imagine a feminist future given the postpandemic, cataclysmic historical moment they/we find ourselves in?

Clara and Kaya, both students of color, began by asking me to define what "white feminism" meant to me and to describe a "real-world" example of its dangers that I have experienced as a feminist of color and a gender studies scholar. My response focused on the following characteristics of "white feminism": the centering/universalizing of white women's experiences/history; the absence of a challenge to white supremacy and imperialism globally; normalizing whiteness in gender studies/analysis/movements for justice; and legitimating the ideology of white women's rescue narrative and the corresponding normalization of women of color/women in the global South as victims in need of saving. Note that these are ideas that preoccupy me in various ways throughout this text. The dangers of these assumptions are many, of course. One of the most visible examples and one I lived through was the weaponizing of white, liberal feminism in the war on terror after September 11, 2001, wherein liberal feminism provided the justification for US imperial ventures in Iraq and Afghanistan (waging war in the name of women's rights), while demonstrating that white women were/are "equal" to men (as torturers, soldiers, and intelligence agents in the US war machine). Sara Farris's work on femonationalism illustrates this particular danger of collapsing white women's liberal feminism into nationalism in an age of growing masculinist, fundamentalist, and authoritarian regimes globally.[7] Another example of white feminism gone awry is the way Muslim women were targeted in a US "homeland security" program called Countering Violent Extremism and trained in the name of women's rights and democracy to inform on their sons, husbands, and brothers. Recognizing Muslim women's agency as "feminist and patriotic" seemed to lead to turning them into allies in the US "war against terror." Both of the above examples signal the dangers of the weaponizing of white, neoliberal feminist ideologies in the service of imperial, heteropatriarchal regimes.

I pointed out that white, Western, middle-class definitions of violence against women erase the multiple forms of violence in the lives of women of color and immigrant women in the West and of women in the global South. The definition of violence against women determines how we understand violence as a feminist issue and how we organize around it. White liberal feminism is embedded in most aid/development narratives, and it leads to projects and programs that are not useful to women in the global South in terms of transforming their/our multiple inequities (e.g., providing electric stoves in India in the context of toxic heteropatriarchal relations and offering beauty/cosmetic education to women in Afghanistan fighting for fundamental rights under the Taliban).

Clara and Kaya's questions about critical race theory and intersectional feminism in the classroom led me to think about and define intersectionality as an approach or methodology. The opposite of intersectionality is, of course, analytical singularity (i.e., an assumption of gender or race as a singular and homogeneous construct). The title of the 1982 book edited by Akasha Gloria Hull, Patricia Bell Scott, and Barbara Smith summarizes this approach to intersectionality: *All the Women Are White, All the Men Are Black, but Some of Us Are Brave.* An intersectional methodology demands that we focus on the multiplicity of experiences/cultures/histories that contribute to our understanding of identity, power, and gender justice. So white women are not just generically white or women: they come from particular ethnic/cultural/class backgrounds; grow up in particular neighborhoods; and inherit ideas, practices, and behaviors from previous generations and geopolitical contexts. It's easier to see that Black and brown women's lives are determined by multiple forms of oppression, but so are white women's lives (it is harder to see this since white women's experiences are universalized and seen as nonracialized). White is a color—and also a race, given the way our society works and the histories of colonialism and racialization we inherit. I told Kaya and Clara that as an educator I always complicate and challenge the power of a single narrative. There are too many narratives and material realities that have been erased for us to continue to believe in a singular hegemonic narrative. So I always want students to ask: What has been erased? What can't we see in the textbooks? And how does making multiple histories visible change the way we understand the subject we are focusing on? This in a nutshell is what it means to understand a feminist intersectional approach to scholarship and pedagogy.

The final question my young interlocutors were interested in was how I would define some of the most pressing or controversial issues we need to be looking at when it comes to gender studies today. This is a good place to map the issues that concern me and are foregrounded in this text. Using a transnational, decolonial, antiracist, anti-imperialist, feminist lens, the key issues that will determine our collective futures include (1) the proliferation of carceral regimes globally that criminalize and incarcerate brown, Black, and poor communities; (2) geopolitical climate destruction and its impact on the world's dispossessed; (3) the militarization of national borders and corresponding imperial projects; (4) the economic and political consequences of the massive displacement of peoples (war, economic, climate refugees); (5) the proliferation of corporatist, racist, misogynist cultures across national borders; (6) the decimation of labor movements; (7) the rise of protofascist, religious fundamentalist governments around the world (rise of the global right); and (8) the policing and surveillance of gendered bodies and sexualities in multiple geographic spaces. In each of these contexts I ask what difference gender makes: How are women, queer, and gender nonconforming communities impacted in each context? What does this analysis make visible in terms of gendered lives, and what does it suggest in terms of gender justice and public policy?

Based on my responses to Clara and Kaya's last question, I analyze three sites of decolonizing, anticapitalist, abolitionist feminist engagement below. In each context it is visionary feminist thinking about material realities and coalitional organizing based in a theorization of epistemic privilege, as discussed above, that shows the way forward. While each context reveals profound layers of gendered violence, histories of insurgent feminist organizing have always suggested what we might call new "freedom horizons." These are the stories of insurgent feminist thought that we need to retrieve in order to inspire future generations of social justice workers.

Insurgent Feminist Futures: On the Urgencies of Freedom and Violence in the Twenty-First Century

I think you have to work with people in such a way that you can facilitate the emergence of a shared common project. You have to address the contradictory "common sense" that we all live with, that Gramsci (1971) speaks of. Unless you can do that, then you are not going to make much headway with constructing new political agendas. To do that, you have to begin with where people are at, but not stay there, and not get sucked into taking up a narrow political position. But rather to jointly develop new discourses and practices for the creation of new political horizons, a new common sense. —AVTAR BRAH, *Decolonial Imaginings*

Avtar Brah's words suggest we must deal with the contradictory "common sense" narratives of hegemony (what we often refer to as "misinformation") in order to imagine and enact new political horizons and agendas going forward. This is precisely the conundrum we face in understanding the challenges of freedom and violence in 2025. How do we define and honor the histories and genealogies, the strategies and tactics, of our feminist foremothers and imagine new and realistic political horizons in the political and economic global landscape of the present? As suggested earlier, I draw inspiration from the CRC formulation of a feminist praxis, anchored in the lived experiences and epistemological viewpoints (critical knowledges) of queer, marginalized Black and brown women in different and connected geopolitical and historical contexts, to suggest that it is this materialist, antiracist, anti-imperialist politics that is necessary for insurgent feminist praxis at the present time.

Given my location and my history of commitments as a feminist of color living in North America, a diasporic Indian, and a member of the 2011 Indigenous and Women of Color feminist delegation to Palestine, I analyze three urgent sites of feminist engagement using a materialist, antiracist, and anticaste comparative framework to explore the meaning of an ethical, mutually accountable solidarity politics. Palestine justice and solidarity work in the United States remains a key site of antiracist, anti-imperialist feminist engagement for me—as it does for Black-Palestine solidarity movements and Indigenous-Palestine solidarity movements especially after Ferguson and Standing Rock. I believe, like many of my feminist comrades, that feminist politics must address the question of justice for Palestine as key to our liberatory agendas.

In the United States, MBL focuses on the issue of multiple levels of US state violence in the targeting of Black queer, trans, and disabled bodies, explicitly widening the lens of state violence to include those who have been marginalized in Black liberation movements. Similar to the radical politics of the CRC, this analytic framing emerges from the lived experiences and epistemic spaces of Black, queer, trans, and feminist communities. And unlike the civil rights and Black Power movements, BLM and MBL chapters across the country do not operate by identifying charismatic leaders, opting instead for a collective, decentralized, grassroots politics. This absence of a vanguard (Old Left politics) does not mean the absence of a coherent analytical framework—and it is this framing, the analysis of state violence from the epistemological point of view of the most marginalized Black communities, that allows for a capacious and inclusive grassroots politics. This focus on state violence and its multilayered impact on Black communities is at once local, national, and transnational.[8] It involves detecting the exercise of power and relations of rule *from* the positions of Black, poor, queer, trans, impoverished, criminalized folks across a range of gender identities and thus has inspired movements across national borders, especially in Europe and Latin America. Feminist praxis that connects questions of the personal and political, of structures and subjectivities, identity and movements can thus map a countertopography of state violence as it makes and remakes notions of national borders and citizenship, subjectivities, and identities. Analytically and politically, then, BLM/ MBL understood in this way is an important example of the connections between local, global, and national contexts. The interweaving of capitalist economic dominance with masculinist, protofascist, supremacist modes of governance is in full view, and just as we develop a countertopography of forms of state violence addressed by MBL, I want to connect this to US complicity in the question of justice for Palestine and to state violence as it impacts Dalit, Adivasi, and Muslim communities in India.

Given the pace at which cartographies of violence, war, and genocide continually shift, there are no conclusive arguments or strategies we can focus on. We must always work hard at understanding deepening gendered violences and regimes of disposability. I want to focus, then, on three geopolitical urgencies in the contemporary historical moment that are key to my geopolitical location and lifework of scholarship and struggle: (1) occupation, genocide, and Palestinian feminist struggles for justice; (2) the carceral state, abolition, and antiracist decolonizing feminist struggles in the United States; and (3) Hindutva, Islamophobia, and caste resistance in India. These are geopolitical urgencies that are woven through this text, but given their shape-changing nature at the present time, I need to begin here. I argue that a decolonizing abolitionist feminist praxis provides the most capacious analytical and strategic framework to demystify the colonial carceral logics of capitalism and its continued reproduction through a politics of disposability. This feminist framework grounded in the theoretical framework of epistemic privilege of oppressed and marginalized communities in each context exposes the connections between imperial regimes, racial capitalism, and struggles around solidarity in the context of a "divide-and-rule" culture of carcerality in the three contexts explored below.

Palestine Is a Feminist Issue: On Occupation and Genocide

In June 2011, I was part of an Indigenous and feminist of color solidarity delegation to Palestine, and it transformed my understanding of the violence of occupation and the significance of Palestine as key to anti-imperialist, anticapitalist feminist struggle. My experience in Palestine led to an ongoing commitment to always teach and talk about Palestine as an urgent example of settler colonialism and imperial dispossession in the context of feminist studies.[9] It is now over eighteen months since October 7, 2023—the beginning of what the US media calls the "Israel-Hamas War" and what the rest of us understand as another Palestinian Nakba and ongoing genocide in Gaza waged by Israel, funded and sustained by the United States.[10] This is also a unique historical moment in terms of global solidarity movements for justice for Palestine evident in the massive student mobilization on US campuses and universities around the world. Since October 2023, more than sixty-two thousand Palestinians have been killed, and over three times that number injured—the majority being women and children. Gender and sexual violence has always been central to imperial projects of occupation and genocide, with ideologies of racialized heteromasculinities and femininity instrumentalized as weapons of war. The Palestinian Feminist Collective states, "In Palestine, the Zionist settler-colonial project is driven by a demographic anxiety that constructs Palestinian women's bodies, sexualities, and reproductive capacities as security threats. Palestinian mothers are coded as 'problems' and are systematically denied reproductive justice and security. Against this backdrop, the Israeli settler state falsely touts itself as a safe haven for women and LGBTQ communities. Their propaganda depicts us as violent and regressive even as we are being violated routinely, indiscriminately, and with no regard to our bodily autonomy."[11] It is a colonial/imperial/neoliberal feminism that underlies the construction of Israel as the "only democracy in the Middle East" and fans the flames of Islamophobia against Palestinians. This very construction facilitates settler colonialism and occupation in the name of "progress"—the now familiar "pink-washing" of imperial violence in Israel. In terms of the trajectory of this volume, the ongoing genocide in Gaza and the repression and treatment of student and faculty movements for justice in Palestine on US campuses illustrate the nexus of part I of this book ("Capitalist Scripts, Imperial Projects, Decolonizing Feminism") and part II ("Neoliberal Academic Landscapes, Transnational Feminisms, Cross-Border Solidarity").

The censorship of critical race theory and feminist/sexuality/trans studies in numerous states in the United States fueled by the conservative right reflects the current repression of Palestine's history and justice on US campuses.[12] As Rod Ferguson argues, "There are real connections between censorship around Black Studies and the one we are witnessing around Palestine. To begin with, the right-wing's attack on intersectionality, Black queer studies, abolitionist politics, and the like is based on the notion that these concepts and topics have no intellectual merits and they are ways of indoctrinating young people."[13] Thus, any discussion of Palestine is falsely labeled anti-Semitic and the critique of Zionism (as an ideology and a national state-building project) is conflated with anti-Semitism (racism against Jews because of who they are). The very fact that the world is witnessing a genocide and the dehumanization of Palestinians in real time and that a critique of Israel, the United States, and some European countries is "disallowed" or seen as anti-Semitic, while we are also witnessing the largest global mobilization of people calling for a ceasefire and end to war that the world has seen, is itself instructive in terms of the urgencies of violence caused by capitalist, right-wing interests around the globe. The outcome of this urgency will no doubt determine insurgent political struggles for generations to come.

There are "Gaza solidarity" student encampments on US campuses and in other parts of the world (in all seven continents) calling for a permanent ceasefire, economic divestment from Israel, and an end to US and European imperial and military support of the war on Gaza. The United States has sent more than one hundred shipments of weapons to Israel since October 7, 2023, as well as billions of dollars in aid.[14] The repression and criminalization of student movements for justice in Palestine mirror the criminalization and incarceration of dissidents and minoritized communities enacted by India and Israel—in fact, the global movements for justice in Palestine address an economic and social crisis that capitalist greed, racialized gendered supremacies, and masculinist right-wing authoritarian political culture have engendered over many decades around the world.

The Indigenous feminist scholar Sandy Grande states, "Historically the university functioned as the institutional nexus for capitalist and religious missions of the settler state, mirroring its histories of dispossession, enslavement, exclusion, forced assimilation and integration."[15] This long history of the politics of disposability, increasing levels of violence against those considered "outsiders/others," and the university and higher education as an arm of the settler-capitalist state and corporate power is now visible in ways never before seen. Is it then at all surprising that the largest student uprising on US campuses in this century has led to levels of repression and criminalization unheard of in university settings?[16] There have been hundreds of Gaza solidarity encampments and solidarity actions around the world. There have also been hundreds of police raids and thousands of campus arrests.[17] Since May 1, 2024, when police moved onto the Columbia University campus, more than two thousand students across US campuses have been forcibly removed or arrested. Here, then, is a microcosm of the entanglement of colonial/imperial projects, racial capitalist structures (read universities) anchored in carceral logics, and the refashioning of the neoliberal university into an explicit arm of the colonialist/capitalist settler state. These encampments are about freedom—calling for university disclosure of financial holdings; divestment from companies violating international law or treaties recognized by the United States and companies that manufacture weapons; recognition of Israel's war and US complicity in the ongoing genocide of Palestinians; and protection of academic freedom and democratic governance processes on university campuses. Students are engaging in popular education; participating in study groups on topics related to decolonizing, feminist, and antiracist histories of resistance; and creating infrastructures of governance at encampments that are based on mutuality, equality, and care (rather than hierarchy and bureaucracy)—thus modeling decarceral, abolitionist horizons for freedom. Here again, it is not coincidental that it is students who provide the most capacious understanding of corporate and military power in university settings and connect questions of democratic governance, freedom of expression, and imperial wars as they play out on university campuses. And it is students who face the repression of the carceral state. Henry Giroux analyzes the corporatization and militarization of higher education, naming this a "pedagogy of capitalist cloning buttressed by the threat of state terrorism."[18] Similar to the antiwar movements in 1968, South African antiapartheid, divestment protests in the 1980s, the mobilizations around Occupy Wall Street, BLM, and encampments in opposition to the Dakota Access Pipeline (DAPL), in this historical moment when the world is witnessing the active attempt to remove Palestinians from Gaza and the West Bank, it is a multiracial coalition of young people, mobilizing their identities as students leading these solidarity movements—essentially showing the world why justice for Palestine is a generational calling for freedom for all. In fact, these Gaza solidarity encampments and the analysis and praxis they embody encapsulate the themes that animate my scholarship: colonial/imperial projects, anticapitalism, neoliberal academic landscapes, and solidarity across borders. While state managers, mainstream media, and corporate donors/boards of trustees at universities attempt to naturalize narratives that collapse critiques of Israel into discourses of anti-Semitism, and use punitive measures to police and criminalize students and faculty on US campuses, encampment communities of resistance loudly proclaim a counternarrative that calls for financial transparency and divestment from militarization and the weapons industry, and a permanent ceasefire in the war on Gaza. This is a call to action and for accountability for US complicity in genocide and military support in the Israeli war on Palestinians in Gaza and the West Bank.

When the solution for all so-called social ills and resistance struggles is "law and order" embodied in the carceral state apparatus, it becomes obvious that the insurgent feminist politics at this time must be abolitionist—rooted in the CRC and in the radical feminist thought of Black, Indigenous, and feminists of color in the global North and South. I analyze this visionary decolonial, abolitionist feminist thought in the context of the United States below.

On the Carceral State, Abolition, and Decolonizing Feminist Struggle

A prison-centered map shows dynamic connections among 1) criminalization; 2) imprisonment; 3) wealth transfer between poor communities; 4) disenfranchisement; and 5) migration of state and non-state practices, policies, and capitalist ventures that all depend on carcerality as a basic state-building project. —RUTH WILSON GILMORE, "Race and Globalization"

Given the widespread, indeed normalized, use of punishment, incarceration, and surveillance in the guise of "law and order" in the United States as well as globally, abolitionist, decolonizing feminist frameworks anchored in the radical politics of Black, global South, and feminists of color are key to the demystification of carceral ideologies and the dismantling of the carceral state. Ruth Wilson Gilmore's lifelong work on abolitionist feminism exemplifies the connections between racial capitalism, the prison-industrial complex, and "carcerality as a state-building project." Abolitionist feminism is a theory, politics, and practice that refuses to consign any human beings to disposability. Angela Davis, Gina Dent, Erica Meiners, and Beth Ritchie claim that an abolitionist feminist framework conjoins a "relationality and interruption" such that abolition is most compelling when it is feminist and feminism is most capacious when it is abolitionist.[19] In fact, carceral logic seeps into all institutions and is naturalized within the United States, aided and abetted by an increasingly right-wing, conservative political establishment and neoliberal capitalism. Carceral nation-states are also national security states, and their reach extends globally. The connections between Israel, the United States, and India, for instance, are fundamentally about carceral practices shared across national borders.

Alisa Bierria, Jakeya Caruthers, Brooke Lober, Amanda Priebe, and Andrea J. Ritchie list "the ways the ideological and structural regimes of carcerality are intimately locked with the logics of debt, reputation and property; the epistemic violence of criminological bioempiricism and 'science'; carceral domesticity and policed sexuality; the exclusive white supremacist rights of privacy and surveillance; regimes of respectability and embodied order; and colonial-capitalist notions of democracy, citizenship, borders, and security."[20] Carceral logics thus reach into all our institutions, our relationships, and even our imaginations, and it is decolonizing, abolitionist feminist praxis that exposes these logics and suggests notions of freedom and liberation that allow us to imagine an epistemology of dreaming otherwise. Given the immense, disproportionate ratio of incarceration of Indigenous and poor people of color in US prisons and the use of incarceration as a strategy of containment and social death for communities deemed disposable, terrorist, or criminal by nation-states around the world, it is the vision and praxis of a transnational abolitionist feminism that suggests the way forward. The United States has 4 percent of the world's population and 22 percent of the world's prisoners.[21] The 2023 US Bureau of Justice Statistical Report on prisoners in the United States at the end of 2022 states that an estimated 32 percent of sentenced state and federal prisoners were Black (31 percent were white, 23 percent were Hispanic, 2 percent were American Indian or Alaska Native, and 11 percent were multiracial or some other race). The imprisonment rate for Black people was thirteen times that for other races.[22] In addition, the US government spends $80.7 billion on public prisons and jails and $3.9 billion on private prisons and jails. These statistics have remained stable for many years. The epistemic standpoint, analysis, and leadership of Black feminists and feminists of color in the analysis and organizing of movements against the carceral state is thus very important. As Mariame Kaba and Andrea Ritchie claim, it is Black, queer, trans, migrant, and disabled communities who experience the highest forms of violence and thus have been at the forefront of defund demands.[23] In the United States, mass movements like BLM and MBL, Dream Defenders/immigrant rights coalitions, Indigenous rights movements around missing and murdered Indigenous women,[24] against the DAPL (#NoDAPL), and global land rights movements all address carceral practices, materialist capitalist dispossession, and gendered violence as key analytic frames in their demands for liberation. And I would argue all these movements are anchored in an understanding of power and knowledge that grows out of the experiences and reflections of these particular marginalized and criminalized communities and is thus key to freedom and struggles for social and economic justice.

Kaba and Ritchie state, "Given the role of the U.S. military as global police, defund demands are deeply connected to global struggles against settler colonialism, militarism, and imperialism, and for migrant justice."[25] After all, policing and surveillance enforce racially gendered economies, modes of existence, sexualities, and relations of power through technologies of surveillance, containment, and control. An abolitionist feminist praxis reveals the intimate power relations between an extractive capitalist landscape that reproduces itself through a politics of disposability of those considered "outsiders," and a sensibility that the distribution of resources ought to be organized through punitivity. This is also a decolonizing framework that exceeds national borders given the history of empire, global capitalism, and transnational governance structures. An abolitionist feminism challenges Euro-American hegemonies and foregrounds subaltern epistemologies anchored in the histories, everyday experiences, and struggles for justice of marginalized communities of women and differently gendered people. Françoise Vergès analyzes the question of cleaning—the ways that capitalism produces material and toxic waste. Her brilliant exploration of decolonizing feminism suggests that "the struggle against the racialization of cleaning and caring while imagining a decolonial politics of cleaning, caring and repairing, shows the way to construct a post-racist, post-capitalist, and post-imperialist, thus post hetero-patriarchal, world."[26] Anticaste feminist praxis in India also foregrounds struggles against the racialization of "cleaning and caring" in relation to a politics of body and purity in movements for caste and gender justice.[27] Some of the most radical feminist collectives globally are anchored in a politics of care and repair. The MAMAS Collective in Chicago is a perfect example of a decolonizing, abolitionist feminist practice based on a politics of care and repair. This collective defines its project as "a Chicago-based feminist of color reproductive justice collective, unapologetically confronting and dismantling systems of state violence—including prisons, war, colonization, imperialism, and migrant injustices. We build power among mother-survivors of state violence, developing mutual care and aid while nurturing resistance and working, in coalition, towards a world rooted in radical justice and love."[28] There are similar collectives around the world in autonomous communities and in many countries focused on collectivity, mutuality, reciprocity, and care, showing us the way to new political and relational horizons.

Similar questions of state violence, racialized/caste politics of disposability and bodily purity, and exploitation of labor animate the analysis and visions of freedom in the work of Dalit feminists in South Asia. I turn to this analysis below. Here too it is a decolonizing abolitionist feminist analysis of caste/class/religious supremacy that suggests a way forward.

Hindutva, Islamophobia, and Dalit Feminist Challenges

As a Savarna feminist who grew up in India but has spent most of my adult life involved in Black and women of color feminist politics in the United States, I take Dalit feminist challenges very seriously. In fact, it is my work within US feminist of color communities that helps me understand and be accountable to the challenges posed by Dalit feminism. On January 22, 2024, India celebrated the consecration of the Ram Mandir in Ayodhya—a grand temple constructed on the very grounds of the sixteenth-century Babri Masjid destroyed in 1992 in the midst of the massacre of more than two thousand Muslims by Hindus instigated by Hindutva leadership, including Narendra Modi (then chief minister of Gujarat, now prime minister of India). The destruction of the mosque and subsequent rebellions ("riots" in government-speak) marked a watershed moment in Indian history (and my relationship to it). This historical event frames a key theoretical and political question for feminists—the rise of masculinist authoritarianism, religious/racial supremacy, and the global right in India and the United States (my two home spaces).

A number of Dalit feminist scholar activists like Shailaja Paik have analyzed the parallel history and connectivities between African American and Dalit movements in the United States and India.[29] Dalit feminists focus on the lived experiences and epistemic location of Dalit women to analyze the unacknowledged racial/caste, economic, cultural, and religious hierarchies within progressive, left, and feminist praxis. Here, too, it is the analysis of the history and materiality of state violence (specifically the policing of bodies, the regulation of sexuality, and the exploitation of labor) as it targets Dalit women that is key to developing an anticaste, feminist framework. Thus, for instance, the Indian socialist feminist movement focused on class and patriarchy while ignoring the issue of Brahmanism, merging issues of class and caste in ways that erased Dalit women's experiences and history of organizing in the 1970s and 1980s. Sharmila Rege (an anticaste feminist scholar) referred to the exclusion of Dalit women's lives as the result of the "savarnization of womanhood and the masculinization of Dalithood."[30] (Shades of *All the Women Are White, All the Blacks Are Men, But Some of Us Are Brave*, 1982.) The parallels between Dalit feminist and Black feminist critique are not coincidental—each movement is situated in the context of racial or caste supremacy: white supremacy and Brahmanical supremacy. And both call for an anticapitalist, antiheterosexist, and embodied feminist praxis without which solidarity across differentially situated feminist communities in national and global contexts remains a distant horizon. Since the 1990s, Dalit feminist engagement with caste and sexuality explicates the history of exploited and dehumanized Dalit women's experiences of sexual violence as central to rethinking the project of "violence against women" as it has been understood by mainstream Indian feminisms over many decades. Issues of economic dispossession, labor exploitation, caste-class privilege, sexuality, and the resultant embodied experience and critical knowledges of Dalit women pose serious challenges to the project of alliance and solidarity within Indian feminist struggles.

The last decades have witnessed the rise of the global right around the world and the consolidation of power by Hindutva forces in India. Gender hierarchies and toxic masculinity are at the heart of these political developments, whereby ideologies and practices of militarized masculinity, sexualized violence, and protectionist discourses of the nation facilitate the rise of authoritarian right wing governance structures consolidated around "strong men" leaders (Narendra Modi, Donald Trump, Recep Tayyip Erdoğan, Vladimir Putin, etc.). There are key similarities in the extremist, right-wing ideologies of Hindutva, Zionism, and Christian/white supremacy—Islamophobia, militarized masculinity, and the creation of all so-called minorities (Dalits, Christians, Muslims, immigrants, queer, etc.) as "outsiders" to be excised from the nation.

The inauguration of the Ram Mandir legitimizes a renewed spate of violence against Muslims and Dalits, just as the war on Gaza normalizes genocide against Palestinians, and Trump and company symbolize the rise and consolidation of white supremacists in government and corporate structures in the United States. Just as in the United States, at this writing there are eighty-six bills prohibiting colleges from having "diversity, equity, and inclusion" (DEI) offices and staff, and 215 campuses in thirty-two states have called for or passed anti-DEI legislation and thus the erasure of critical race, queer, and gender studies and rewriting history of struggles for racial and gender justice, in India the National Council of Educational Research Training, which advises the central and state governments on educational school policies, removed key aspects of Muslim history and Dalit history, as well as any account of the 2002 Gujarat riots (Hindus targeting Muslims) from high school history textbooks.[31] While there is less information on contemporary Zionist rewriting of history, the very fact of the founding of Israel in 1948 on the historical land of Palestine and claiming it as the sacred right of settlement for Jews fleeing prosecution in Europe is indicative of one of the key ideological and material tactics of supremacist states—the rewriting and erasure of Indigenous communities, histories, and memories. This is of course a key strategy of settler states globally.

The history of the building of the Ram Mandir in Ayodhya on the grounds of the demolished Babri Masjid is also a textbook case of the masculization of contemporary Indian politics and the consolidation of Brahmanical supremacy. Dalit feminist scholars have long challenged the mainstream Indian feminist movement around questions of erasure and Brahmanical supremacy and the collapsing of caste and class in feminist analysis of violence against women. Sunaina Arya and Aakash Singh Rathore, drawing on Dr. B. R. Ambedkar, describe Brahmanical patriarchy as a "specfic modality" of patriarchy based on the structure of caste, a patriarchy that is state-sanctioned especially in the context of Hindutva governance. Within this structure, they suggest that "lower caste women are most prone to violence as they face oppression at three levels: 1) caste, as subject to caste oppression at the hands of 'upper' castes, 2) class, as laborers subject to class-based oppression, also mainly at the hands of 'higher' castes who form the bulk of landowners, and 3) gender, as women who experience patriarchal oppression at the hands of all men, including men of their own caste."[32] It is this very caste-specific intersectional sexual violence against Dalit women that mainstream Indian feminists have not attended to in their theorizations of violence against women as an ongoing and profound feminist challenge in India. It is the conjuncture of endogamy, labor exploitation, caste violence, and Brahmanical partiarchy that Dalit feminists focus on. The body politics underlying caste—the politics of purity, propriety, and sexuality—must then be key to the analysis of sexual and state violence in any South Asian context, just as questions of sexualized race and racialized class/gender must be central to any analysis of the laboring bodies of Black and brown women in the global North. Arya and Rathore claim that in fact Dalit feminist thought is subject both to masculinist scholarship, given the patriarchal structure of the Indian academy, and to what they call a "Brahmanical feminism," which is a caste-based feminist tradition of scholarship. These challenges are fundamental and urgent ones for feminist politics in India as caste hierarchies and Islamophobia form the very backbone of Hindutva ideology.

The demolition of the Masjid was carried out by Kar Sevaks (all Hindu men) under the leadership of Hindu men of all the political parties involved, and it was accompanied by a well-documented reign of physical and sexual terror inflicted on Muslim women.[33] The collapse of the idea of India as one of the largest democracies in the world, and of the Indian nation-state as no longer secular-democratic but a Hindu Rashtra (nation) symbolized by the Ram Mandir and representations of Modi as the rightful heir to Hindu gods, signals the triumph of authoritarian, masculinist rule with urgent repercussions for feminist organizing. The global shift to the right, with its corresponding authoritarian, masculinist ideologies and racist politics of extermination and exclusion of "outsiders" from the nation-state, remains one of the key urgent challenges for transnational, decolonial, feminist praxis. Dalit feminist and anticaste analysis and organizing are important instances of interfaith, multiracial, intergenerational solidarity across borders evident in grassroots organizations like Equality Labs, Severa, Coalition of Seattle Indian-Americans (CSIA), and India Civil Watch International.[34]

Confronting Power: Pedagogies of Insurgent Feminism

Our strategy should be not only to confront empire, but to lay siege to it. To deprive it of oxygen. To shame it. To mock it. With our art, our music, our literature, our stubbornness, our joy, our brilliance, our sheer relentlessness—and our ability to tell our own stories. Stories that are different from the ones we're being brainwashed to believe. The corporate revolution will collapse if we refuse to buy what they are selling—their ideas, their version of history, their wars, their weapons, their notion of inevitability. Remember this: We be many and they be few. They need us more than we need them. Another world is not only possible, she is on her way. On a quiet day, I can hear her breathing. —ARUNDHATI ROY, *An Ordinary Person's Guide to Empire*

Inspired by Arundhati Roy's invocation of refusal, what does an antiracist, decolonizing, anticapitalist transnational feminist praxis consist of at this time when colonial legacies and global inequities are no longer invisible and building solidarities and movements across borders is more urgent than ever before? What does it mean to craft insurgent knowledges through our writing, our art, our cultural productions, our activism, and our pedagogies? Simply put, an insurgent feminist lens requires understanding that racialized gender is key to mapping borders, histories, and movements, and asking the question: How and why do women, queer, and gender nonconforming people matter in understanding and responding to this moment of global pandemic and protest?[35] Insurgent knowledges are knowledges that demystify the circuits of power and draw on historical legacies of resistance to create spaces where democratic, anticolonial, nonhierarchical, nonexploitative relationships, identities, and communities can be imagined and practiced. Insurgent knowledges are not merely alternative knowledges—they are knowledges that contest dominant paradigms and habits of being. They are knowledges that do not suffer from a paucity of the imagination but can enable the conditions for social and economic justice on the widest possible scale. Insurgent knowledges must contest the normative, individualist, free-market-oriented paradigm of the consumer-citizen and make possible a collective, justice-based, differentiated understanding of citizenship across national, racial, and gender divides. Given the challenges I have mapped, the following are some key formulations that constitute pedagogies and practices of dissent and refusal. I want to talk about these formulations as theoretical and pedagogical imperatives, as epistemic strategies we can deploy in our classrooms and our everyday journeys through educational and cultural spaces—hence, an insurgent feminist primer![36]

a. Connect educational/cultural spaces to national and transnational institutions of rule and oppositional social movements (talk about the corporate/prison/ cyber/military-industrial complex).
b. Make power hierarchies, labor relations, knowledge/disciplinary hierarchies, research funding, financial aid priorities, and so on, transparent and connect to questions of social control and collective struggles *outside* educational and cultural institutions.
c. Engage in institutional ethnographies that historicize and contextualize questions of difference in institutional and curricular terms. Issue "state of the institution" reports. Form watchdog groups to monitor corporate practices and investment portfolios—call for disclosure and divestment.

d. Actively resist the privatization of social justice commitments—ask what "public" means, how citizenship, democracy, and justice are addressed by university mandates. Make our institutions accountable to the public good defined in social justice and redistribution of resources terms—not politics of presence or charitable acts toward communities.

e. Make market logic and national security priorities of higher education and the state transparent in all curricula. Create and build collectivities of dissent—study groups, watchdog groups, unions, and mentoring collectives that nurture the will to critique/dissent. Organize!

Insurgent Visions: A Road Map

Insurgent Visions combines single and coauthored essays, as well as an extended interview, and is organized into two parts: (1) "Capitalist Scripts, Imperial Projects, Decolonizing Feminism" and (2) "Neoliberal Academic Landscapes, Transnational Feminisms, Cross-Border Solidarity."

As the book title suggests, my thinking over the last decades has woven together all the themes/topics/concepts in the sections above, and it is the result of deep involvement in radical transnational, antiracist, anticapitalist feminist communities in the global South and North and my location as a feminist scholar-activist in the US academy. As in earlier work, I always think and imagine new worlds alongside communities in struggle. I believe our best work is always indebted to dialogue, thinking, and organizing across borders; thus for me collaboration is as much a form of radical political work as it is a genre of writing and producing knowledge.[37] The three collaborative chapters in this collection as well as the interview/dialogue in the first chapter are then as important as the single-authored chapters. Each chapter in *Insurgent Visions* encapsulates feminist struggles at a particular historical moment and location and maps the intricacies, challenges, and potentialities of solidarity across borders in imagining and enacting new, liberatory feminist horizons. Each chapter involves historical, contextual analysis, exploring genealogies of structures, policies, movements, and identities that suggest decolonizing projects in multiple sociopolitical and pedagogical spaces.

Part I, "Capitalist Scripts, Imperial Projects, Decolonizing Feminism," foregrounds the structures, ideologies, and practices of colonial legacies, racial capitalism, imperial projects, and the challenges faced by a decolonial feminist praxis committed to cross-border organizing and solidarity. Chapter 1 is a conversation about my intellectual and political genealogy and the intellectual trajectory that led to my theorizing the significance of race, colonialism, and the state in anticapitalist feminist critique. Chapter 2, cowritten with Sarah Miraglia, demonstrates how neoliberal economic policies are fundamentally gendered and argues that restructuring policies commodifying public services has effectively "reprivatized" women, reifying their subordinated, invisible work under the guise of "empowerment." Chapter 3, cowritten with Linda Carty, continues the analysis of neoliberal economic structures and the challenges posed to radical transnational feminist solidarity. The chapter reflects on a survey conducted among thirty-three multigenerational feminist scholar-activists from Asia, South America, the Caribbean, North Africa, Europe, and North America, honoring the voices, theorizations, and multiple genealogies of our feminist interlocutors, constructing a dialogue that foregrounds the similarities and the differences in our collective thinking and praxis as it has evolved over the decades. Chapter 4 analyzes the political and epistemological struggles that are embedded in radical critical, antiracist, anticapitalist feminist praxis at this time. Focusing on three geopolitical sites, the US-Mexico borderlands, Gaza and the West Bank, and India/Kashmir, I argue that there is a new/old world order in which neoliberalism, imperial practices, and militarization proliferate under new guises of development, humanitarianism, and peacekeeping, revealing the contours of securitized states that function as imperial democracies. The ideologies and practices that constitute and legitimize these imperial democracies fundamentally include gendered logics (such as the rescue narrative, militarized masculinity, and "the condition of women"). They also operate *on* and *through* the body, via what I call the "biomilitarization of the body," in which particular and predictable (immigrant, brown, poor, Indigenous, etc.) individuals exist under constant surveillance and fear of incarceration. Given the current wars, occupations, and dispossession that are ongoing in Gaza, Kashmir, and the US-Mexico border, I believe this chapter offers a comparative analytic framework that continues to be relevant.

Part II, "Neoliberal Academic Landscapes, Transnational Feminisms, Cross-Border Solidarity," focuses centrally on US higher education and the challenge of transformative antiracist, anti-imperialist feminist knowledge projects. Chapter 5 raises key questions about the genealogy and material investments of the discipline of women's and gender studies in the United States and its ties to empire building. Using the case of Abu Ghraib, the prison-industrial complex, the Bush/Cheney war state, and the history of women's studies as empirical supports, this chapter outlines the ways in which colonialism and empire traffic in women's bodies, relying on particular narratives of race, gender, sexualization, and nationalism (including citizenship) to consolidate and reproduce power. Chapter 6, cowritten with M. Jacqui Alexander, continues this genealogical mapping, this time mapping the "transnational" in feminist studies. We begin by naming the US neoliberal academy as a site of empire consolidation as well as knowledge production about globalization and the transnational. From our privileged space within the system, we suggest an analysis attentive to "hierarchies of place." In other words, we pay attention to what types of knowledge may be produced from within the academy as well as to the other (nonacademic/movement) spaces that produce feminist knowledge, and what the voices from these (lesser-valued) spaces are saying (and doing). To be accountable to hierarchies of place—a form of power—in the study of the transnational means integrally including knowledge from everywhere: from outside the academy, from diverse voices, and from a variety of epistemological perspectives. Chapter 7 extends my analysis of the neoliberal academy, focusing on critiques of my work and the ways this "travels" across national borders and geopolitical sites. I explore how my work is utilized in the differing neoliberal contexts of Sweden, Mexico, and Palestine. I argue that for feminists invested in projects of social justice, the concepts of "the decolonization of knowledge, the politics of difference and commonality, and historicizing and specifying women's struggles and identities in the context of anticolonial, anticapitalist struggles within a neoliberal global culture" have proved fundamental. On the other hand, to those invested in maintaining the status quo, my ideas are more often misread. In other words, for those who need them—the insurgents, the marginalized, the radicals working for change—my political commitments within the theorizing are clear and gainfully utilized. For those who don't "need" the work in concrete material contexts, however, it can still be read as essentialist theory, useful in the abstract. Finally, chapter 8 returns to my earlier work, and the construct of *cartographies of struggle*. As an analytic concept, I argue that cartographies of struggle allow us to grasp how power works through interconnected histories of (1) racial capitalism and labor flows, (2) colonial legacies of heteronormative nation-states and projects of citizenship, and (3) transnational/cross-border movements and advocacy for economic and social justice. Chapter 8 argues that we build a transnational feminist praxis by addressing three interwoven conceptual and political cartographies in these times of pandemic and protest: border crossings, interconnected histories, and intersectional social movements/ethical solidarities.

Notes

1 See my earlier book *Feminism Without Borders.*
2 See "Combahee River Collective Statement," in Eisenstein, *Capitalist Patriarchy.* See also Yamahtta-Taylor, *How We Get Free.*
3 Kannan, "Third World Women's Alliance."
4 See Alcoff et al., *Identity Politics Reconsidered*; and Moya and Hames-Garcia, *Reclaiming Identity.* For instance, Satya Mohanty argues, "If we define the notion of epistemic privilege in this way, as the product of the labor of living in oppressive social conditions, we can see how realist theorists reclaim and rehabilitate the much-needed notion of experience—ordinary, everyday experience—as a materialist one, as an aspect of a wider cluster of views about knowledge and social identity" ("Social Justice and Culture," 18–27). See also feminist philosophers' theorization of standpoint theory in Harding and Narayan, *Decentering the Center.*
5 See the documentary film *Crossroads*, by Clara Fong and Kaya Srivastava Liu.
6 See Ahmed, *Living a Feminist Life.*
7 See Farris, *In the Name of Women's Rights.*
8 See Ransby, *Making All Black Lives Matter.*
9 See the statement from the delegation: BDS, "A Call to Action from Indigenous and Women of Color Feminists."
10 As Ruth Wilson Gilmore says, "To describe is also to produce." See her "Race and Globalization."
11 Palestinian Feminist Collective, "Shut Down Colonial Feminism on International Day."
12 See *Inside Higher Ed*, "Higher Ed's Top 10 Developments of 2023."
13 Ferguson, "An Interruption of Our Cowardice."
14 *Tricontinental*, "The Students Will Not Tolerate Hypocrisy."
15 Grande, "Refusing the University."
16 Tuck and Yang, *Toward What Justice?*, 47. On April 30, 2024, the day before May 1 (May Day, a holiday that honors workers' struggles around the world), hundreds of New York City police officers entered the Columbia University campus at the behest of the president, Baroness Minouche Shafik. They were there in full riot gear to arrest and remove students who had occupied Hamilton Hall (renamed Hinds Hall in honor of a six-year-old girl killed in Gaza) and to provide "law and order" and protect the private property of Columbia University. The world watched this militarized takeover of the campus in real time on all the major news outlets (CNN, MSNBC, etc.). Columbia University students were the first in the United States to build a peaceful Gaza solidarity encampment on their campus, declaring it a liberated zone for political education, care, and community advocating for justice for Palestine and other humanitarian crises around the world.
17 See "An Interactive Map of Gaza Solidarity Encampments Around the World," Palestine Is Everywhere, accessed May 20, 2024, https://www.palestineiseverywhere.com.
18 Giroux, "Campus Protests Are Fighting Militarism and Corporatization."
19 Davis et al., *Abolition. Feminism. Now.*
20 Bierria et al., *Abolition Feminisms.*

21 Prashad, *Struggle Makes Us Human*.

22 "Prisoners in 2022—Statistical Tables," Bureau of Justice Statistics, Office of Justice Programs, November 2023, https://bjs.ojp.gov/document/p22st_sum.pdf.

23 Kaba and Ritchie, *No More Police*.

24 See Native Hope, "Missing and Murdered Indigenous Women (MMIW)," accessed November 26, 2024, https://www.nativehope.org/missing-and-murdered-indigenous-women-mmiw.

25 Kaba and Ritchie, *No More Police*.

26 Vergès, *Decolonial Feminism*.

27 My thanks to Taveeshi Singh for pointing this out.

28 "Mothering Is Radical," MAMAS, accessed May 20, 2024, https://www.motheringisradical.com accessed.

29 S. Paik, "Building Bridges."

30 Rege, *Writing Caste/Writing Gender*.

31 See the DEI Legislation Tracker in the *Chronicle of Higher Education*, accessed May 20, 2024, https://www.chronicle.com/article/here-are-the-states-where-lawmakers-are-seeking-to-ban-colleges-dei-efforts. Similarly, a report issued by twenty-two Indian diaspora organizations names the dangerous role played by the BJP (Modi's Bharatiya Janata Party) in rewriting history by presenting Muslims as having no ties to India. See Wire Staff, "Ayodhya Ram Temple Inauguration Sets a 'Dangerous Precedent.'"

32 Arya and Rathore, *Dalit Feminist Theory*, 15.

33 Raveendran, "Ayodhya Issue Reflects the Increasing Masculinization of Politics in India." For current debates around feminism in India, see feminisminindia.com.

34 Equality Labs is a Dalit feminist civil rights organization that "works to end caste apartheid, gender-based violence, Islamophobia, and white supremacy through advocacy, education, digital security, and collective healing" (https://www.equalitylabs.org); Savera is a platform "bringing together an interfaith, multiracial, anticaste coalition of organizations to build a new world" against supremacist politics (https://www.wearesavera.org; see its report *HAF Way to Supremacy* on the Hindu American Foundation's far-right connections); and Coalition of Seattle Indian-Americans (CSIA) led the efforts to make Seattle the first US city to ban caste discrimination (Sarkar, "Meet the Activist Coalition"). India Civil Watch International is "a non-sectarian left diasporic membership-based organization that represents the diversity of India's people and anchors a transnational network to building radical democracy in India" (https://indiacivilwatch.org/).

35 See chapter 8 for an extended discussion responding to these questions.

36 This is my own small version of Sara Ahmed's brilliant primer *The Feminist Killjoy Handbook*.

37 This commitment to dialogue and collaboration is the basis of a video archive project with my colleague Linda Carty: Feminist Freedom Warriors, http://feministfreedomwarriors.org.

PART I

Capitalist Scripts, Imperial Projects, Decolonizing Feminism

PART II

Capitalist Scripts,
Imperial Projects,
Decolonizing Feminism

1

ANTICAPITALIST FEMINIST STRUGGLE
AND TRANSNATIONAL SOLIDARITY

Interview with Jesper Nordahl

I.

I should start by saying something about my own intellectual and political genealogy, which is crucial in understanding the kinds of questions I am asking and the kinds of analysis that I am trying to get through. Growing up in India, it was very clear to me that if I was interested in questions of freedom or liberation, they had to take on decolonization as a deep intellectual epistemological question. Even though I grew up as part of the postindependence generation, all we had at that time was formal decolonization, which meant we weren't necessarily thinking about how colonization affects people beyond self-governance at the state level. So questions have to be about, for example, how people who are formally colonized and who have been subjected to various forms of domination think about decolonization—at psychic levels, at social levels, in terms of racialized gender ideologies, and in terms of the knowledges being produced. The kinds of things that are taught in the school system become very crucial in terms of how people can imagine themselves. So I thought about these things, growing up there and then experiencing a different colonized culture, which was in Nigeria, where I taught high school. In Nigeria, I again had to think about and justify to myself why teaching Keats and Shelley and Shakespeare to Nigerian students for whom this was a very far stretch was important, not that it was not for me when I was in school in India. But I think the combination of those experiences brought home the significance of thinking about history, and specifically colonial legacies, in any liberation project.

When I came to the United States, one of the things I had to do almost immediately was to learn the script of race and racism in the United States. And this was a new script for me. It is not that I did not understand a little bit of it, because I had lived in Nigeria as an Indian in a Black country with Europeans in a very dominant role, but the script of American racism is very particular. To understand it, as somebody from the outside, as somebody from the South, and to find my place within it, I needed to teach myself about the counternarratives, or the histories from below of this country. I needed to do this to understand how racial and economic domination worked and where I fit in as an immigrant and as a person from the South. And so that kind of thinking that I had learned coming of age in India, about colonial legacies, then comes together with thinking about what those legacies mean in the context of a hegemonic culture in the North. The questions become about how you think questions of the profoundly gendered structures of society together with colonial legacies, capitalist scripts, racialized ideologies, and nationalisms. How do you keep those things together? And how do you keep this complex framework in your mind, as your analytical starting point, to make sense of and understand the world? And *then* to use that as a frame to understand what is going on. So a lot of my work then began by asking this question—intellectually, subjectively, and politically.

What Am I Reading in Terms of Feminist Theory?

By centralizing questions of colonial legacies, capitalist scripts, and gendered and raced ideologies, I was able to think differently about what hegemonic feminist theory (however we define that) is teaching me. What it was teaching me was that there was a way in which there was a particular kind of focus on gender as nonracialized, as nonclassed, and also as taken for granted as US American. I realized that there was no real space for thinking about marginalized constituencies of women who in the North are very often poor, working class, and of color and are often peasant working-class workers in the South. In the feminist theory I read in the 1970s and 1980s, there was not a space for understanding these communities of women as critical communities with agency, who have their understanding of how they are located in the situations they are in. That is, they have an understanding of reading power. What I started finding was that the kind of feminist theory or gender analysis that I was subjected to ended up colonizing these groups of women to construct this notion of the free liberated Western feminist subject. Socialist feminists, while paying attention to questions of class and women workers, very often did not pay attention to questions of colonialism and race. So while there was a piece of socialist feminism that was important, in the reading of capitalism and understanding how capitalism and capitalist values become naturalized in the world we live in, in effect these understandings allowed people with privileges to construct people without those privileges either as pure victims, or as people deserving of charity, or as people who have no critical understanding of power and how to fight it.

That seemed to be what I was reading. So that is some of how I got to thinking about what it means to speak of global capitalism and corporate globalization, right now, and *toward* the possibility and the potential of transnational anticapitalist feminist struggle. That is how I get to this place of asking questions like, for instance, How do historical colonialisms construct themselves and their relations of rule based on racialized gender? This is an important question. And how does that then get picked up in the decades following? And how do capitalist relations of rule utilize those gendered and racialized colonial legacies? To, now, once again, create surplus labor; to once again create third world poor women as the preferred workforce.

II.

Can we talk about anticapitalist struggle without understanding the importance of race, gender, and colonial legacies in that struggle? To me, that is a crucial question.

One way to think about this question is, in the world we live in now, how does the colonial traffic in the imperial? It seems to me that imperialism, militarism, and globalization—capitalist corporate economic globalization—are hand in hand right now. We need to understand how those three systems, as modes of operation and practices, interconnect with and sustain each other, and how at the heart of some of those practices are gendered and heteronormative sexual politics and ideologies. That gets cemented. So the kinds of imperialism and militarism we see now require a construction of masculinity. It requires thinking about mobilizing the old colonial ideologies of white men rescuing brown women from brown men. It is a very old trope. It gets mobilized again, over, and over. That trope is very crucial in creating hegemonic consent. We now have an incredible amount of literature on colonial legacies of racialized gender in different contexts in the world. To not disconnect that work from the work that is happening now, which people would call antiglobalization work or anticapitalist work, is an important task. So on the one hand I think that the whole tradition of European Marxism, and the left probably, that a lot of the critiques of the left, both in India and in the United States, have come from women within those struggles who have made it very clear that the way the revolutionary subject is defined, or even the reading of how power works, is faulty—because it is not gendered. Some of the more interesting union work happening right now in the United States is with the service industrial employees union. In this struggle, some unions in the United States figured out that they cannot ignore the fact that women are the dominant workers in certain industries, like the health and service industries. And secondly, that immigrant labor is fundamental in this country to certain industries. So you cannot then go in and organize women and immigrants on the same kind of platform because their experiences are not the same. So the moment you start paying attention to questions of gender and race, your practical politics have to change.

And then if you pay attention to the practical politics and theorize from there, then you have a way to intervene in the larger discourses. One of the ways that capitalism, in the United States at least, is naturalized or normalized, meaning people breathe the values that are created in the air around them and think that that is what democracy is (rather than as connected to an economic structure which has a particular value system attached to it), is by mystifying how power functions, by making it invisible. By not allowing us to see it and see that there are false categories that get created, this is one way that that mystification works.

When we allow ourselves to think in some of those rigid categories, of workers who are nongendered, or not located in any place, placeless, then we are keeping the whole system going. The way change occurs is if people can think very carefully in the place that they are, about what is happening, in the most detailed forms. What is happening to the community that they are a part of, and how is that connected to what is happening in the world? There are real continuities. Globalization and capitalism have flourished for centuries now. So I do not think that there has been a marked break in that. I do think though, that now, with the almost monopoly of certain corporations and the power of transnational governance institutions like the World Bank and the International Monetary Fund (IMF)—which are again governed by particular Western countries—with that and with the fact that the largest economies in the world are now corporate economies and not countries, there has been a major shift in terms of economic and therefore political power.

Some people argue that nation-states are much less important than corporations today. I would say that nation-states continue to play a very significant role as the mediating force between corporations and the way labor is organized in any country. In various parts of the South, for example, free-trade zones are only possible because the state is making them possible. So without the state, there would be no free-trade zones. The state provides a lot of the surveillance and policing mechanisms that are then required by corporations to engage in the level of exploitation that they engage in. And the level of profit-making that results from it. So the role of the state is still essential, if changed.

People have talked about this incredible shift from privatized patriarchal relations within the family to what is referred to as "public patriarchy." So the factory or the corporation becomes the patriarch who is taking care of the women who are employed. And people wonder, is this better or is this worse? Well, some of the research shows that it is better in the sense that women have some income and perhaps therefore have a little bit more autonomy than they have had previously. On the other hand, is this liberation? No, because public patriarchs have similar paternalistic, controlling, surveillance relationships in place for women as do private patriarchs. An interesting question then, in the shift from private or familial patriarchal structures to this kind of less public, more corporatized patriarchal structure, is whether in fact that shift means that there is really an accelerated form of control that happens in the name of young girls getting salaries, getting money, or participating in beauty contests: all the kinds of ideologies that then support the naturalization of capitalist culture and the consumerism that has to be present for capitalism to function well. In other words, does the "liberation" possible in the shift from the private to the public patriarch entrench and strengthen both unequal gender relations *and* an expanding, aggressive capitalism?

Part of what is interesting to me in this question is how we, wherever we are located, very rarely think of our roles as consumers as being central to the way capitalism works. Our participation is crucial. Here is another gendered lens, which is how capitalist corporate companies go after women as consumers. To be a consumer at the level of having access to lots of brands of things becomes a sign of freedom to choose versus any kind of understanding of what it means to live as an individual who can make choices about your own life, on your own, which you cannot. You can choose among products; you cannot choose a lot of stuff about your life. Capitalism provides an illusion of choice, an illusion of liberation, while in fact I think there has been an exacerbation, an acceleration, of forms of exploitation and colonization, which are continuous. I mean the kinds of strategies that are used sometimes are old strategies of containment, of harassment, of physical violence. The same sorts of things that the British, and the Spanish, and everybody else used to subdue subject populations are now happening in different sites.

And because media is so corporately controlled, almost everywhere in the world, most people do not get to see what is happening in terms of struggles and pushbacks that are happening by marginalized people all over the world. Maybe similar corporations are being fought back against, or the same corporation in different sites. And yet, if you do not see it, you do not connect the dots. Then the struggles seem like these isolated struggles that people in Mexico have, and people in India have, and people in Sri Lanka have, and they are not concerted or connected in any way. Some of the most interesting forms of resistance currently are the transnational connections that are happening among women workers, but also among women in sex work, specifically, and the prostitution that is happening transnationally.

All these conduits of crossing are now in place, which are very much part of this particular stage of corporate globalization. Certain bodies can cross under certain conditions, and it seems like this is freedom. That you are *free* to cross versus you *have* to cross to sustain yourself and your family back home.

III.

I want to talk a little bit about something else, which shows something different about what is happening now with corporate globalization, and that is the growth of the global prison industry. It is a global prison industry. Through the seventies, eighties, and nineties, the counterpart of structural adjustment in the South was privatization in the North, and specifically in the United States. The same kind of economic restructuring has happened here as has happened there. There has been a period of structural readjustment and economic readjustment that has happened in this country, and the primary form it has taken is of course deregulation and privatization. And the growth of the global prison industry in that sense is very, very instructive. At the time when, in the eighties and the nineties, in the United States, when people were losing their jobs, there was all kinds of furor about economic depression, economic downsizing, all those things. The prison industry was in an economic boom, exactly at the same time. And in the 1990s, while the crime rate in the United States went down, the prison population doubled. People now are talking about the privatization of prisons, which means the taking over of the prison system by private corporations, and for-profit corporations. There were no privately owned prisons in the United States before, I think, something like 1983, and now it is a booming industry. It is huge. There are prototypes of privatized prison systems that are being exported to other countries. Mexico is one, and Malaysia is another, as is Colombia.

But right now, I am going to talk specifically about the United States, and what I see as the present condition here, which is that there is a real dovetailing between domestic and foreign policy, of the Bush war state right now, and the prison state. We have for a long time been creating both internal and external enemies, and very often they look alike. Right now, corporate globalization—corporate rule in this country—goes together with the militarization of everyday life, and of the imperial project outside, imperial wars outside. So private prisons become a part of the way corporate America specifically flourishes, and the way it ties into its larger imperial aspirations. There are levels of surveillance now in place that are unprecedented. So health services, state health services, hospitals, school systems, and welfare offices are all under surveillance and managed in terms of internal threats (for example, school shootings and responses). So who is an internal threat becomes a very big question. Phones are being tapped. Military recruiters go into public school systems to recruit young people for the military, and they especially target schools in low-income areas with large populations of students of color. Also, this is a very gendered practice, because it immediately constructs notions of what kinds of masculinities are desired masculinities, and what it means to be a real, strong man.

The prison and military systems are also raced, and the military or the prison are today especially options for young men of color, young African Americans and Latinos. There is something like two-thirds of African American men who are either in prison, on parole, or in some way connected to the prison system. In effect, such policies are disappearing entire generations of groups of people. Connected to this, there is a rise of private and public immigrant detention centers, privatized immigrant detention centers all along the California, Texas, and Mexico border. And again, what do privatized detention centers do? They look to fill beds. Federal prisons are now full of immigrants.[1] Further, there has been a recent shift in thinking about rehabilitation as the object of going to prison, to basically criminalization, permanent criminalization. Because the point is to have people in prisons like the Marriott, filling beds.

Why is this relevant for feminist work? Well, because similar racialized and gendered ideologies are being mobilized as have been used to justify a number of other interventions, and women are the fastest-growing population in prisons. This is not just in the United States, but globally. Jamaican women, Mexican women for whom the only form of income is to carry drugs either for their boyfriends or for somebody else in power, across borders—and who get caught and then get thrown in jail and then stay there for a very long time. So the people who bear the brunt of these policies are poor women from the South, usually.

There is a continuity between the war on drugs and the war on terror, so it is logical that, in fact, poor women are the people who get most caught in the system. They are still the most marginalized; they are still vulnerable in many ways. In the United States, the Southern states have the largest growing private prison industry in the country. You can understand how this is all connected because prison labor is cheap labor or free labor sometimes—which is why prison abolitionists such as Angela Davis speak about the prison-industrial complex as the continuation of slavery. So you have private corporations, and you do not have any public control or state control. And the prisoners are part of chain gangs; they are part of the labor force for huge numbers of corporations in the US South.

So it is a continuity with slavery in many ways. There is even a place in North Carolina that used to be a plantation in the 1850s, which had some of the largest numbers of enslaved people and is now a private prison. Slavery was outlawed, and supposedly it is done with, but it is now taken over by the Corrections Corporation of America and made into a private prison, which houses largely young African American men who have been shipped, outsourced, from the North, from Connecticut. So here in effect is a whole other incarnation of labor patterns that have very long histories in this country and are devastating for many communities of color.

So you asked me, from where I sit, what are some of the more interesting, important, and crucial struggles around the prison industrial complex in this country? This is where a lot of young people of color are involved in fact. It is interesting because it is not yet seen as part of the antiglobalization movement or struggle where it seems to me that it is perfectly compatible and connected. This is the other thing about anticapitalist struggle. We need to widen the range of how we understand the profoundly devastating effects of capitalist exploitation because the surveillance industry and the criminalization industry are connected to the way labor is organized in this country, and to the way it is organized around the world. The fact that different countries, and often authoritarian regimes in different countries, are now reproducing the same kinds of prison systems, and privatizing prison systems in the same ways, shows us that we are moving in this very dangerous direction. The organization that I work with, Grassroots Leadership of North Carolina, is trying to prevent private industries and corporations from coming in and taking over prisons. So they work with the communities on the ground, work with legislators, and put pressure on local county state governments. And it is precisely in the US South because the South is such an important place in this country for prison privatization. For example, our organization participated in a coalition with a student group, where students in different universities organized against companies that were connected to the Corrections Corporation, which is the largest prison privatizer in the world. The target of the organizing was Sodexo, which provided a lot of food services to prisons and is also one of the most important food suppliers to universities. Students organized to boycott food services and Sodexo, and Sodexo pulled out. So there have been coalitions among different groups in different sites to target particular corporations and the building of immigrant detention centers and private prisons.

The challenge is to get people to see the fact that the community does not want this entity to exist. Privatization threatens democracy. Where private good substitutes for the public good is a profound way in which corporatization and globalization are working now. If one does not fight it, if you do not see that this is something that permeates everywhere, then we lose the battle. Because if we buy into the capitalistic rhetoric of competition, of you privatize something then the competition increases the output and it is more efficient, and you do not keep in mind that when you privatize something, then as a citizen you have no rights in relation to what the private company is doing, we lose the battle.

Privatization is a huge issue. Right now, people are privatizing absolutely everything: educational systems, health systems, medical systems, public parks, transportation services. And in all of this, there are struggles in this country, pushing back at that level of privatization. And there must be, because such privatization deeply threatens the understanding that democratic citizenship is about the ability to participate in decision-making about your life, and about having accountability between you as a citizen and your government's structure, whatever the structure is, and that this is undercut by this form of privatization. People who are part of this move are very aware of this and are brilliant at coming up with language that shifts the terrain of struggle or discourse, or even understanding, to somewhere else. The language that we use here really matters. So you do not talk about people losing rights, you talk about people getting more efficient services. You do not talk about accountability; you do not talk about the fact that in privatized spaces it is people who have wealth and money who have a say. And people who do not have wealth and money have no say, have none whatsoever. So your citizenship is determined by your wealth and your class privilege. It is not guaranteed just because you happen to live in something that calls itself a democracy. This has nothing to do with the kind of rights that you are afforded. So we must take on privatization in a central way. We cannot see it merely as an economic solution or something to do with efficiency rather than as eroding some very central ways of thinking about the public good, public responsibility, public relationships, and all of those things. It is quite insidious.

IV.

I am not squeamish about militant tactics, so in other words, I do not think one can be a nice girl and make any revolutionary change. I do not think that deliberate destruction or violence against someone else is necessary to create militant tactics and get attention from the media, if that is part of what one is trying to do. I think that the Seattle demonstrations were interesting because, first, it was a coalition of different sets of people and communities. The fact that this happened, and the organizers were able to bring so many people together, was amazing and crucial because it was one of the first things that happened in the United States after the sixties that made people sit up and think, "Oh well, there *are* enough people who are thinking critically about what is going on and who are willing to take certain kinds of stands." So one of the effects of that, if you were paying attention and if you cared about these things, was to show people that the state and the transnational institutions do not have absolute power, necessarily. In terms of people's hearts and minds, that power is not there. Seattle made it clear that dissent on a mass scale was possible. Making this visible/clear is one of the most important things about those mass demonstrations when they happen in different contexts. The more recent Occupy movements globally also illustrate this point.

As we mount our protest, we are also struggling with the fact that the media is so corporatized. For more accurate information you have to go to alternative media sources, which many of us go to, but everyone cannot, or doesn't know that they need to. You have to have certain kinds of access to find alternative sources. The US state is the most depressing state, it is very unabashedly an imperial state right now, and whether the elections next year (2008) will change, I do not know, I do not think so. I think the same kinds of policies will continue. I think there will be a difference if there are Democrats in power. I think one of the differences will be that perhaps the religious right will be less powerful. The recent spur in fatherhood initiatives and faith-based initiatives is a very important place to look at how normative heterosexuality is being rethreaded and recast in popular culture. It is just the perfect place to look at it. Or the "Don't Ask, Don't Tell" policy regarding gay and lesbian people in the military, which is another place to look at how heterosexualization is a very important part of the state apparatus, especially in states that are corporatized and imperial states. You know, those are part of the rule in practice. And you have to see it. You have to pay attention to the connections between all of them.

Thinking about the US state, I cannot exactly say "what would be successful," but I do know that there are struggles and there are people in different places that are coming up with alternative economic arrangements—a different kind of basis of subsistence than we are in the North. And I think that those everyday practices are as important to pay attention to and to be clear about. An example of this in the North is called community-supported agriculture (CSA), which is farmers who farm on the basis of support from an entire community that commits to subsidizing the farming, small farmers, and buying the product whatever the product is, whether it is huge or little. It is a very small thing, but it pushes back against agribusiness, it pushes back against certain kinds of ways in which the world is governed by corporatized institutions. So everyday practices or certain kinds of alternative institution building within various communities is very crucial.

From what I know about struggles around the world, many of the struggles that poor women have been involved in all over the world have to do with their neighborhoods and communities. When it is a struggle that affects an entire neighborhood, it is always the women who are in the leadership positions. You can look all over Latin America, you can look in the United States, lots of other places. So one of the struggles in this country, which has been led by poor women of color in inner-city areas, is the struggle against environmental pollution, where privatized corporations come into what is seen as an economically devastated area to set up shop. Most often, such corporations come to inner-city areas or even rural areas, which are seen as economically devastated with no possibility of anything else. The assumption is that if there is economic devastation, then there is no political power among the people in that context, so the corporations can turn that area into a toxic dump. So some of the most urgent but also successful struggles against what is called environmental racism have been by these poor women of color based on the devastation of their communities due to toxic dumps. And they have managed to in some cases get corporations to move, to take it out of there. The creation of urban toxic dumps is also enabled because other sources of industry have also fled. In Syracuse, Lockheed Martin moving away is an example of this effect.

Looking at the role of corporations in harming communities, it very quickly also becomes evident that there are many connections between corporations and militarization. I think of the different industries that are connected to the making of a highly militarized society, one where it is assumed that the only way to have security is through militarization and policing. Since I came to this country in the eighties, I have never thought that I have lived in a democratic society or democratic culture. There are certain formal mechanisms of democracy that work in this country, that are protected in this country, which are very important, and which are not available in some other parts of the world. But what is democratic culture if there is a *belief* that there *is* freedom of assembly, speech, and so on, and yet there are certain things that because they are not in the landscape that you grew up in you cannot even imagine, or speak, or fight? In authoritarian regimes, the power is very blunt and clear, so on some level, it is easier to name and resist. Pedagogically, one of the things that has happened in the United States in the last decade is that now the exercise of power is so raw around us, that it is now actually possible to talk about US culpability, accountability, and all these things, whereas before it was not so easy. So the imperial projects are right out there, and now you can say so and be differently heard. It is no longer possible to just say, OK democracy exists here, and you know, we are bringing democracy elsewhere.

You cannot bring democracy to anybody. People struggle for it on their own. You win it. You achieve it; you cannot be given it. If you take some of the things I said earlier about decolonization seriously, then you see that a colonizing power moving out of a country does not mean that the country is free in terms of people, in terms of how people think, in terms of how people feel, or what they can imagine for themselves. So what they often put in place is a neocolonial regime, which is of course what many of my experiences in India and Nigeria have been, which have been very nationalist and masculinist at the same time. Further, we need to make the distinction between the people of a country and the government of a country very clearly, because the government many times does not represent the interests of the people at all. It is only representing its own interests.

In short, there are many large struggles ahead of us, and I think that one of the ways to think about *winning* struggles is to be clear about the fact that these struggles are happening around the world, in various places, right now. Centering the ongoing history of resistance teaches us that profound changes are possible if and when people respond and resist. I do believe in revolution. What that means in different sites and different contexts requires thinking carefully, because it may not look the same, and it may not be the same, in different places and at different times. So the Zapatista movement is a revolution, but will we be able to reproduce the Zapatista movement in the United States? I do not think so at all. The contexts are too different. Indigenous communities in the United States have a very clear critique of colonization and genocide by the US state historically and a claim for sovereignty. But it is also the case that they are working within the context of a US national landscape, which is very corporate and consumer-oriented. So the struggles and the models that Indigenous communities come up with in the United States are very different from one another, and from others, and the tactics are different. The struggles mounted by Indigenous peoples in the United States come from a very different history of struggle than, for instance, the struggle for civil rights in this country. Where the struggle for civil rights was a struggle to become part of a polity that treated Black people as less than equal, for Native Americans the struggle is not about civil rights, because they reject the United States as the nation they want to belong to. So there are very different genealogies of struggle and very different kinds of histories and tactics that people end up following. Who we are matters in our struggles, and where we come from matters as well.

I sense that all these things are crucial. No one thing is going to get us what we want. It is important to always look at a situation carefully, to look at the history of the situation, and to look at the relationships within that context and ask the question: What are the stories that I have been told about this, and how have the stories left out particular things that I need to know to understand and figure out what form of resistance will work here? In my context as a teacher, I have found that some of the most radical activities that I can engage in are to provide students with alternative narratives and histories to the ones that they take for granted. Doing this shakes up the paradigm that has been normalized.

In the same way as you have the trope of third world women as victims, you can turn the question on its head. If you did not think about women workers in Sri Lanka, India, or anywhere as victims, but began from the place of agency that prioritizes what they see, how they organize, and how they analyze what is happening to them, then you can use that to complicate the narratives that you have always taken for granted. From this place, you can ask questions about what a just society looks like. Or what kind of values do you have about human life? Is one more valuable than the other? Those kinds of questions become the ethical questions made possible by taking women's agency seriously. I think one of the effects of the naturalization of certain capitalist values (competitiveness, the assumption that success means wealth, that wealth and success are just and merited, that being able to be a good consumer is a major value, that private ownership is not questioned) is that those things become naturalized. Naturalizing such values undermines any kind of notion of interdependency, collaboration, inequality, or the connection between privilege and domination. That connection gets severed. This is one way in which capitalism is naturalized. People stop seeing the fact that their wealth has something to do with the fact that huge numbers of people are poor. But if you start from the other place, right? You start from the place of people who are fighting those forms of domination, and then what you see, what is real, and what you view as important has the potential to shift.

When you start from this place, you also have the potential to look at the power structure differently. You can start posing questions about what the cost of privilege is, and whether you are willing to live with that cost. This question has the potential to get "successful" people—by capitalist standards—to make some different choices about their own lives and what they will do with them. Part of the way that privilege works is by reproducing itself. It constantly reproduces itself. So by thinking about your privilege, in connection to others, you are going to interrupt that pattern. So resistance needs to work at all kinds of different levels. The best resistance is that which begins in the place where you are at. This is a motto for all organizers. You begin where you are. You look around you, and who is around you? And who are the people that you are in touch with? And what are their lives like? And what would it take for them to change? Is that the group that you are working with? Then, what does it take for this group of people to come to some collective understanding of the conditions of their lives and how the conditions of their lives are connected to the conditions of lives of people in different places in the world? Rooting resistance in such questions is the best way that people can organize. Organizers who can do this are generally successful.

This is very much the history of labor in this country, and it is very much the history of race and gender struggles. It is fascinating to look at women's resistance in this country because particular groups of women from different communities have historically occupied different parts of the labor market. And they have been segmented. It is important and insightful to understand how race and gender are integrally connected to the history of capitalism and labor and the building of the United States as a nation. So the United States becomes a nation through those three interconnected histories: race, gender, and labor. Particular groups of people get exploited, and superexploited in certain ways, and that is connected to a whole other set of people who are exploited in a whole other different way. The trajectories of race and gender still shape labor. There is still sweatshop labor, there are still exploited women in Silicon Valley, and there is still the preponderance of piecework, which is a huge part of what is happening with immigrant labor specifically, women workers, and immigrant women in the United States. The way that this level of superexploitation works is through the mobilizing of gendered and racialized ideologies that naturalize—and devalue—certain kinds of labor. This reality is why an anticapitalist, socialist, or Marxist analysis that does not pay attention to how race and gender are mobilized in the service of profit fails to understand what is going on and fails to find a way to effectively organize across those boundaries.

In the early twentieth century in this country, the Communist Party was successful. It was one of the few groups that were successful in organizing Black and white workers together, in the shipbuilding industry, I think.

But, again, you know what happened to the Communist Party. It is no longer a strong player! There has always been a lot at stake in workers from different racialized and gendered groups and identities finding ways to work together and organize together because they have always been separated by the ways that capitalism functions. So I think there is no way to even talk about any form of a proletariat without racing and gendering it right now, and also understanding it geographically in terms of the way people are located and how they are connected to larger systems. In the university setting, we live in a culture where many people are attentive to and are trying to not be racist, and yet all you have to do is to look at how different people are concentrated within the workplace—with women of color working in the food industries on campuses all over the country and white men in the positions of the highest power, to see that the labor patterns are still segregated. There are not that many differences when you look at working conditions in the North and in the South for particular groups of women workers who are seen as the most expendable and exploitable sources of labor. This makes "sense" because poor women are where the most profit can be extracted, and the assumption is that these are the most powerless people. And if they are powerless, then they cannot challenge us.

Therefore, I think that some of the most important struggles are transnational—as women workers who struggle across borders.

V.

Living in the United States for this long, it is my responsibility to engage in what is happening here, and what is happening here has devastating effects on everyone around the world. This is the weird thing about living here. It is the most hopelessly depressing thing because things are happening around you that are just phenomenally oppressive, and it is also one of the most urgent and important things to live here now because there is so much work to be done here. And you cannot *not* do the work. I may feel like an outsider, and I am an outsider, but I am still on the inside in the sense that there is a certain amount of power I can have. And there are privileges I have. The question then becomes, What am I doing with my power and my privileges? To me, that is the question the people who live in the United States need to ask. What are the privileges that you have, and what are you doing with those privileges? And not just for yourself, because that is easy. Everybody can do it for themselves, but what are you doing for what is happening in the world, and for what the United States is doing in the world?

Notes

The book *Anticapitalist Feminist Struggle and Transnational Solidarity: Chandra Talpade Mohanty*, by Jesper Nordahl (2019), is based on a transcript of a video interview Jesper Nordahl conducted with Chandra Talpade Mohanty in Ithaca, New York, in March 2007. For the video, see https://vimeo.com/28572566. For information on the book, video, and Jesper Nordahl, see www.jespernordahl.net.

1 See Urbina, "Using Jailed Migrants as a Pool of Cheap Labor."

2

GENDERING JUSTICE, BUILDING ALTERNATIVE FUTURES

with Sarah Miraglia

We want guaranteed access to basic services such as telecommunications, energy, health and water. Moreover, we want to live in a world without war, with social justice, with equity, where men don't dominate women, where children don't have to work in cane fields or in factories, where children don't roam the streets without hope. With this desire, when our various organisations come together, we know this movement has a bright future. America is destined to be the continent of hope and life. And our struggles will show that, though we might not experience it in our lifetime, we will have added a grain of sand to the pile. —ERASTO REYES, "The Power That Makes Pitchers Overflow and Rivers Flood Their Banks"

Erasto Reyes reminds us of a vision for social and economic justice that fuels continuing struggles for liberation in the twenty-first century. While neoliberal cultures inevitably place capitalist interests above the needs and hopes of people, it is people's movements (anticolonial/anti-imperial, peasant, ecological, labor, women's, peace and justice, antiglobalization, etc.)

that have exposed the fault lines of neoliberal capitalism and placed questions of democracy, equity, and justice at the center of struggles for emancipation. A decade into the twenty-first century, we face an unprecedented consolidation (and crisis) of social, economic, and political power fueled by the conjuncture of relentless neoliberalism, masculinist religious fundamentalisms, rampant militarisms, resurgent racisms, and the criminalization of minoritized populations in many countries. This chapter argues that gender equity and women's agency are core components of envisioning anticapitalist struggles for social and economic justice in general, and for enacting alternatives to privatization in particular.

The first part of the chapter, "Gendering Neoliberalism," interrogates the politics of economic restructuring, arguing that neoliberal reforms have effectively worked to reprivatize women through "empowerment" projects that entail the commodification of public services and participatory projects. The rest of the chapter, "Gender Equity in Imagining Alternative Futures," counters the disempowering effects of commodified public services, suggesting that rather than seeking to "empower" women, alternatives focus on women's agency in struggles for social and economic justice. Our review of gender equity in alternatives to privatization highlights the complex nature of working in and through established governance structures and within institutional settings and argues for models of action that work to create the infrastructure necessary for women's strategic interests. Finally, we introduce an analytic framework that allows us to see women's agency through their struggles around the body, the environment, and diverse economies—through place-based struggles that originate in the lived experiences of women struggling against neoliberal reforms.

Feminist scholarship and activism in the last several decades have shown conclusively that gender is constitutive of economic and political structures of governance, that gender ideologies and representations consolidate hierarchical relations of rule globally, and that people's subjectivities and identities are profoundly gendered. Thus, any project that seeks to confront the hierarchical and unjust relations of rule embedded in processes of privatization and commercialization must engage with the everyday politics of gender. Fundamentally, a gendered analysis assumes attentiveness to unequal male/female power relations and a commitment to gender justice—that is, strategies to eliminate the subordination and impoverishment of women. Gendered analysis does not assume that women are uniformly or universally subordinated or that women in different places, spaces, and cultures face identical challenges.[1] Class, caste, sexuality, religion, culture, ability, and race/ethnicity/indigeneity all intervene to position women in different *and* similar relationships to power and inequality. In addition, patriarchal histories of colonialism, racism, and capitalist exploitation position communities of women in the global South and North in different, yet comparable, relationships to each other, to the state, and to transnational governance structures. Women in the global South bear the brunt of the current economic order.

Speaking of the Americas, Ericka Beckman suggests that, while "'Old' forms of domination such as patriarchy, capitalism and racism remained in place ... neoliberal economic and political arrangements have exacerbated the feminization of poverty across the region."[2] In other words, neoliberal economic policies further cheapen women's labor in the workplace, simultaneously increasing their labor in the home via the dismantling of social services in particular, and the welfare state in general. Privatization and commercialization constitute key aspects of neoliberal restructuring in the global South. Privatization recasts the principles of democratic governance, leading to the abdication of responsibility and a shift in power and accountability from governments to private corporations, transforming the "structures of entitlements" in ways that are most injurious for the poor, especially poor women who subsidize the environmental costs of overconsumption.[3] Power relations of gender, class, and race/ethnicity are reconfigured through the mechanism of feminization as devaluation. What many analysts refer to as the "feminization of labor" operates through a devalorization of the labor and skill involved in performing tasks, simultaneously reducing wages for jobs considered "feminized."[4] The feminization of labor has led to the marginalization of men in the workforce, and this loss of a male income leaves households with very few resources for survival, pushing more families into poverty. Thus, gender analysis and questions of women's rights and agency remain central to envisioning and enacting alternatives to privatization in the global South.

This chapter suggests a relational, complex understanding of gender. We speak of gender (1) as a theoretical lens and an epistemological project (gender in relation to meaning systems—ideologies, theories, paradigms); (2) as an apparatus of governance embedded in institutions of rule (gendered structures, practices, and forms of social reproduction), and (3) as lived cultures—gendered subjectivities, self- and collective identities.[5] Our analysis is anchored in an antiracist, materialist feminist framework that links everyday life and local gendered histories and ideologies to larger, transnational/global structures and ideologies of capitalism through a gendered "placed-based" framework.[6] This particular framework draws on historical materialism and centralizes a differentiated notion of gendered struggles anchored in the bodies, environments, and economies of the most marginalized communities of women—poor and Indigenous women in affluent and neocolonial nations, and women from the global South.[7] We suggest that an experiential and analytic grounding in the lives and struggles of marginalized communities of women (urban poor, working-class, peasant, Indigenous, etc.) provides the most inclusive paradigm for advocating gender justice in the creation of alternatives to privatization. We agree with Ben Fine and David Hall in their call for public sector systems of provision that utilize an "approach that needs to be contextually driven rather than as a . . . universal theory."[8] However, our call for a particularized framing is coupled with a vision of gender justice that is both expansive and universal. We envision a world that values and promotes gender justice within households and the larger polity, a world in which legacies of colonialism, violence, poverty, and deprivation are acknowledged and actively resisted. We work and struggle for a postcapitalist world, for what many people refer to as a "solidarity economy"—one that values cooperation and interdependency above profit and greed. Our work is dedicated to the feminist struggle for gender justice—to an expansive and universal vision, anchored in the differences and specificities of women's lives. In our discussion of alternatives to privatization, gender justice (the elimination of hierarchies and unequal power based on gender) is central to socioeconomic practices and structural arrangements that value equity in access to resources, participation, leadership, and the politics of knowledge.

Some of the questions pertaining to a gendered analysis of privatization and commercialization include a *gendering* of the left critique of neoliberalism in Africa, Asia, and Latin America; a critique of global restructuring in terms of the gendered impact of policies/practices and implications for gender equity; and, finally, a focus on the ways in which women cope, adjust, resist, and advocate for their communities and on their own behalf (i.e., women's agency). In concrete terms this gendering of the left critique includes a shift away from treating "the poor," "the worker," or "the peasant" as homogeneous identity groups, to being attentive to how gender, race, ethnicity, and nation inflect and constitute each identity in ways that shape the opportunities and constraints faced by women and men positioned differentially in hierarchies of power, privilege, and exclusion utilizing an intersectional approach. For example, the particularities of poor, Indigenous women's lives in Latin America are different from (and similar to) the lives and struggles of poor male peasants in South Asia. While each group may be "poor," the challenges faced by the different communities can only be understood if the gender, race, and ethnic particularities are taken into account. These are some of the questions we address in what follows.

Gendering Neoliberalism: Global Restructuring and the Politics of Development
Colonial Legacies, Neoliberal Frameworks

Colonial legacies and patriarchal structures, as well as ideologies and practices of masculinist, class, and race/caste supremacy, underlie social relations and institutions that constitute neoliberal economic and political orders. Legacies of colonialism include capitalist processes of recolonization that consolidate and exacerbate relations of domination and exploitation by making use of existing social divisions to further the goal of profit maximization.[9] As Gita Sen suggests, "Faced with intransigent social structures and rigid hierarchies such as those based on gender, race, or caste, the expansion of commerce builds on these hierarchies, altering and reshaping them in the process, and transforming the life experiences of those involved."[10] In fact, it is colonial legacies of racialized patriarchies that underlie the division of labor in contemporary capitalist cultures. Maria Mies theorizes colonization and "housewifization" as linked processes of racialized gender that were instituted by colonial powers during the eighteenth and nineteenth centuries to extract maximum profit from women's labor in the colonies and at "home."[11] Thus, while slave women's "productive" labor was valorized, and reproductive labor controlled because it led to the loss of profit, bourgeois women in the metropole were subjected to a process of housewifization that valorized their reproductive roles, withdrawing them from the public sphere, simultaneously constructing gender regimes of public/private spheres. It is these very processes of race, class, and gender differentiation in the service of capital exploitation that traffic in the present. Since the 1970s, US feminist economists have critiqued the notion of "hegemonic economic man" (a self-made man: narrowly self-interested, competitive, individualistic, and motivated by greed) that developed historically in nineteenth-century Europe and the United States. The "economic woman" required by this hegemonic notion of masculine personhood tended to be the full-time homemaker-wife, a racialized, class-specific, and heteronormative notion of womanhood.[12] However, while public/private distinctions have been the basis of gendered regimes since post-fifteenth-century colonialism, an intersectional approach that is attentive to race and class particularities suggests that women in the global South, and poor, immigrant, and women of color in the global North do not fall neatly into the homemaker-wife or "economic woman" designations.

Neoliberalized global restructuring has drawn on these colonial legacies to consolidate the current regime of international debt, development aid, and the so-called structural adjustment of the economies and governance structures of developing countries. Marianne Marchand and Anne Sisson Runyan argue that global restructuring reworks practices and meanings of masculinity/femininity by shifting the boundaries and meanings of public/private, domestic/international, and local/global.[13] Feminist scholars of global restructuring claim that the relations of domination and the economic and political hierarchies instituted by neoliberal cultures are profoundly gendered and could not be sustained without the gendered symbolism and metaphors that serve to "naturalize" the gendered division of labor that underlies processes of economic restructuring. The withdrawal of government responsibility for social welfare has resulted in the transfer of these obligations to women, a process that Florence Babb refers to as women "absorbing the shocks" of adjusting economies.[14] In essence, women subsidize processes of economic liberalization, through both unpaid labor in the home and paid labor in formal and informal work.[15] It is erroneous, however, to construe public and private spaces as discrete spaces. As Kathryn Pitkin and Ritha Bedoya suggest, "Production and reproduction overlap and often occupy the same space in women's lives."[16] Women's work in the home is increased in a number of ways that are often directly related to changes in the public sphere. They have to work harder to collect water, provide food, ensure health, and supplement household incomes due to cuts in health, education, and food subsidies and the privatization of water, which often has detrimental effects on the poorest women.

Over three decades of feminist activism and scholarship in the global South, from the early critiques of the impact of economic development on poor third world women by DAWN (Development Alternatives with Women for a New Era) to more recent analysis by the Feminist Initiative of Cartagena, point to the profoundly negative effects of mainstream development policies and Structural Adjustment Programs (SAPs) anchored in neoliberal paradigms.[17] The 1980s to early 1990s witnessed the sustained engagement of development discourse by feminists via the UN world conferences on women and the entry of women's movement activists into international governing bodies and NGOs focusing on women's issues. Wendy

Harcourt argues that this engagement of international governance structures by women's rights advocates resulted in a "professionalization" of development and a proliferation of NGOS on women's issues leading to a depoliticization of radical gender justice projects and the creation of a management apparatus of development.[18] It is this particular development discourse, backed up by UN statistics, texts, case studies, and reports, that partially fueled the managerial and bureaucratized neoliberal policies, in turn discursively producing a generic, gendered female body with a particular set of needs and rights, thus potentially erasing all the differences among women. The radical feminist critiques of SAPS and of privatization as a legacy of SAPS and the IMF/World Bank policies thus resulted at this time in an organizational focus on "gender mainstreaming" (as evidenced through static measures of gender parity in development plans and projects and/or women's participation in the private sphere), not gender justice (an analysis of gendered power hierarchies that unearth and destabilize the roots of gendered forms of inequality; a project often regarded as meddling in the "cultural" affairs of "other" nations).

From Gender Mainstreaming to Women's Empowerment:
Reprivatizing Women Through Health, Water, and
Electricity Projects

Gender mainstreaming was agreed on as the "global strategy for the promotion of gender equality" in the 1995 Beijing Platform for Action (the Fourth World Conference on Women).[19] In some ways, gender mainstreaming represents the gains made through the persistence and struggle of thousands of women around the world whose activism and advocacy persuaded international organizations to rectify gendered silences and omissions in international policies.[20] But it also represents ongoing negotiations and contestations between women-based/feminist groups and the members of the UN system, and ostensibly the larger development industry.[21] While the goal of gender mainstreaming was to bring women's issues to the center of development agendas and to move away from "the earlier 'add women and stir approach,'" it has fallen short of actually transforming gendered inequalities in development plans.[22] As Maitrayee Mukhopadhyay argues, "Feminist concerns with the political project of equality are being normalised in the development business as an ahistorical, apolitical, de-contextualised and technical project that leaves the prevailing and unequal power relations intact."[23] Despite—and partly because of—the attempts to make gender politically viable within international organizations and NGOS, gender mainstreaming has more often than not failed to rectify gender inequalities, though it has spurred on debates surrounding methods and strategies. This policy dialectic—the relationship between activists, advocates, and planners—has generated a new/old paradigm emphasis on "women's empowerment" as a strategy for gendering development.

The empowerment approach, we argue, is gender mainstreaming adapted to a neoliberal ideological agenda. On the surface, women's empowerment is concerned with promoting equality of access to resources, and power in decision-making for women, but in practice it works to conceal deep-seated social, political, and economic inequalities that need to be addressed to make real, meaningful change. Empowerment approaches tend to individualize gender equity, subject gendered interests to tests of market efficiency, and essentially *reprivatize* women through a marriage of "efficiency, productivity and empowerment."[24] This marriage of objectives is enacted on the ground through the commodification of resources and the decentralization of resource management, which also is a process of commodification as it relies on the "free labor" of community members to enact the project.[25] The introduction of commodified public services, it was argued, would increase access for millions. On the whole, this prediction has not played out in practice. Millions continue to lack access to safe drinking water, sanitation, electricity, and health care. Worse yet, not only have women not gained access to these vital services, but also in many cases they have lost government subsidies for them and/or the total provision of them. The gap between what can be paid and what commodified services cost and/or the loss of the service altogether is filled in by women's labor. In very concrete ways, neoliberal policies have "privatized social reproduction" by reprivatizing women's labor.[26] In the following pages, we highlight some of the problematics of this approach.

The Costs of Commodified Public Services

One means of commodification is the introduction of user fees and "full cost recovery" programs into systems of public service delivery. Cindi Katz identifies this process of commodification as one that moved from pricing schemes that valued "social equity" (paying what one could afford) to "economic equity" (users must pay for the full costs of the resource).[27] Proponents of this system argue that user fees compel consumers to make judicious choices in their use of the good. What aren't accounted for in these models are the consequences of an inability to pay. In the field of health care, for example, Priya Nanda found that women's rates of utilization of health care decreased dramatically in several African nations after the introduction of user fees, thus jeopardizing women's health.[28] Nanda similarly shows that maternal death rates increased by 56 percent in the Zaria region of Nigeria as a result of an inability to pay user fees. In this case, women could not afford maternity care and thus suffered the consequences of unattended births. Commodified services have multiplicative effects as well. Rebecca Brown's study of water privatization in Tanzania shows how an inability to pay for water makes HIV/AIDS care increasingly difficult, particularly in Tanzania, where home-based care for HIV/AIDS patients is policy.[29] In this case, an inability to pay for water jeopardizes women's safety as at-home caregivers. Thus, not only is the patient's health put at risk but so too is the health of the caregiver.

In the electricity sector, neoliberal reforms have had similarly detrimental effects because planners have tended to focus on supply-side concerns that value profit over equity and prioritize industrial consumption.[30] The supply-side focus has marginalized the energy needs of women through a lack of policy attention to biomass fuels, which are largely used by the poor in both rural and urban settings.[31] Women's health is put at risk by the lack of attention to biomass fuels; they are tasked with the responsibility of collecting biomass fuels and also with cooking responsibilities that have particularly adverse, though well-known, health effects.[32] The World Bank, for example, "classed indoor air pollution in LDCs [least developed countries] among the four most critical global environmental problems."[33] Beyond indoor pollution, the use of biomass fuels puts women at risk of injuries related to collecting firewood and inhibits school participation by young girls who often work alongside their mothers to collect biomass energy sources. In these ways, women's labor becomes a subsidy for supply-side electricity reforms.

The costs of supply-side reforms are often compounded by the rising costs of energy and by the loss of government fuel subsidies.[34] Taken together, these reforms work to further marginalize rural populations in poverty where electrification requires costly infrastructure that investors are unwilling to take on given low expectations for a return of profit.[35] The gap between rural and urban electricity access is the greatest in sub-Saharan Africa (SSA), where Hall shows that 54 percent of households in urban areas have access versus 8.3 percent access in rural areas.[36] Though significant, the gap between rural and urban access is crosscut by race, class, and gender inequalities. For example, W. J. Annecke's research on the South African electricity sector notes: "The 46% of households that are not yet electrified are usually those housing poor, black women in rural areas, further marginalized as a result of their lack of access to electric power."[37] Additionally, David McDonald argues that, though connections have been made possible, millions of South Africans continue to live without electricity because they are unable to afford the service under cost-reflexive pricing schemes.[38] These findings suggest that increasing connections may work to bridge the rural/urban gap in service, but poor communities will continue to lack adequate access when economic efficiency is valued over social equity.

One of the primary arguments for the commodification and/or privatization of public services is that it will allow governments to save money. However, actual savings have been the exception rather than the rule. Such was the case in Buenos Aires when the International Finance Corporation (IFC) provided funding to distribution companies to reduce electricity theft by terminating "illegal" connections. The terminations resulted in lawsuits being brought against corporate distributors, which argued that privatization deprived people of basic services. The lawsuit ended with the government subsidizing the costs of hookups for the unserved populations.[39] As such, while the urban poor received electricity in Buenos Aires, it was the actions of the government—not the corporation—that ensured such access. As this case illustrates, government spending on energy has often increased rather than decreased, leaving fewer resources available for the provision of basic welfare services.[40] In another example from the health sector, Santa-Olaya Bernal and colleagues show budget cuts resulting from economic restructuring work to inhibit the provision of legalized access to abortion.[41] Though Mexican political leaders have signed on to statements that call for greater access to reproductive health care, they are able to sidestep this controversial issue by arguing that they lack adequate funding to materialize that mandate.

The Gender and Politics of "Community" Participation

The participatory approach to resource management coconstitutes a process of donor-driven decentralization of governance and has become the sine qua non for development agencies. Participation, it is argued, creates commitment to a project; ensures efficiency, accountability, and transparency, democratizing decision-making through bottom-up processes; and enables empowerment for women and marginalized groups.[42] The focus on decentralizing management, feminists hoped, would open the door for women to gain measures of control over natural resource management and, ostensibly, access to natural resources.[43] However, these hopes have not fleshed out in practice. Instead, feminist advocates and activists point out that women's relationships to water are essentialized according to a gendered division of labor, communities are conceptualized as homogeneous in their interests, and households are treated as a congruent unit of interests. Finally, there are also critiques of the meaningfulness of participation, which can vary greatly from "nominal" to "empowering," with direct consequences for how a project is structured and to what degree it meets the needs of all community members.[44]

Much of the development work on gender and water tends toward an essentialization of women's relationships to water and fails to trouble the socially constructed division of labor informing these roles.[45] In mainstream policy literature, women's uses of water are typically limited to their uses in the domestic sphere, including washing, cleaning, and reproductive work. The essentialization of women's uses of water casts their activities as predominantly rooted in their "natural" role as caretakers.[46] Taking for granted the idea that women primarily use water for domestic purposes fails to question the socially constructed division of labor. Ruth Meinzen-Dick and Margaret Zwarteveen provide a useful corrective, arguing that women's uses of water should not be seen as a product of their natural gender roles but as produced by a naturalization of gender inequality.[47] They ask if policymakers would observe different uses of water for women if there were structures in place that allowed such uses. The essentialization of women's uses of water is representative of narrowly construed resource management schemes. These abstractions make it easier to design a universalized approach, but the flattening out of difference forecloses the potential for these projects to produce meaningful changes in women's lives.

Treating the community as a homogeneous entity has serious consequences for the structure of a community-based group and the distribution of benefits. Without a nuanced approach to the community, privileged community members are more likely to become the primary contacts (referred to as "elite capture") for participatory projects, perpetuating and/or exacerbating "naturalized" inequalities.[48] For instance, in the Chhattis Mauja irrigation scheme in Nepal, a local woman leader volunteered to act as a village leader, called a *muktiyar*. Though she was given the position, she was forced to resign after five months because the villagers would not accept a woman in this position.[49] In this example, the leadership position was made available to women, but the project planners didn't account for male resistance to a woman in a leadership position. Beyond male/female gender inequalities, an intersectional approach further compels a consideration of relations between women. For example, Nandita Singh's study of village-level water management committees in rural India found that although the majority of women were vastly underrepresented at the meetings, upper-caste women were more likely to have their needs met because, unlike lower-caste women, their interests were represented by male family members.[50] The result was that in two different instances, hand pumps were located in places considered to be the province of upper-caste members. The lack of accountability for the poorest members means that the benefits of community-based projects tend to accrue to more powerful members in a given community, with gender being mediated by race/caste/class.

As with the water sector, energy sector projects treat communities and households as unitary in their goals and interests. As a UNESCAP (United Nations Economic and Social Commission for Asia and the Pacific) report argues, "Technologies and innovations that are actually targeted for women are based on perceptions and preferences of men."[51] Similarly, Annecke reports, even when the benefits of energy interventions are meant to accrue to women, the unequal status of women permits male community and household members to reap the benefits of those projects.[52] Margaret Skutsch and Elizabeth Cecelski add an intersectional dimension to this discussion by arguing that within groups of women, it is also necessary to give attention to the energy uses of various classes of women or women from different castes.[53] As Cecelski notes, the benefits of rural electrification programs tend to accrue to wealthier families, including, of course, women. In these ways, to homogenize groups of women, as mainstream development projects often do, is to miss opportunities to provide equitable services to those who need them most.

Community-based projects also operate at the household level, where, similar to homogenization at the community level, an assumed "congruency of interests" between men and women means that women's interests aren't adequately represented in the project.[54] Project planners are more likely to meet with male members of the household and are sometimes apt to not speak with women at all.[55] This model also assumes there is a "male breadwinner" in each family, which conceals a number of realities faced by women. In the agricultural sector, access to water is often dependent on ownership of property. However, many women are prohibited from land-ownership, which by extension prohibits them from owning the water sources (natural or constructed) on that land.[56] This, in turn, effectively erases the fact that women—as well as men—are also farmers, either by themselves or alongside husbands or children. Women are further marginalized when landownership determines the selection of participants in community-based agricultural groups, as was the case in a project designed to optimize the scarce water supply in Llullucha, Peru.[57] The project was organized by the Instituto de Manejo de Agua y Media Ambiente (IMA) (a government entity), which chose a participatory approach that engaged the local *comuneros*, a group of registered landowners and an all-male group. Through this focus, the IMA effectively excluded women from participation. The result was that women protested the irrigation system that didn't allow water to flow into the water holes that they used to care for livestock. As a consequence of women's protests, project planners were forced to alter their plans.[58] Similarly, in the energy sector, the disenfranchisement of women at the household level has contributed to the devaluation of women's labor expenditures and the neglect of women's energy needs.[59] For example, Joy Clancy and colleagues find that male control over household funds often means that investments are not made in technologies that would make women's tasks easier or safer.[60] As these examples make clear, energy policies are not gender-neutral, as is assumed by energy experts. The failure of these experts to include gendered analyses reverberates in the reprivatization of women's labor.

Finally, participation can also be problematically construed solely as economic exchange. This approach to participation reprivatizes women (and men) in the form of consumer-citizens whose participation consists of market transactions rather than meaningful democratic participation. For example, in the water sector in Mexico, José Esteban Castro argues, "the prevailing notion of user participation is mostly limited in practice to the expectation that users would become obedient customers who pay their water bills punctually."[61] O'Reilly similarly highlights the role that gender plays in the making of a modernized citizen-consumer by focusing on a water project that invoked modernization as a justification for women's empowerment through the commodification of water in Rajasthan, India. As argued by Kathleen O'Reilly, "The promotion of modern water by project staff ran parallel to a marketing of modern womanhood and consumerism coded as 'women's participation.'"[62] In these examples, the rhetoric of participation operates as a thin disguise for the imposition of commodified service delivery.

In each of these sectors—water, electricity, and health—the imbrications between gender and neoliberalism have produced perverse consequences that pay lip service to gender equality while advancing projects that undermine that goal. Women's workloads have increased through the removal of government subsidies, and they are reprivatized through participatory projects that fail to meet their needs but require their participation. Empowerment through participation is often a pretense that furthers project goals but conceals the fact that women actively negotiate access to resources in their everyday lives. An alternative approach to gendering resource management would be attentive to the practices that women already employ to gain access to resources. As argued by Bina Pradhan, alternative models should work to "find out how or in what ways women influence decisions even under conditions of structural subordination."[63] Rather than impose an empowerment agenda, we argue that alternative models would do well to seek out what Faranak Miraftab calls "invented spaces of participation," or those spaces "characterized by defiance that directly challenges the status quo."[64] Like Miraftab, we argue for attention to women's agency in the context of gender justice and imagining alternative futures—not in defending a patriarchal status quo or in the service of conservative social movements. Starting with women's transformative agential practices is a "bottom-up process" that builds on and broadens the agency that women already express. In the following sections, we review projects that recognize and build on women's agency, as opposed to projects that seek to *give* empowerment.

Gender Equity in Imagining Alternative Futures

The previous sections briefly reviewed feminist scholarship on neoliberalism and global restructuring, and privatization and commercialization in the water, health, and electricity sectors in the global South. The remainder of this chapter focuses on alternatives, taking up the central question of envisioning and enacting alternatives to privatization (and commercialization) that centralize gender equity and gender justice. Struggles against private incursions are galvanizing new social movements that join together the efforts of diverse communities. These movements draw on and build up processes of participatory democracy that compel state actors to take seriously their mandate to govern in a manner consistent with the needs of the people. In this way, processes of privatization and commercialization should also be regarded as processes of politicization.[65] Thus, as suggested earlier, engaging the perspectives and experiences of those most marginalized by capital provides a fuller understanding of how capital operates and points toward strategies of resistance that can fundamentally transform social inequalities from the ground up.

We have sought a variety of sources to inform our analysis of gendered alternatives, but locating sources that systematically review gendered alternatives has not been an easy exercise. While there is a growing body of literature that documents the rise of social movements against commercialization (most notably in regard to water and sanitation), there are far fewer resources that explicitly address the role of gender, particularly as it relates to race, nation, ethnicity, class, and/or caste. Many of the reports and articles we found give gendered concerns only a passing mention, noting that women are most affected by neoliberal policies but failing to explicate how they might become agents in the process of constructing alternatives. Many of the feminist analyses of gender in relation to the restructuring of health, water, and electricity center on critiques of processes associated with commercialization, not necessarily on creating alternatives. In most cases, we do not see women presented as agents and changemakers. Our work here pieces together the stories of resource management projects that include partnerships between community-based groups, NGOs, governments, and international organizations that have made specific efforts to confront inequalities based on gender, race/ethnicity, class/caste, and/or Indigenous identities.

Writing about empire in the neoliberal age, Arundhati Roy argues passionately that no act that confronts empire is too small.[66] She urges us to resist by identifying "its working parts, and dismantle them one by one. No target is too small. No victory is insignificant." It is in this very spirit that we craft our vision of gender justice in the context of neoliberalism, global restructuring, and privatization. Fundamental to this vision is the recognition that women have been key to late twentieth-century social movements—Indigenous, feminist, antiracist, anticolonial, environmental, labor, peasant, LGBT, and antiglobalization, creating and cross-pollinating more just, democratic, and sustainable economic values, practices, and institutions that many see as the basis of a new "solidarity economy."[67] Feminist economists have long argued that the values of a solidarity economy—cooperation, equity in all its dimensions, economic democracy, local and community control, and sustainability—are commensurate with global struggles for gender justice.[68] While place-based struggles and contextual approaches to women's resistance to privatization and commercialization are key to understanding larger struggles for gendered economic justice, it is the universal principles embodied in the right to equity and dignity in varied economic practices, the right to clean, sanitary, and sustainable living arrangements, the right to develop relationships and households based on autonomous sexual choices, the right bear children or not, and even the right to leisure for working-class/poor women that constitute the broad parameters of our vision of gender justice. Thus, documenting forms of resistance, and evidence of alternative visions in the terms we have laid out in this chapter, is itself an important contribution. Our hope is that activists, scholars, advocates, and practitioners will take up the tactics and strategies outlined below in pursuit of this vision of gender equity and more just and democratic systems of governance.

*Governance Practice, Institutional
Settings, and Women's Agency*

From the Chipko Movement to protect the forests in northern India to Las Madres del Plaza de Mayo in Argentina to the Cochabamba Water Wars, women have been a formidable source of power and protest, but women have also seen their victories usurped as protest movements take on formalized structures.[69] Maxine Molyneux's analysis of "women's emancipation" as it was taken up by the Sandinista government after the Nicaraguan Revolution provides insight into the processes that give rise to the subordination of women's interests.[70] Molyneux distinguishes between "practical gender interests" and "strategic gender interests." Practical gender interests ease the hardships for women struggling under conditions of poverty but do not subvert the systems of inequality that perpetuate their subordination. Challenging those systems requires the development of strategic gender interests, those based on an "analysis of women's subordination and from the formulation of an alternative, more satisfactory set of arrangements to those which exist." Thus, strategic gender interests work toward undoing gendered divisions of labor, male violence, and unequal political representation.

In many ways, commitments to gender and participation have been used as a charitable front for profitable endeavors. The necessary focus on women's experiences has been overlooked in the process of developing "toolboxes" of gender mainstreaming techniques designed to expedite and streamline the process of creating new markets for commercialized water, sanitation, health, and electricity services, and although there are clear critiques of the role of international financial institutions (IFIs), the analysis is a bit murkier in regard to the work of the UN bodies and the international NGOs that have taken shape around issues of gender inequality. Speaking of the gendered health initiatives emerging through global platforms, such as the United Nations International Conference on Population and Development (ICPD), Harcourt notes the complexities of women's engagement with international bodies: "While such global processes open up new spaces for women's solidarity and network building with the new communication technologies and new economic resources, it is also pushing women into new forms of poverty."[71] Broad policy commitments do not easily lend themselves to concrete, practical actions, and are made more tenuous by the predictable tensions between stated interests in gender equality, programmatic commitments to a market-based system of service provision, and (in the case of health care in particular) the rising power of fundamentalist religious authorities.[72] Harcourt's observation suggests that meaningful change does not begin at the top but must be generated from the ground up, at local levels of experience and organizing.

Beyond protest and critique, people's movements are beginning to construct alternative practices and paradigms for access to and management of resources. The struggles over access to water, health, and electricity are also struggles for creating inclusive models of democratic governance that empower people.[73] The question for us is how and to what extent women and/or woman-based groups have been or can be part of the process of imagining and creating alternatives. Though it is certainly the case that community-managed resources are more accountable to the needs of people, it is also the case that gender, class/caste, religious, and racial/ethnic relations inform processes at the community level. Nina Laurie's analysis of the roles of women in the Cochabamba Water Wars illustrates the contradictory gender relations embedded in this iconic struggle.[74] Laurie found that while women were active members of the Cochabamba protests, they were also solely responsible for the reproductive work that was necessary to maintain the protests—cooking, providing water, and attending to families. Thus, while women were centrally involved in the water wars, gendered ideologies and expectations may remain unchanged.

Opening Doors: Rethinking Women's Participation and Decision-Making

The challenge is how to open doors, doors and not windows, doors and hopefully big doors so we can take over decision-making spaces. That doesn't mean just being present; I am tired of that kind of tokenism in which women leaders are delegated to the same domestic role within the board of directors in the water organization as in the homes. It's not enough to say that women hold a leadership position. We must ask: what is the quality of this post or what kinds of decisions are they allowed to make? —ANA ELLA GÓMEZ, "A New Definition of Hope"

Ana Ella Gómez calls attention to the necessity of an approach to gendering alternative movements that goes beyond formal statements and participatory quotas, beyond visibility to the power to make decisions. The larger question here is how to move from the politics of representation to a politics of equity and justice. We have argued that gendered assumptions are embedded in systems and institutions, naturalized into discourses, practices, and policies that structure access and resource management and give shape to the presumed roles and alleged capabilities of women that are deeply ingrained in local, state, national, and international contexts. Because gender is so integral to these processes, gender inequalities cannot be undone by simply ensuring that women gain numerical parity with men. Instead, a feminist approach is one that challenges gender inequalities in a way that builds on and develops women's agency.[75] The examples we review take steps not merely to bring women to the table but to enhance the power they have over decisions that affect their lives.

Bringing women to the table in meaningful ways has been a major challenge for woman-based groups and gender advocates. A particularly trenchant issue has been the resistance of male community members to the increased public presence of women. There are, however, examples of women's groups and project teams that have effectively stifled male resistance and even induced male appreciation for women's active roles in resource management. The work of the Self-Employed Women's Association (SEWA) in India has been invaluable in this respect. The struggles over women's meaningful participation were brought into sharp relief through SEWA's "Women, Water and Work" campaign, which later became the "Millennium Water Campaign." The campaign covers eleven districts in five hundred villages and seeks to bring women into water projects as active participants in the locally operated water boards and committees. Women were initially hesitant to serve on these boards, and male villagers were even more resistant. As described by Smita Mishra Panda, "[Men] were critical of women entering the public domain on this issue, and several went so far as to say they would not drink water from a source created by women. Many threatened not to work on water harvesting structures that would be managed by women. Some men openly said women would make financial blunders and force them to mortgage their lands (as all land titles are in men's names) to repay their debts."[76] Regarding itself as a "militant" organization, SEWA continued to facilitate the inclusion of women on water user committees despite this resistance. SEWA's persistence worked to increase women's agency in the water project but also within communities and homes. As Panda reports, the spheres of activities that women engage in have broadened to include new woman-based institutions with strong links to governance structures.

Male resistance to women's roles in public spaces isn't unique to SEWA's experience, but in some cases it has been so strong as to require alternative sites for women's participation. Such was the case in a community-based water management committee in the Ghogha region of Gujarat, India, where a women's "self-help group" (SHG) was created. Sara Ahmed looks at one example of an SHG in the Ghogha region that was formed by Utthan, a local NGO that facilitates the participation of local communities in the construction and maintenance of water supply systems.[77] The Utthan project facilitators explicitly sought to increase the role of women in decision-making realms but found that male resistance was quite formidable. In the village of Neswad, women reported that male attendees would complain to their husbands about their wives' participation, thus acting as a form of social control on women's participation. Utthan opted to form an SHG, which, Ahmed asserts, "provides a 'safe' place for women to voice their priorities and articulate their opinions."[78] In this case, the SHG operated as a site for women to voice their concerns and a stage from which to launch concerted actions that benefited women in particular, and the community in general.

A Rural Energy Development Program (REDP) in Nepal, a joint effort between the Nepalese government and United Nations Development Programme (UNDP), also wanted to increase the role of women but recognized that specific efforts would need to be made to sensitize men to women's increased presence in the public arena. The project focused on creating community organizations (COs) that formed the basis for the functional groups, which are the decision-making bodies in regard to community energy needs. The REDP project considered it important to organize gender-differentiated COs in order to provide a space for women to voice their concerns, noting that "in mixed groups, women only tend to nod their heads in unison rather than genuinely participate in discussions and decisions."[79] Woman-only COs are drawn into decision-making processes through the functional groups, which require membership of both male and female COs. The results of this project suggest that women have made gains beyond greater access to energy sources. In several districts, women manage the micro hydro schemes, and in some cases husbands watched the children while their wives participated in the training to become managers. While gains appear to have been made through this project, the focus on gender is not met with a necessary focus on the role of caste in the villages where, as the report notes, caste hierarchies exist. It isn't clear how or if the project conceptualized gender in relation to class/caste in this project.

In some cases, women have organized themselves in attempts to fill the gaps in service left by unresponsive governments. In Northeast Brazil, a group of women began to notice that the Olho d'Agua River, located in Santa Cruz da Baixa Verde, was drying up, largely due to the effects of large-scale irrigation projects. The river was a lifeline to the women who made their homes along its banks. The Rural Women Workers Movement of Sertao Central (MMTR) and the Rural Workers Labour Union (STR), a municipal-level union, began to organize themselves and the community in order to save the river from "dying."[80] At the time of Adelia de Melo Branco and Vanete Almeida's writing about the project, it was in its initial stages but included plans to contact each of the families affected as a mobilization strategy, conduct workshops with all members of the community with the assistance of gender and environmental experts, and involve local authorities in the project once a broad-based coalition had been formed. Though the project began through the efforts of women, men also became involved in the activities, believing that saving the river will contribute to the sustainability of the community. In 2002, the project planners also began to make alliances with the Federation of Agricultural Workers (FETAPE), a state-level union organization. This project illustrates the process of women forming activist groups at the community level while also making strides to connect to broader political goals and organizations. This strategy allows community groups to make connections to large-scale political processes through a bottom-up process of collective action.

While beginning with women's everyday experiences is necessary to the process of creating alternatives that are accountable to women, the continued marginalization of women's interests compels partnerships with groups and organizations outside of the local context in order to obtain funding, access to media, and technical assistance. Gender budgeting advocates, for example, take this approach to organizing for women's interests. Gender budgeting initiatives (GBIs) draw from the contestatory framework of Latin American public budgeting (PB) programs but build on them by denaturalizing the assumed gender neutrality of the budgeting process. PB is a model of economic governance that devolves power over financial decision-making to local levels of governance where communities and civic groups engage in setting budget priorities and overseeing expenditures. PB experiments began at the municipal level through the work of community leaders and the Brazilian Democratic Movement (MDB) in São Paulo and Santa Catarina within the context of an authoritarian Brazilian government.[81] In this context, facilitating the participation of the people served to put pressure on an unresponsive government and worked to create systems of governance that were responsive to the needs of people. PB thus emerged as a challenge to the absolute power of strong, centralized governments, and these early examples set the stage for future attempts at redressing unequal and unaccountable government budgets. While the value of PB has surely been demonstrated in the Latin American context, the assumption that budgets are gender-neutral instruments has largely remained in place in those initiatives.[82]

Since the mid-1980s, a series of budget initiatives have been launched in over sixty countries that extend the critical and participatory elements of PB beyond the assumed gender neutrality of conventional budgeting practices.[83] These initiatives are models of collective action that include the efforts of international organizations; national, state, and local governments; and NGOs working at the grassroots level. Gender budgeting facilitates an analysis of budgets at multiple levels of governance but can also be used to analyze the spending priorities of nongovernmental entities.[84] The implementation of gender budgeting initiatives at local levels of governance has particular relevance because decentralization has meant that public services are often provided at these local levels.[85] In regard to creating alternatives, gender budgeting can be used to pressure local governments to be accountable to agreements that have been made at the international level. For example, Prabha Khosla notes that feminist organizations in Mexico have made use of gender budgeting to illustrate the gaps created by unfunded mandates made by Mexican authorities through the ICPD.[86] In this way, gender budgets deal "directly with the responsibility of governments to international commitments to women, namely equality in the distribution, access, and funding of public resources."[87] The application of gender budgeting processes to groups and organizations working to create alternatives can work to ensure that women's needs are met and that women's labor is properly accounted for by alternative systems.

What seems evident from this review is the gap between international agreements on women's equality and national action on these agreements. However, gender justice activists continue to utilize these agreements in their work. The new (as of 2010) UN entity, UN Women, was created to address this precise gap, to pressure nation-states to address questions of gender equity in economic, political, social, and cultural arenas. What is also obvious is the existence of male resistance and patriarchal cultures at all levels in women's struggles for democratic and just alternatives. These structural issues and institutional cultures need to be addressed directly in imagining and enacting alternatives. Alternatives that are gender sensitive, that centralize women's experiences in the origin of the project, that define women's roles as leaders and decision-makers and defend this position through the life of the project are likely to be more effective than projects that are not attentive to these issues. Additionally, alternatives that provide women with economic assistance and security (as SEWA does), and those that provide women with skills, knowledge, and political education to mobilize their strategic interests are likely to have the most lasting impact in terms of gender justice.

Democratizing Knowledge: Critical Literacy and Alternative Pedagogies

At the heart of creating alternatives that are responsive to issues of equity and access for women is the question of knowledge production. How do we come to know what the best arrangements are for all women? Given that neoliberal policies assume a "generic and oppressed" third world woman, the task for feminist research is to excavate the ideological basis of these assumptions and privilege the lived realities that are concealed by them. A productive and sustainable approach to gendering alternatives compels us to recognize that "knowledge *is* produced by activist and community-based political work—that some knowledge can *only emerge within these contexts and locations*."[88] This approach thus addresses the question of what gets to count as knowledge and who counts as knowledgeable, and suggests a reprioritization of subaltern knowledges and experiences.

Mainstream development projects have focused their efforts on training communities and groups in the methods of resource management developed by academics and practitioners situated in the global North. This approach often valorizes "Northern-centric" models of resource management, obscures the biases with which development practice operates, "evades the question of whether 'modernity' is desirable . . . [and] neglects the issue of local, subjugated knowledges."[89] Whereas mainstream development projects assume an approach that is "universally rational and efficient," Indigenous approaches are sensitive to local environmental conditions and have created complex modes of distribution that can accommodate the needs of diverse constituents.[90] Paul Trawick argues a similar point in his analysis of the problems associated with the privatization of water systems in Peru, where water laws were based on "rational" use models that "failed to achieve an equitable and efficient distribution of the resource."[91] By contrast, he argues, the models that have been employed in the Andean region since precolonial times are models that are attentive to the local geographic terrain and the equity concerns that exist in the region. While we need to be careful to not romanticize the "equitable community," learning about Indigenous methods of resource management provides a means of acquiring cultural competence in structuring alternatives.

Practitioners working in the health care field have similarly critiqued the top-down approach to knowledge production. Alternative approaches to health care have, in some cases, sought to remedy this situation in order to build sustainable systems of delivery that make sense for the communities in which they work. The Zimbabwean coalition Community Working Group on Health (CWGH) is an example of a health research, education, and advocacy project that works to undo the "one-way transfer of knowledge from technocrats to the community" in order to make health education more relevant to the local context.[92] Its work takes on the gender neutrality of "traditional" (meaning technocratic, top-down) information, education, and communication (IEC) approaches to HIV/AIDS education and awareness that do not address the "unequal gender power relations, and notions of masculinity and femininity that shape expectations [and] . . . erode women's and girls' ability to negotiate safe sex, make informed choices regarding reproduction, and enjoy control over their bodies."[93] By contrast, the CWGH works extensively with men and women to bring issues of sex and sexuality to the fore in order to adequately address issues of power and inequality between men and women that endanger women's sexual health, freedom, and choice.

The CWGH also trains community members in the process of collecting local data that can then be used to advocate for themselves in the policy arena. It is the belief of the CWGH that information generated by the community is more likely to be credible to the community, and this facilitates the advocacy efforts of the communities it works with. This is similar to the goal of the AMANITARE (African Partnership for Sexual and Reproductive Health and Rights of Women and Girls) coalition in Africa, which works to "create a knowledgeable constituency that would act as a pressure group to influence health and legal professionals, political institutions and society at large."[94] The CWGH, in fact, takes the research process one step further to include "report back sessions." During these sessions, the results of the research are discussed with community members, and resolutions may be made to address the concerns that arise in the project. For example, after hearing the stories of several women who made use of dangerous methods for abortion, and listening to the reasons why they would seek an abortion, one community opted to campaign for the full legalization of abortion. These examples of efforts anchored in women's everyday lives and struggles provide models for the development of alternatives that embody women's strategic interests, focusing as they do on education, accountability, and women's leadership.

Similar efforts have been made by gender budget advocates who call attention and create resistance to the gendered impacts of macroeconomic policies related to trade, investment debt repayments, and market liberalization, policies largely regarded as gender-neutral and/or policies that have been depoliticized by neoliberalism.[95] One such initiative is the Gender and Economic Reforms in Africa (GERA) program. GERA began in 1996 and consists of African women researchers, advocates, and activists who are particularly concerned with extending gendered analyses of budgets beyond national budgetary processes. GERA is also concerned, however, with the process of knowledge production and thus works toward bringing women into the research process with the understanding that "research is an important means of empowering women and marginalised groups."[96] Importantly, GERA's work moves beyond empowerment as the appropriation of women's experiences to coordinating women's voices and experiences into a cohesive source of opposition: "GERA advocates for African gender researchers and activists to re-claim the concept of gender mainstreaming, so that it plays the role of a political tool for women's empowerment, instead of a technical device for legitimising inequitable trade and economic policies."[97] The GERA approach to reclaiming gender mainstreaming is to organize a pan-African network of active and engaged activists, researchers, policymakers, and scholars who can work together to transform economic policies and processes.

Gendering alternative, democratic structures of governance and resource management demands that alternative methods of presenting and sharing information also be developed. In an innovative example, a "hand pump technology" project in rural Costa Rica produced educational materials that explicitly strove to destabilize gender binaries.[98] The educational materials consisted of manuals that illustrated the process of building and maintaining hand pumps. In the manuals, women and men were each pictured in nontraditional gender roles (i.e., women were installing hand pumps and men were caring for children), there was equal male/female representation throughout the manual, and gender-neutral language was also used. In addition to the strategic use of gendered images, the manuals were also created in a manner that allowed people who could not read to follow the steps necessary for building and repairing the hand pumps.[99]

In this way, the relatively simple task of producing educational materials becomes an important route to destabilizing gender binaries and educational hierarchies. Similarly, the South African Women's Budget Initiative (WBI) has employed strategies to democratize participation in gender budgeting exercises. What these examples show is that while resource and budget management has been construed as the realm of educated bureaucrats, these modes of management have worked to exclude laypersons from active participation in the legal and economic structures that affect their lives. But activist groups are deconstructing the mantle of bureaucratic authority that has stifled the participation of citizens. Such is the case in Ecuador, where a coalition group of activists are in the process of drafting a new constitution: "What's been really important is that this new constitution has been created by a group of citizens, environmentalists, women, economists, architects, farmers, and social leaders. We've broken with the notion that the constitution is only for lawyers, only for constitutionalists."[100] For those groups that have sought to democratize resource management, knowledge has to be created by all and extended to all.

In all sectors a lack of gender-disaggregated data has been perhaps the greatest barrier to designing policies that are responsive to women's needs. This is true at both the macro and micro levels of policymaking. As such, feminist researchers have sought new methods of data collection that work toward illuminating women's contributions. At the micro level, GBIs work to make visible women's unpaid labor in the home and in the community, to enumerate the extent to which their unpaid labor bolsters economies, and to quantify the impacts on women of the reductions in public services.[101] Debbie Budlender and colleagues have identified an approach to gender budgeting that allows for data collection at the micro level in order to fill the gaps created by the neglect of women's work in national indicators called the Community Based Monitoring System (CBMS).[102] The CBMS approach facilitates the collection of disaggregated data at the level of the community and household, and is conducted at the lowest administrative level of governance in order to provide the most detailed information to local-level government planners. The value of this approach is that it covers a relatively small area but captures data and information that are neglected by state and national surveys. In regard to gender budgeting, the CBMS approach facilitates a data-backed discussion of the productive and economic value of women's unpaid labor.

While the CBMS approach does not appear to directly draw women into the process of negotiating budgetary priorities, a method identified as the interpretive focus group (IFG) may assist in that process. The IFG was developed by Lisa Dodson and colleagues as a means of bridging the "interpretive" gap between researchers and participants of differing social locations and is a model of practice drawn from feminist participatory action research (FPAR).[103] Though the CBMS approach strives to make visible the economic contributions of women's unpaid labor, the gap between researcher and participant may work against the process. The IFG provides a means of overcoming this distance by involving participants in the analysis of their responses. Dodson and colleagues argue that IFGs have two central purposes: First, they include participants in the research process through the final stage; second, they ensure the accuracy and appropriateness of the researchers' evaluation of the data.[104] Thus, the CBMS approach in tandem with the IFG provides a methodological approach to acquiring gender-sensitive data that are also accountable to the differences between women. To further the relationships between women, the findings from the CBMS as analyzed through the IFG may also be shared among various groups of women in a process of knowledge sharing. These methods of research provide a model for building alternatives that are grounded in the needs of those groups that are marginalized by neoliberal development policy and discourse. They also work to train these groups in the process of advocating for what they want and need. In this way, alternative research practices create alternative models of citizenship and action that are necessary for building accountability into alternative models of resource management.

The value of knowledge sharing for the creation of alternatives is that it works to make connections across communities whether those communities are geographic or social. These knowledge-sharing exercises permit the cross-fertilization of understanding, both in terms of similarities of struggle but also in terms of strategies for resistance. Again, SEWA's "Women, Water and Work" campaign serves an instructive purpose here. The campaign included groups and organizations from eleven districts and five hundred villages, and the vastness of the project meant that information sharing was an important part of the overall success of the program. To facilitate this part of the project, SEWA organized monthly information meetings that were held in selected villages where the successful initiatives had occurred. As noted by Panda: "This is essentially a lateral learning process between members providing them with an opportunity to learn from each other as well as visit different parts of the state to get a first-hand knowledge of how water problems have been tackled by other women. Thus, this is not only an exposure visit meant to build capacities of women, but also an empowering experience."[105] We suggest that projects that frame gender equity as an epistemological project, in terms of the transformation of practices and institutions, and as lived culture, are the most successful in addressing women's strategic interests. It is this framework of envisioning alternatives that emerges in the conceptualization of place-based struggles in the discussion that follows.

Gender Justice and Place-Based Struggles

Our objective, even if it is unconscious, is to reactivate the processes of participation, to re-appropriate in our own hands our own resources of our own communities, contexts, territories: From the little, without the big. Related to "the big," related to the general themes, to grand values, grand issues, universal struggles, but, within the dynamics of the small, of the quotidian. —INTERVIEW, PORTE ALEGRE, 2003, quoted in Michal Osterweil, "Place-Based Globalism"

The critique of the managerial and bureaucratized development apparatus, and of the NGOization of the women's movement discussed earlier, led to a distancing by some women's rights scholars and activists from the UN establishment. As many feminist activists have become disillusioned with the UN system, they have moved to a more effective, transformative gender justice strategy of place-based politics.[106] This strategy grows organically out of women's struggles as they materialize in and through particular sites. To bring together these collective struggles under a framework that allows for cross-comparison and analysis, Wendy Harcourt and Arturo Escobar developed the Women and the Politics of Place (WPP) framework.[107] The WPP framework argues that the place-based practices of women involved in social justice struggles invoke related transformations around the body (e.g., women's movements that involve sexual, productive, and reproductive rights), the environment (ecological and environmental justice movements), and the economy (social and economic justice movements). In other words, the WPP framework makes capacious use of "place." It refers not only to place as territorially based but also to place as a site of struggle for gender justice, particularly in relation to women's bodies, their environments, and their economic activities. Importantly, place is also attentive to difference, diversity, and specificity in relation to these struggles as well to larger, global processes. It is to the imbrications between global processes and the politics of place that we now turn.

Placed-based movements and activism should not be regarded as place-bound.[108] Instead, the framework suggests that places act as prisms that refract global economic and governance structures, bending and shaping them in ways that make sense within the politics of particular sites and in different communities, what Michal Osterweil calls a "place-based globalism."[109] This is not to suggest that global processes exact a determined force on the ground. Rather, it is a recognition that global processes become part of the terrain on which women struggle, and this perspective compels us to see the ways that women are politicized and act through these changes. The defense of one's right to survive in the face of the overwhelming valorization of markets compels new strategies and modes of resistance that challenge left political organizing as well as hegemonic development discourses and practices and create new modes of globalized struggle. Recognizing the power of place privileges local and translocal modes of resistance to totalizing theories of global processes and seeks to valorize those movements. As sites where global processes are materialized, the analytical value of a place-based framework lies in thinking through place as a unit of analysis.

The pertinence of a place-based framework is borne out by the scholarship on antiprivatization water movements and the creation of alternatives to privatization, which can be read as place-based, economic justice struggles—what others have called "territory based" or livelihood struggles.[110] For instance, Danilo Urea, a Colombian, says that water struggles lead to a reappropriation not just of water sources but also their territories: "We are told that 'territory' means the land, but really territory means the construction of a life profoundly rooted in our natural heritage. The river, the watershed, the mountain, all this forms part of what we mean by territory, and all of it is profoundly linked to culture. So, for our communities, organizations, and movements in Latin America, the defense of territory is fundamental; protecting territory is protecting culture, and water runs through both."[111] Similarly, Susan Spronk discusses territorially based organizations versus class-based organizations in antiprivatization struggles in Bolivia, where membership is based on participation in daily struggles and the focus is on living conditions and neighborhood issues, not workers' rights.[112] All the preceding are examples of struggles that grow out of lived realities, that draw on Indigenous knowledges and participatory decision-making in the context of larger struggles for equity and democracy.

As *Changing the Flow: Report on Water Movements in Latin America* illustrates, the recent water wars engaged in place-based local and regional movements, leading to a new vision of water democracy based on principles of equity and access in resource management; exchange in technical and Indigenous knowledges across linguistic, cultural, and national borders; ecological and environmental sustainability; and community participation based on reciprocity and collective and inclusive recognition. Women are centrally involved in these struggles, although they tend to not be visible in leadership positions. As Marcella Olivera from Red Vida (Bolivia) states: "It is true that the role of women is more invisible but that doesn't signify that it is less important in the element of water. Red Vida is a network propelled by women. It's a network where there's a diversity of organizations, everything from unions to non-profit organizations to grassroots organizations, but women are the driving force. I think it's rich that women have appropriated the defense of water. On our continent, at least, the face of the movement is the face of a woman."[113] Envisioning alternatives to privatization that address questions of gender equity necessitates attentiveness to the ways in which women have organized around their own practical and strategic gender interests.

This model contrasts sharply with the formal leadership structure and official platforms generated by older forms of internationalism that required a centralized strategy of action detached from the specificities of place and gendered realities; it suggests the need to shift to a model of organization embedded in what Dianne Rocheleau describes as "rooted networks" of people involved in place-based politics anchored in vertical (class/race/gender hierarchies) and horizontal (cross-national/cultural/linguistic borders) resistance networks.[114] These rooted networks signify a place-based globalism that Osterweil argues "is not simply a tactical or technological perspective for effectively reaching the global scale; it also constitutes an ethico-political vision, a basis for revisioning political practice at a global scale without succumbing to a totalizing or universalizing approach that ignores or negates difference and specificity."[115] Using the WPP framework of place-based globalism or the notion of rooted networks of people involved in antiprivatization struggles allows us to be attentive to gender in all the ways that we argued earlier constitute a materialist project: as knowledge/ideological frames, as institutional practices, and as lived culture. This feminist framing reorients our theoretical and methodological lenses, allowing us to *see* women and to centralize their/our everyday lives so that the prisms through which we understand global economic processes are gendered.

What these cases illustrate is a move away from coalitions based on homogenized identity politics to coalitions rooted in place-based struggles that kaleidoscope difference and diversity into powerful social justice movements. This is illustrated by Brazil's National Environmental Sanitation Front, which brought together unions, public municipal sanitation workers, neighborhood committees, and peasants, an entire cross-class/gender/race coalition in defense of water.[116] Similarly, in Ecuador, the constitutional "Human Right to Water" was written by a group of "citizens, environmentalists, women, economists, architects, farmers, and social leaders."[117] When we look specifically at the gendered aspects of place-based organizing, we can see a critique of the domestication of women in stereotypically gendered ways through the commodification of water, electricity, and health and the reconstitution of a public/private divide. In contrast, we argue that the politics of place offers a way to rethink and reconfigure alternatives that are accountable to women's struggles in access to and control over municipal services. Our approach centralizes the agency that women express in their everyday lives, which are not usually lived through the public/private binary that is assumed in neoliberal policies and practices. The structure of alternatives that we argue for would recognize and build on the agency that women enact through practices of survival and resistance, and that often occur in places that are neither wholly public nor wholly private. Countering the re-privatization of women, then, calls for an imagining of new publics that work against the neoliberal model of atomizing resource management along the lines of a public/private divide, and through which women are able to exert autonomy and influence. Alternatives cannot be just technical projects; they must also be projects aimed at creating transformative publics.

Postscript: Toward Gender Equity Projects in Alternatives to Privatization

As privatized and commercialized systems of service delivery fail to deliver on their promise of increased access, a new moment is opened up that is ripe for antiprivatization activists. The crisis of global capital is a moment of opportunity for its critics. Imagining and enacting alternatives that do not re-create race/class/caste/gender/Indigenous inequalities means that women from marginalized groups must be at the center of analysis. This approach makes use of the framework of WPP to understand women's livelihood strategies. This is an epistemological project that seeks a nuanced understanding of women's practices of accessing health, water, and electricity services. This approach is open to traditional research methods so long as feminist methodological concerns shape the research process. In a very general sense, feminist researchers engage strategies that "excavate" women's experiences. This process of excavation is one that strives to "elicit accounts and produce descriptions . . . of practice and thought that are part of female consciousness but left out of dominant interpretive frames."[118] Thus, it requires an approach that moves away from generalizations to specific accounts of the social divisions that mediate structures of access and distribution.

Concretely, there must be a commitment to including women in numbers that are either equal to or greater than those for men. Beyond numerical parity, however, there must be a commitment to advancing women's agency within these groups. We suggest the inclusion of a gender justice advocate as part of the project team who can mediate discussions in favor of women's active participation, someone who is willing to do the difficult work of redistributing power within male-dominated groups. There is also a need to accurately account for women's labor contributions in the health, water, and electricity sectors. One means of accounting for women's unaccounted-for activities is to employ a time-use study that is attentive to women's work in the household as well as their income generating activities. In a similar approach, Diane Elson argues for analyses of "waterpoints" that can illuminate the patterns of water usage by particular women.[119] Time-use or waterpoint studies can work to illustrate the analytical value of a place-based approach by employing these methods in multiple settings in order to empirically understand the similarities and differences of women's lives in different contexts. More generally, seeking alternatives that are accountable to gendered inequalities requires coalitions with women's groups—the "invented spaces" of participation that emerge organically in response to threats to women's lives. Engaging with women and women's groups at multiple levels of social hierarchies entails a commitment to producing empirical studies of their activities, their goals, and their modes of resource use and management. We are advocating for a bottom-up process that recognizes and seeks to augment women's agency in order to create alternatives that are accountable to multiple constituencies. These are only a handful of options that may be employed for those seeking to document or conduct new studies on gendered alternatives to privatization. Given the lack of attention to women in resource management, the possibilities are virtually endless.

To conclude, this chapter suggests that women's experiences, specifically the experiences of women who have been reprivatized through the commodification of municipal services, should be the most basic unit of analysis when thinking through questions of equity and access in regard to alternatives. This involves a commitment of energy and resources to gain a deep understanding of the community that is intended to benefit from the alternative service, including attention to the relevant identity categories such as class/caste composition, wealth distribution (measured in local terms, i.e., land, income, etc.), educational levels and disparities (by wealth and gender), gender composition, religious orientations, and racial/ethnic divisions. We have argued that in terms of gender justice, alternatives to privatization and commercialization cannot be narrowly circumscribed but must be envisioned as part of a larger struggle for women's rights and economic and social justice. Women cannot be treated as a "special interest" group—economic gender justice and nonprivate service delivery systems are a core aspect of a larger anticapitalist struggle and a universal vision for equity and freedom. Taking women's interests as central to building alternatives requires us to move beyond the liberal frame of "gender mainstreaming" and the neoliberal frame of "women's empowerment" to an approach that recognizes and builds on women's agency. This shift begins in the lives of women, learns from their perspective, and formulates policies that are attentive to local, place-based struggles as they exist within structures of privilege, power, and inequality.

Notes

This chapter was originally published as "Gendering Justice, Building Alternative Futures," with Sarah Miraglia, in *Alternatives to Privatization: Public Options for Essential Services in the Global South*, ed. David A. McDonald and Greg Ruiters (Routledge, 2012).

Many thanks to Amanda Wilson for getting us started with an initial bibliography on the work of MSP on gender and alternatives to privatization, and to David MacDonald and Gregg Ruiters for useful and productive feedback on this chapter.
  1 Mohanty, "Under Western Eyes"; Davis, *Violence Against Women*; Moraga and Anzaldúa, *This Bridge Called My Back*; Jayawardena, *White Woman's Other Burden*.
  2 Beckman, "Eighth Encuentro."
  3 On structures of entitlements, see Elson, "Gender Awareness in Modeling Structural Adjustment."
  4 See Samson, "Producing Privatization," for an analysis of the feminization and racialization of street-cleaning work in Johannesburg, South Africa.
  5 Marchand and Runyan, *Gender and Global Restructuring*; Sangtin Writers, *Playing with Fire*; Ahlers and Zwarteveen, "Water Question in Feminism."
  6 Harcourt and Escobar, *Women and the Politics of Place*.
  7 Mohanty, *Feminism Without Borders*.
  8 Fine and Hall, "Terrains of Neoliberalism," 66.
  9 Alexander and Mohanty, *Feminist Genealogies, Colonial Legacies, Democratic Futures*, xvii.
  10 Sen, "Gender, Markets and States," 821.
  11 Mies, *Patriarchy and Accumulation on a World Scale*.

12 Matthaei, *Economic History of Women in America.*

13 Marchand and Runyan, *Gender and Global Restructuring.*

14 Babb, "After the Revolution."

15 Benería, "Structural Adjustment Policies."

16 Pitkin and Bedoya, "Women's Multiple Roles in Economic Crisis," 47.

17 Sen and Grown, *Development, Crises, and Alternative Visions*; Members of the Feminist Initiative of Cartagena, "In Search of an Alternative Development Paradigm."

18 Harcourt, "Global Women's Rights Movement."

19 Panda, "Mainstreaming Gender in Water Management"; Manase et al., "Integrated Water Resources Management."

20 Panda, "Mainstreaming Gender in Water Management."

21 Mukhopadhyay, "Mainstreaming Gender."

22 Subrahmanian, "Making Sense of Gender," 89.

23 Mukhopadhyay, "Mainstreaming Gender," 100.

24 Cleaver, "Choice, Complexity, and Change," 294.

25 Aguilar, "Water as a Source of Equity." This is what Elson, in "Gender Awareness in Modeling Structural Adjustment," refers to as the "cash and committee" approach.

26 Roberts, "Privatizing Social Reproduction."

27 Katz, "On the Grounds of Globalization."

28 Nanda, "Gender Dimensions of User Fees."

29 Brown, "Unequal Burden."

30 Clancy et al., "Gender-Energy-Poverty Nexus"; Dutta, "Mainstreaming Gender in Energy Planning and Policies."

31 Batliwala and Reddy, "Energy for Women"; Clancy et al., "Gender-Energy-Poverty Nexus."

32 Holdren and Smith, "Energy, the Environment, and Health"; Reddy et al., "Energy and Social Issues."

33 Cecelski, "Enabling Equitable Access to Rural Electrification," 18.

34 Clancy et al., "Gender-Energy-Poverty Nexus."

35 Zomers, "Challenge of Rural Electrification."

36 D. Hall, "Energy Privatization and Reform in East Africa."

37 Annecke, "Still in the Shadows," 291.

38 McDonald, "Electric Capitalism."

39 World Resources Institute, *Power Politics.*

40 Bayliss, *Privatization of Electricity Distribution.*

41 Bernal et al., "Effects of Globalization."

42 Beall, "Decentralizing Government and Decentering Gender"; Resurreccion et al., "Officializing Strategies."

43 Meinzen-Dick and Zwarteveen, "Gendered Participation in Water Management."

44 Agarwal, "Participatory Exclusions, Community Forestry, and Gender."

45 Sultana, "Water Resources Management"; Meinzen-Dick and Zwarteveen, "Gendered Participation in Water Management."

46 Cleaver, "Analyzing Gender Roles," 61.

47 Meinzen-Dick and Zwarteveen, "Gendered Participation in Water Management."

48 Sultana, "Water Resources Management"; van Koppen, "Water Rights"; Karim, "Gendered Social Institutions"; Boelens and Zwarteveen, "Andean Water Reforms"; Resurreccion et al., "Officializing Strategies."

49 IFAD, "Gender and Water."

50 Singh, "Women's Participation in Local Water Governance."

51 Dutta, "Mainstreaming Gender in Energy Planning and Policies," 21.

52 Annecke, "Still in the Shadows."

53 Skutsch, "Gender Analysis for Energy Projects"; Cecelski, "Enabling Equitable Access to Rural Electrification."

54 Upadhyay, "Gendered Livelihoods."

55 Udas and Zwarteveen, "Can Water Professionals Meet Gender Goals?"; Clancy, "Market Empowering Women?"

56 The Inter-Agency Task Force on Gender and Water (GWTF), "Gender, Water and Sanitation: A Policy Brief," notes that globally, women own titles to 2 percent of private land.

57 Delgado, "Irrigation Management."

58 Delgado, "Irrigation Management."

59 Reddy et al., "Energy and Social Issues."

60 Clancy et al., "Gender-Energy-Poverty Nexus."

61 Castro, "Poverty and Citizenship," 764.

62 O'Reilly, "'Traditional' Women, 'Modern' Water," 962.

63 Pradhan "Measuring Empowerment," 54.

64 Miraftab, "Invited and Invented Spaces of Participation," 4.

65 Naples, "Changing the Terms."

66 Roy, *Ordinary Person's Guide to Empire*, 66.

67 See the work of the Intercontinental Network on the Promotion of the Social Solidarity Economy (RIPESS), and of the World Social Forum (WSF), both founded in 2001. For definitions of the solidarity economy, see Jenna Allard and Julie Matthaei, "Defining the Solidarity Economy," accessed January 10, 2025, http://avery.wellesley.edu/Economics/jmatthaei/transformationcentral/solidarity/definingsolidarity.html.

68 Allard and Matthaei, "Introduction"; Nelson, *Economics for Humans*.

69 Safa, "Women's Social Movements in Latin America."

70 Molyneux, "Mobilization Without Emancipation?"

71 Harcourt, "Building Alliances for Women's Empowerment," 6–7.

72 Shiva, *Earth Democracy*.

73 Balanyá et al., "Reclaiming Public Water."

74 Laurie, "Gender Water Networks."

75 Ahlers and Zwarteveen, "Water Question in Feminism."

76 Panda, "Women's Role in Local Water Management," 8.

77 Ahmed, "Negotiating Gender Equity," 76.

78 Ahmed "Negotiating Gender Equity," 79.

79 Winrock, "Assessment of Rural Energy Development Program."

80 Branco and Almeida, "Women, Mobilization and the Revitalization of Water Resources."

81 Souza, "Participatory Budgeting in Brazilian Cities."

82 UNIFEM, "Gender Responsive Budgeting."

83 Budlender and Hewitt, *Engendering Budgets*.

84 Villagomez, "Gender Responsive Budgets."

85 Budlender and Hewitt, *Engendering Budgets*.

86 Khosla, *Water, Equity and Money*.

87 Villagomez, "Gender Responsive Budgets," 4.

88 Alexander and Mohanty, "Cartographies of Knowledge and Power," 27 (emphasis added).

89 Wieringa, "Women's Interests and Empowerment," 841.

90 Boelens and Zwarteveen, "Andean Water Reforms," 753; Adams et al., "Water, Rules and Gender."

91 Trawick, "Against the Privatization of Water," 985.

92 Chigudu, "Community-Based Participatory Research."

93 Chigudu, "Community-Based Participatory Research," 263.

94 Ochieng, "Supporting Women and Girls' Sexual and Reproductive Health and Rights," 41.

95 Çağatay, "Gender Budgets and Beyond."

96 Randriamaro, "Challenging Neo-Liberal Economic Orthodoxy," 45.

97 Randriamaro, "Challenging Neo-Liberal Economic Orthodoxy," 48.

98 Aguilar, "Water as a Source of Equity."

99 Aguilar, "Water as a Source of Equity," 129.

100 Martines, "Keepers of Water," 27.

101 Khosla, *Water, Equity and Money*.

102 Budlender et al., "Gender-Responsive Budgeting."

103 Dodson et al., "Researching Inequality Through Interpretive Collaborations."

104 Dodson et al., "Researching Inequality Through Interpretive Collaborations," 826.

105 Panda, "Women's Role in Local Water Management," 7.

106 Harcourt, "Global Women's Rights Movement."

107 Harcourt and Escobar, *Women and the Politics of Place*.

108 Harcourt and Escobar, *Women and the Politics of Place*, 5.

109 Osterweil, "Place-Based Globalism."

110 On "territory based," see Spronk, "Roots of Resistance."

111 Urea, "Protecting Territory, Protecting Culture," 7.

112 Spronk, "Roots of Resistance."

113 Olivera, "Struggle for Life."

114 Rocheleau, "Legacy of Mama Tingo."

115 Osterweil, "Place-Based Globalism," 186.

116 Melo, "Alternatives for Another, Possible World," 29.

117 Martines, "Keepers of Water," 27.

118 DeVault, *Liberating Method*, 65.

119 Elson, "Gender Awareness in Modeling Structural Adjustment."

3

MAPPING TRANSNATIONAL FEMINIST ENGAGEMENTS

Neoliberalism and the Politics of Solidarity

with Linda Carty

A transnational feminist movement needs to be led by women from the South, and to be aware of and concerned about the negative impacts of neo-liberalism. —PEGGY ANTROBUS, BARBADOS

The major difficulty is to create transnationalism that is not just at the top, so to speak. Beyond this, there needs to be much more work—theoretical and organizational—on how women can actually support each other's movements in an effective way that does not play into colonialism. —LINDA MARTÍN ALCOFF, UNITED STATES

Precisely because the divide is expanding, it is imperative that the feminist movement at least retain solidarities, that it give up forever the notion of a so called first world and a so called second or third world. . . . My sense is that feminism needs to be alive to that crucial thing, difference, and it needs to battle against all kinds of hierarchies, it needs to build solidarities where they are necessary, and to continue to work separately where that is important. —URVASHI BUTALIA, INDIA

Possibly, one of the ways to generate transnational solidarity within feminism is to take advantage of the internal fissures of neoliberalism in order to erode its foundations, that is, its way of administering politics and economy by constructing fragmented global markets. The possibility of transforming these failures into strengths for an active global society can be an opportunity for feminists of color. —MARA VIVEROS-VIGOYA, COLOMBIA

As antiracist, anticapitalist feminists from the global South, now living in the United States and committed to the politics of solidarity and radical antiracist, feminist knowledge production, we embarked on this ambitious project wanting to map transnational feminist engagements by talking with key feminist scholar-activists with decades of political/intellectual involvement in feminist movements and knowledge production.[1] While we knew this could be only a particular (and partial) story, we were interested in a generative dialogue and wanted to map a critical feminist geography of knowledge production, organizing, and solidarity building across multiple layers of difference in the current neoliberal context. The quotes at the outset of the chapter encapsulate some of the themes and dilemmas that emerged in our survey of a small number of feminist scholar-activists: the importance and difficulties of transnational feminist praxis in the context of neoliberalism; the politics of difference; and the coloniality of North-South divides and the radical necessity of building solidarities across multiple borders. There is a vast literature on feminist movements and feminist knowledge production in different sites.[2] However, we were especially interested in how our respondents crafted and reflected on feminist realities on the ground— basically mapping how feminist knowledge production over the last few decades is connected to the place-based lived realities of feminist praxis.

To this end, we surveyed thirty-three feminist scholar-activists from Asia, South America, the Caribbean, North Africa, Europe, and North America.[3] Most of our respondents have histories of organizing and scholarship that date back to the 1970s—and each and every one continues to be committed to the urgencies of feminist politics in the contemporary context of neoliberalism and increasing impoverishment and violence against women around the globe. Some, like Nawal el Saadawi and Angela Davis, have been involved in radical anticapitalist, feminist social movements since the 1960s, while others, like Himani Bannerji, Islah Jad, Zillah Eisenstein, Teresa Cordova, and Honor Ford-Smith, describe their feminist genealogies in the context of organizing in location-specific feminist struggles of the 1970s and 1980s. Our respondents include women in their forties to eighties in age. Like the two of us, many of our respondents are anticapitalist, antiracist feminists with a history of organizing across racial, sexual, national, and religious divides. Since this group of scholar-activists is based within our own interconnected transnational feminist communities, we cannot claim that this is a representative sample of any sort. For instance, while we have a broad representation of feminists from the Caribbean, South Asia, United States, and Canada, we have only a couple from North Africa. While antiracist white feminists (Eisenstein, Pratt, and Peake) are key participants here, the generational specificity of this collective has as much to do with our own networks as with the significance of the historical transformations in feminist struggle (from the 1960s to the present) that many of our respondents participated in and indeed led.[4]

In this chapter we honor the voices, theorizations, and multiple genealogies of our feminist interlocutors, constructing a dialogue that foregrounds the similarities and the differences in our collective thinking and praxis as it has evolved over the decades. We were interested in a collective mapping rather than a comprehensive review of feminist genealogies so we could understand how far women have come in creating a better world for themselves in this phase of capitalism and so that we can get a sense of what feminists across the globe are thinking about the challenges we face at this historical juncture. We thus asked our respondents four questions designed to understand how they view the last thirty to forty years of this collective feminist activism and how they see the knowledge that it has produced as influencing their thinking and current work. We posed deliberate questions about neoliberalism and the future of feminist activism:

1 When we talk of the production of feminist knowledge, we understand that it includes the notion of working through the intersections of race, class, gender, and sexuality to configure a different kind of feminist praxis that is more relevant to women's lives globally. From your knowledge of the communities in which you've worked, what is your assessment of how this has worked on the ground?
2 In reflecting on your work as a feminist over the last two or three decades, how would you say your thinking has evolved on the relevance of feminism as praxis in economically marginalized communities or communities of color?
3 What do you see as the challenges ahead in relation to neoliberalism and the obstacle it poses to solidarity among feminists of color on a global scale?
4 Considering the North-South divide that seems to be expanding, what do you imagine a transnational feminist movement needs to look like in this era of extreme conservatism in neoliberalism to be effective?

Needless to say, our survey elicited deep, complex, thoughtful, and challenging responses to the questions. And while it is impossible to construct a single map or story of our collective feminist genealogies, it is in fact possible to identify important, parallel narratives of feminist activism. Rather than focus on each of these four questions, we have chosen to explicate one particular thread that runs through all responses: the anatomies of dispossession and violence in the age of neoliberalism and the particular, connected challenges this poses to feminists located in various geopolitical sites around the globe. It is this particular contemporary context that illustrates most clearly the sociopolitical analyses and feminist knowledge production mirrored in different corners of the globe and allows us to sketch a materialist map of transnational feminist engagements and possibilities of an ethical and just solidarity across borders based on attentiveness to power and historical specificities and differences.

The chapter is divided into two large sections, with a concluding discussion that focuses on two site-specific radical social movements that emerged around the same time in late 2012. The first section discusses how feminists across geopolitical sites confront the growth and consolidation of neoliberal states and transnational processes of exploitation.[5] The key question it addresses is how feminists understand, engage, and resist the multiple violences of neoliberal cultures in their own place-based struggles for gender justice.

The second section looks at how various scholar-activists define feminism for themselves and in their own locations; their thoughts on the significance of difference and power; and the North-South divide and their reflections on building and sustaining solidarities across colonial, racial, sexual, class, and national borders. Throughout the chapter, rather than summarize or edit responses, we have chosen to quote at length from our respondents. The text we want to create is one where the dialogue between us all as feminist scholar-activists is primary, not the Carty-Mohanty interpretation of the responses of our sisters and comrades. Given the key historical and current role of many of our respondents in local and transnational social movements and knowledge production, we honor their voices in their entirety, creating not a seamless third-person narrative but a capacious, conversational text that moves between geopolitical spaces and different voices, between histories and cultures of feminist organizing.[6]

The chapter's conclusion focuses on two site-specific social movements that emerged in late 2012 in India and Canada (Bekhauf Azadi and Idle No More, respectively). An analysis is offered of these ongoing women-

and feminist-led social movements as exemplary movements confronting gender injustice and neoliberal practices, inspiring the transnational solidarities that are key to antiracist and anticapitalist feminist struggle at the present time.

For the last four decades, feminists have been confronting a series of neoliberal policies by states in both the global North and South that have been wreaking havoc on women's lives across race, class, sexuality, and ethnic divides. Neoliberalism—an ideology and a political and economic practice—is marked by an increased concentration of international finance capital, the so-called liberation of capital markets that turned over every aspect of the economy to free-market operations, the widening of free-trade policies that benefit only the (already privileged in the already) wealthy countries, and the celebration of individual entrepreneurial freedoms that ultimately lead to the strengthening of private property rights. It is more or less a celebration of capital markets being left on their own to function without government regulation. It gained traction in the middle to late 1970s with a tightening of the reins on liberal democracies in the North, specifically their social programs, and the loosening of regulations on their capital markets. This occurred simultaneously with the (often violent, forced) dissolution of socialist states in the global South, specifically in Chile, Tanzania, Argentina, Nicaragua, and even smaller countries like Jamaica and Grenada in the Caribbean. The rise of these socialist states was attributed to Keynesian economics and political policies that encouraged too much government regulation in the market and allowed too much power to organized labor and social movements such as antipoverty struggles, women's rights, civil rights, and Black Power in both the North and the South.

In the global South, they followed on the heels of anticolonial struggles and created nervous tension in the US government and particularly in capital markets in the North. The demise of these social movements came with the rise of neoliberalism as a doctrine that was embraced and run by the Ronald Reagan regime in Washington, DC, and the Margaret Thatcher regime in London. Both the United States and Britain implemented policies that saw the state embark on a new mission to enshrine the security and longevity of neoliberalism. Unlike the state in more liberal phases of capitalism, the neoliberal state bears no commitment even to be present as partially socially responsible for its citizenry. Rather, the belief is that individuals must be allowed and encouraged to market their entrepreneurial skills in an environment that is marked by free markets, free trade, and strong property rights that will encourage further growth and accumulation of capital.

In this environment the role of the state is to protect and guarantee the value of money, property, and markets, not the well-being of individuals or individual rights.[7]

This is the environment in which feminists in both the North and the South have been functioning over the last thirty to forty years as we have watched all areas of life and the resources for human well-being fall under the control of the market. Market principles govern women's existence even though so much of women's lives cannot be packaged neatly for the market. Most of women's necessary labor, though commodified as part of the reproduction in social production, is not as easily quantifiable because it takes place in the family, that private institution that fuels capitalism. It is feminists' assessment of and responses to these forced neoliberal market changes onto women's lives that we seek to address in this chapter. Across the globe the gains that women have made have been championed by feminists who have been at the forefront of women's struggles and mobilization demanding those gains. Of course, we have been there as well when states introduced neoliberal policies that have been hacking away at those rights.

We have been witnessing conservative extremists capturing control of more and more states in the global North, just as we have seen capital markets collapsing as a result of policies that extremist state managers have put in place. It means that many of the experiences that were once known only to the poorest populations in the South are now visible in the North as well.[8] A climate has developed whereby more and more of the gains in women's rights are being seriously threatened as neoliberal states appropriate gender discourses in their attempts to explain away or justify the erasure of women's rights. In this hostile environment, we find women of color creating deeper solidarities across borders and at the intersections of color, class, and ethnicity to more effectively forge a battle against the attack of neoliberalism.

Much of the transnational feminist knowledge production and on-the-ground organizing by women of color critiques the feminist and other social movements. These critiques have impacted and changed the larger sociopolitical landscape as well as intellectual contexts and have thereby transformed the feminist movement itself. Indeed, the questions being asked today reflect transnational feminist theorizing that is directly linked to and often emerges from community engagement. This chapter focuses on the knowledges produced by transnational feminists that engage globalization and neoliberalism as factors that have impacted women's lives in tangible ways and have pushed them into deeper organizing for change.

Confronting Neoliberal Culture and State Practices

Feminist scholars have produced a great deal of knowledge that engages neoliberalism as another phase of capital concentration within the ever-transmutable production system of capitalism. The exception at this particular moment in history is the intensification and expanding role of the market in all aspects of social life and how so much of it impacts women's lives most severely for all the obvious reasons. That scholarship exposes the neoliberal state in both the North and the South as most pernicious for women's organizing because it is so adept at appropriating the discursive elements of those struggles and undermining the actual attempts to forge a politics of change.[9] It means that women must engage these challenges in their different locales, understanding that their sociality is not predicated on what comes out of Washington or London, for example, but by holding their nation-states more accountable for the conditions and quality of life in their countries. This requires creating solidarity across difference and national boundaries to have an effective transnational impact. Solidarity in this sense requires an understanding of the fact that neoliberal culture in the North can have a very different meaning than it does in the global South. Too often in the global North, we can lose sight of what women are enduring in the South and get caught up in a discourse of the North advocating unworkable solutions for the South. On this question of challenges that neoliberalism poses for feminists of color globally, Sara Ahmed draws attention to the differential effects of neoliberalism:

> I think one of the main challenges is to dispel the myth of the West as liberator. . . . I think our task in creating solidarity is to open our ears rather than our mouths. Whilst I think privatization and atomization are major problems, I also think "neoliberalism" is often used too quickly in the West to diagnose everything. I think we need to become aware of how our own diagnostic languages might be part of the problem. One of my interests, for instance, is in how individualism is often identified as a conservative ideology; sure, it can be but so too can community (defined as the restriction of sympathy to our kind; class loyalty; patriotism; even multiculturalism can all be understood in these terms). I think it can even be a Western idea that the individual is a Western idea. So while I am for a defense of the public, of the commons, for instance, I think this has become too easy and too glib within the Western academy. When you have been

owned, being your own can be radical. I think feminism of color is more attuned to this radical history of own-ness than others.

This provocative idea speaks forthrightly to what for many may be a discomforting truth in feminism—that historical differences across class, like race but more so than sexuality, engender privileges of which feminists must remain cognizant. It is this awareness of the multiple negative roles of neoliberalism and feminist commitment to engage in a praxis of countervigilance that will create solidarity among feminists across these divides. Linda Peake, a white antiracist feminist who has worked for over two decades with the women's organization Red Thread in Guyana and who understands these struggles all too well, expresses a statement of solidarity with Ahmed as manifested outside the academy:

> Neoliberalism has also reinforced divides outside the academy through the deepening of access, or not, to liberties and privileges. Many feminist activists in the Caribbean have been forced, for economic survival reasons, to become increasingly engaged in the NGOization of development. As an example, I again quote from the chapter by Karen [de Souza] and myself: "Feminist academics in the North have privileges; even when they are not equally distributed, they are likely to be available in greater supply in a country such as Canada relative to those for feminists of all classes in a country such as Guyana. These privileges come from political liberties that include the freedom of speech and freedom from persecution; from economic liberties that include freedom from hunger, homelessness, and poverty; and from social liberties that include access to facilities, education, and training, as well as access to information, and often access to monies. In addition to these privileges, it has also been argued that the increasing institutionalization of feminist academic research in departments of Women's Studies has resulted in a situation that serves to profit individual women's careers rather than promoting social change. The academic feminist label, for many activist organizations, now has the baggage of careerism, of maintaining the status quo, and of rising to the top rather than aiming for transformation.[10]

Failure to recognize these differences between women as feminists can be the real hair in the eyeball, so to speak, of any attempt at true global feminist solidarity. Indeed, it can serve to create divides among women in the same country and for sure across national boundary lines.

The Caribbean scholar Rhoda Reddock speaks of the need for a feminist political economy critique in understanding the impact of neoliberalism on economies of the global South:

> In my opinion, this approach which was foisted on the South through structural adjustment policies and [the World Trade Organization] WTO and [the General Agreement on Trade in Services] GATS has now backfired, so we will see how this will unfold in the future. A transnational feminist movement would have to be reactivated that once more incorporates feminist political economy into its analysis. This approach must also raise questions about the continuous overconsumption on which these economies are based and the impact through the criminalization and destruction of communities, which is certainly the case in many parts of the English-speaking Caribbean and Latin America. The impact of these developments on women, men, and social and gender relations in our societies [has] been devastating.

In response to the same question on the impact of the neoliberal culture on organizing and solidarity work by feminists of color, Beverly Bain, speaking of the Canadian context, writes:

> The neoliberal agenda continues to have severe economic, social, and political impacts on the lives of women of color globally. The restructuring of capital has meant that women of color have seen gains and losses. Women have gained access to jobs that are unionized in the service sector such as teaching and nursing. However, with job restructuring and downsizing, women are facing the wrath of governments that are intent on breaking the backs of those unions. Women—in this case marginalized women of color—are forced to take jobs that involve long working hours that are part-time and irregular without benefits or the possibility of a pension.
>
> The Federal government under [Stephen] Harper in Canada has introduced severe cuts to the Women's Program, which provides funding to women's groups. One of the major contradictory effects of the neoliberal agenda to feminism and feminist and women of color organizing is the incorporation of our activism into state institutions. Here I want to talk a bit about working in the violence against women's movement for the past thirty years. As part of a group of feminists of color working on the ground to end violence against women, we were struggling simultaneously inside the black and color patriarchal communities to

recognize gender and in the white feminist movement to recognize the intersections of gender and race. As black women and women of color in struggle, we have always occupied the insider-outsider position in the Canadian women's movement and the nation. This position has been placed upon us but is often embraced as a way to mediate the deleterious effects of black and other forms of nationalism, racism, patriarchy, and sexism.

In the struggle to make known the differing impacts of sexual and physical violence in the lives of women of color, we saw these experiences culturalized in institutions and treated as extraneous to the experiences of violence and sexual assault of white women. In fact, while we as black women and women of color were successful in bringing an intersectional analysis based on gender, race, and class to the antiviolence movement, the discourse of the black, brown, and native rapists continue[s] to drive the antiviolence agenda within the women's movement and institutionally.

Speaking in a similar vein and most cogently about the seductiveness of neoliberal culture in undermining the feminist agenda, Urvashi Butalia shows how the practices manifest in a similar way in the South: "Neoliberalism is very seductive and all pervasive. One of the challenges is its emphasis on the individual and on individual achievement. For feminists and women in our parts of the world it also offers access—through the media and in other ways—to a dream world of consumer goods where access to these often becomes a symbol of empowerment and consumer access changes and often replaces the language of human rights. Suddenly, human rights becomes passé."

Himani Bannerji follows up with the incisive cautionary note that we should be mindful of the destructive features and challenges of neoliberalism:

The challenges ahead in relation to neoliberalism must be taken up without being lost in the discourses of freedom, democracy and difference at a superficial level. It is assumed, for instance, that pleasure and self-fulfillment, dreams and desires, might be acquired through the market without admitting that the very form of the market destroys the quality of our pleasures and fulfillment.

Two other challenges that neoliberalism presents us with are war and dispossession or "primitive accumulation." Both involve vast numbers of people, a substantial portion being women and children. Militarization is the coercive violent dimension of neoliberalism, where any barrier to corporate markets must be mercilessly crushed. We see examples of this in the cases of Iraq, Afghanistan, and different countries in Africa. How are we to deal with these situations as feminists? The issue of primitive accumulation or dispossession of millions over the world as a result of encroachment by giant capitalist enterprises is also a gift of neoliberalism, since the state's responsibility for the citizens is continuously erased in favor of private enterprise, causing loss of lives and livelihoods of small producers, poor workers, and landless people in the agricultural sector. . . . Is the anti-state approach of Northern feminism, which recommends the growth of the private sector or inserts itself as organizers and service providers for people who are victims of land grabs and other dispossessions, an adequate response to all this? To create solidarity among feminists requires an understanding of and agreement among feminists of both North and South regarding capitalism and neoliberalism. With respect to the role of the state, we need to see in what way it can empower the people as opposed to empowering capital. Feminists need to ponder their attitude to social and state formations.

In this current phase of capitalism, we witness the state facilitating transnational neoliberal agendas in both the global North and South with policies that seek to undo all of the feminists' gains of the last four decades. Feminists are aware of this and understand how these actions make the North-South divide so much less significant today than it has ever been. We understand that solidarity across this divide is crucial. Therefore, in their articulations of organizing and struggle to combat the state's agenda to undermine their activities through the likes of, for example, hiring feminists to advance its own goals, feminists ponder mechanisms to get the focus back on questions and issues of social justice. Teresa Cordova captures this well as she speaks to how much the state's actions threaten solidarity:

> The challenges ahead involve, first, the realization that the neoliberal push is a powerful one. The logic of capital accumulation, the privatization of governments, and trade liberalization are, by their very nature, exclusive. Pushing people out of the formal labor force while concurrently destroying their subsistence and localized economies exemplifies this.
>
> The biggest challenges: How do we push against these powerful forces? How do we survive in the face of those forces? Most especially, how do we create alternatives that push against the logic of those

dominant forces? How do we ensure that those alternatives are based in values of community, love, and the collective? From those values will stem justice and well-being.

A threat to our solidarity is that if we fail to understand the logic and dynamics of domination and how they get played out, we are more likely to perpetuate it, even among ourselves. An even bigger threat to our solidarity is if we forget to love one another.

Angela Davis directs us to some of the more sinister though astute actions of the state in both the North and the South that can seriously threaten global feminist solidarity and organizing if feminists fail to recognize that the neoliberal state can be very seductive in its pernicious activities to quash imagined enemies. In the structuring of an antiracist and anticapitalist feminist engagement, feminists cannot afford to lose sight of the fact that the state is the real enemy here:

> Liberal feminism—in the twenty-first century we can say neoliberal feminism—has always coexisted with variants of feminism that have been more critical of capitalism and of the state on which capitalism depends. In this century, we have witnessed unabashed manifestations of what we might call imperial feminism. The US wars on Iraq and Afghanistan were in part justified by the putative need to protect women from cultures that supposedly thrived on the oppression of women. [This of course led to] imperialist wars to save women from their oppressors. The state of Israel has gone so far as to engage in public relations campaigns that portray Israel as the most democratic country in the region because it respects women's equality and because it is a safe haven for LGBT communities.
>
> Palestinian Queers for BDS [Boycott, Divestment, Sanctions] have spoken back with their critiques of this process of "pinkwashing," which reveals the shallowness of the democracy Israel purports to represent and the neoliberal appropriation and domestication of feminist social movements. The feminist dictum that "the personal is political" acquires new meaning under the dominance of neoliberalism, and global solidarities among feminist movements that are determined to resist the seductions of neoliberalism will have to be cautiously constructed.

Joan French speaks specifically to actions of the state that underscore regional and class differences in the very diverse feminist movement. She argues that these can obscure women's view of the need for global feminist solidarity across differences and across the North-South divide:

> Because of the diversity of the feminist movement, there is divergence and contention, and huge differences will exist. There is little common ground between the woman struggling to join the army to go to Iraq, whatever her color, even if she considers this a feminist action, and the women in Pakistan joining their efforts in support of a transgender candidate whom they assess will represent their interests as small agricultural producers as well as women—though the latter may empathize with the former's income-earning motives. At the same time, the alienation and marginalization of communities (in particular the youth and women within them)—a result of neoliberal structural adjustment and related economic reorientation policies—has affected all countries to differing degrees. The counterstruggle is on everywhere, and it includes the women of the feminist movement in processes that are often complex and riddled with contradictions and ebbs and flows of consensual action, as in Egypt. The parallels in consequence, despite the difference in geographical location, allow for common cause if the origin of the problem is adequately identified and if the basic principles of an alternative founded in equal rights and equity are clear and the specific insertion of each country or area into the global economy is analyzed from these perspectives and guides the continuing struggle. The differences cannot be avoided—struggle inevitably involves some confrontation and evolution in the interplay of differences. The important thing to note is that so far feminists have not, like men, sought to kill each other to dominate, with the exception of those who join the armies of destruction. Feminists generally have developed the use of other methods, often still necessarily confrontational but more humane . . . and in my view more likely in the long run to create a ubiquitous and more effective movement for change. In this area of strategies of feminism, little has been produced for the Caribbean, with the possible exception of the work of Rhoda Reddock, a foundation member of the Caribbean movement. This remains an area for more specific knowledge production in terms of strategies, their successes and failures, and the lessons learned.

The negative impact of state policies on women's lives in particular, specifically in the creation and sustenance of war and the knowledge production and organizing that feminists continue to mount in the face of the challenges of annihilation, cannot be overstated. In speaking to this, Aida Hernandez points out:

> I think that besides the economic and political impact that neoliberal globalization is having in the global South, and more specifically in the lives of poor women and children, we are also currently subjected to the hegemony of military powers that have not only massacred hundreds of children, women, and elderly but are also endangering the survival of humanity by provoking an arms escalation in the name of disarmament, by violating all forms of international legality in the name of democracy, and by legitimizing the use of violence in the name of peace. (See the military intervention in Afghanistan, Palestine, and the narcotics war in Latin America.)

While looking at the need for global solidarity among feminists, including those of color, and the challenges being posed to the latter by neoliberalism around the globe and while being mindful of hierarchies within difference that feminists must address as obstacles to solidarity, Zillah Eisenstein states:

> The challenges of neoliberalism to women of color across the globe are part of the privatized depoliticized struggles of the moment. Women of all colors, including white women, are becoming poorer while a few women from each color also are becoming more privileged and wealthy. I think the greatest challenges stem from the complex differentiated experiences of women of all colors and the new class inequities and alliances that are developing within any category of womanhood. Allies need more critique and recognition of the new differences being created among women across the globe. And this happens despite geographical divisions. I am not sure North-South holds as a helpful organizing tool today in the way it did earlier.

Reflecting on the differences among feminists that we can agree stand in some ways to aid the neoliberal state in co-opting feminist struggles, thwarting solidarity among feminists who seek to challenge neoliberalism, Honor Ford-Smith posits some possibility in answer to the question. She suggests that feminists begin by

> building and articulating visions, analyses and narratives of struggle, justice, hope and possibility that folks can support BROADLY through alliances and supportive networking as communities of interest

while remaining attentive to hierarchies of difference and differences in needs locally and globally and in all ways.

[It is necessary also to] identify and work toward specific struggles on issues that folks can support from a variety of sites without fragmenting into isolated pockets.

She posits that we can forge solidarities among feminists globally by "keeping questions of redistribution of wealth and alternative economies central to social movements and integrating these with other concerns—especially in North America where identity politics seems to be a privileged ingredient for progressive mobilization and where the notion of alternatives to capitalism seem to be extremely marginal."

Leila Farah also points to issues of difference among feminists that need to be engaged to challenge neoliberalism. She notes some resistance to this challenge and the implications:

Building global solidarity for feminists is challenged by the separation between those who cannot, will not, or don't know how to undo their own privilege and relocating what is considered knowledge and resistance outside of academe and US-based activist circles. Since all institutions are complicit with the neoliberal project in many ways, those who straddle academic lives and employ feminist praxis within communities outside of the hallowed halls often are positioned to act as intermediaries, breaking the age binaries of formal and informal education and knowledge production, bearing a great burden in repositioning and reconciling these multiple spaces. Unfortunately, that increasingly seems to be women of color who are non–US-based originally, who are fighting to deepen US theorizing intersectionality beyond the demographical categories promulgated in US feminist spaces [witness the discussions at the 2012 National Women's Studies Association Annual Conference, for example].

There are many levels on which neoliberal culture is being crafted and utilized by the state, sometimes with the unintentional complicity of feminists, who serve to undermine and in some cases chip away at longstanding antiracist principles and insurgent knowledges that feminists of color developed. Indeed, as we observe the neoliberal state in the North implement severe cutbacks in public education, social services, health care, and other programs that benefit the poor and women and children most, we have seen a changing landscape that threatens to render feminist organizing as ineffective. The material conditions of women's lives are being transformed by the neoliberal culture and state. Also, the ideological underpinnings of the insurgent knowledges legitimizing challenges that brought about improvements in those conditions are being changed as well in ways that threaten the very foundation of radical feminist organizing.[11] The impact of neoliberalism on social movements is as destructive as feminists have long feared. In recent times, we have witnessed the state either co-opting some of the organizing feminist struggles against it or entirely appropriating the language of resistance to many of its policies and practices that have been intensifying the hardships of the poor, especially among women, while simultaneously increasing poverty.

At the same time, in some regions of the North, as feminist activists have found funding for their organizations drying up, the state in these regions has taken to the practice of employing feminist activists in their capacity as organizers but has managed in the process to neutralize their agenda. Beverly Bain notes the poignancy of this in the case of Canada as she writes about the obstacles and challenges neoliberalism poses to feminist organizing. She describes the difficulty of feminist of color organizing under neoliberalism with loss of funding and the suspicion that feminists of Arab and South Asian descent are potential terrorists:

> The usurpation of feminist language such as "empowerment" and "change the shift from anti-racism discourse to diversity discourse" [has] created tensions and made the work among feminists of color working inside state institutions and those in feminist of color communities extremely difficult. . . .
>
> The persistent gender essentialism on the part of white feminists in the North toward women in the South and in particular Arab Muslim women continues to be a source of tension between many feminist of color and white feminists in the North.

She notes: "The ascendancy of whiteness that pervades discourses of race, gender, and sexuality that privileges whiteness over all else in this current global context of its ongoing War on Terror has become even more pervasive. This heteronormative, racist, and colonial discourse that exists in the West has served to further privilege white middle-class feminists and LGBT groups[s] treating them as exceptional citizens."

Speaking to the issue of how neoliberal governments have become adept at appropriating different kinds of discourses of struggle and rights, Aida

Hernandez points to the importance of feminists using their knowledge to counter this:

> Cultural criticism provides us with tools for confronting the "collateral damage to language" that John Berger describes as one of the consequences of military aggression. The discourses on absolute freedom, infinite justice, long-lasting freedom, and axes of evil were taking the meaning out of concepts and affecting the possibility of imagining. These collateral damages are also affecting the capacity to imagine other possible futures. Something similar has taken place with the way neoliberal governments have appropriated discourses on cultural rights. In the case of Mexico, we have seen new government rhetoric emerge in recent years that has appropriated and conceptually limited terms such as culture and gender in response to pressure from the national indigenous movement, and under the influence of a broader international movement in favor of indigenous rights and gender rights. For example, the Mexican government used a Zapatista phrase, to promise "Never again, Mexico without you" in the government's National Program for the Development of Indigenous Peoples for 2001–2006. The concepts of cultural rights, multiculturalism, gender, women's rights and equality are now an essential part of the rhetoric of power, emptying them of the transgressive meaning they could have had as the causes for which social movements are fighting. Deconstructing these discourses, revealing the strategies of power of which they are a part, and recovering the profound meaning of these concepts are tasks that can be fulfilled by socially committed feminist social scientists. Grass-roots globalization is already a reality, and it is the only international force that seems to be decisively opposing the hegemony of the militarist US government. As social scientists, we have a great deal to contribute to this process of grass-roots globalization

In some instances, though, the neoliberal state appears to find some groups' protest language more "acceptable" than that of others: the predominantly white and male LGBTQ activists, for example, who have been for the last few years waging a battle with the US state to grant them the right to marry. Much of their language of gay rights, including the right to marry as equality under the law, has been appropriated by the state. While the long-standing homophobic US state has now acceded to the demand, this action begs the question: What exactly is its acquiescence to this otherwise unacceptable group and its demand that is so acutely incongruous with the puritanical religious principles on which it is based? Is it true that the group's class and gender are of greater value to the state than that of its working-class peers and may have been responsible for the group's sexual orientation being of secondary concern? Indeed, more than a few managers and corporate executives have emerged from this group in recent times. It can be argued, therefore, that despite the deeply entrenched homophobia within the United States, the LGBTQ rights social movement continues to advance seemingly unimpeded. That this is a predominantly white movement underscores the fact that class and gender always being mediated by race makes the movement, although critical of the state, more acceptable to that neoliberal institution. However, the LGBTQ movements that focus on economic and social justice for queers of color are clearly unacceptable and criminalized by the state as in the instance of the struggle around CeCe McDonald, a Black queer transgender activist, who was the focus of a large antiracist mobilization (see the discussion by Minnie Bruce Pratt later in this chapter). Indeed, much of the language of the state on the crucial debate of LGBTQ people for equal rights and privileges has been developed by the movement and was either adopted or appropriated by the state.[12]

Feminist Praxis and the Prospects for Solidarity

One of the points of agreement among the scholar-activists interviewed for this study is thus the need both to rethink and to complicate the North-South divide and to be attentive to the neoliberal state and transnational practices that are organized along this divide—in other words, to analyze and challenge what the divide reveals at this time. Feminists must understand how globalization of capital further globalizes poverty (A. Davis); deep class divides and alliances and the creation of new differences among women (Z. Eisenstein and B. Guy-Sheftall); new and continuing wars, incarceration, surveillance, and warehousing as new colonial state practices (I. Jad, J. Oparah, and A. Hernandez); a growing gap between countries in the South (U. Butalia, A. Trotz and Andaiye, and M. Okazawa-Rey); and the creation of new spaces for feminist struggle in the context of the consolidation of neoliberalism within and across North-South divides (M. Viveros, P. Antrobus, Richa Nagar, and M. Okazawa-Rey). Each one of our interlocutors affirmed the significance of place-based and cross-border feminist praxis. Honor Ford-Smith, reflecting on her decades of feminist engagement, described herself as a situational feminist—that is, as a feminist in some settings, but not in others. This "situational" positionality has to do with the meanings and broad usage of the term feminist in certain settings, the way the term gets taken up, battles won and lost in the past and present and by whom. It also has to do with what strategies might work in given situations and whose alliances might bring about particular changes. . . . I have reached the realization that we continue to fight, that there is unlikely ever to be one great big hallelujah rupture, and that all struggles are long, with imperfect and incomplete victories that are conditional—this is what living means.

A number of feminists around the globe describe their feminism as a doing (B. Bain); as a praxisizing feminism (M. Okazawa-Rey); as relational and dialogic (S. Ahmed, A. Davis, H. Ford-Smith, L. Farah, J. French, T. Cordova, and I. Jad); as intersectional (G. Wekker, E. Crespo-Kebler and Ana Irma Rivera Lassen, F. Sadiqi, S. Ahmed, U. Butalia, and A. Hernandez); and as rooted in a place-based, contextual analysis that is anchored in overarching feminist principles (J. Wedderburn and M. Okazawa-Rey). Avtar Brah says:

> In the context of the North-South divide, transnational feminism needs to revisit the old debates about the specificity of patriarchal and capitalist gender systems that prevail in different parts of the world. Politics of solidarity would need to emerge from such appreciation of "difference" and analysis of global modes of exploitation and patriarchal inequalities. For those of us in the North, we have to have a deep acknowledgment of the intersectional modalities of power—around racism, class, gender, ethnicity, religion, sexuality—between us and women in the South. From our previous experience we know that it is not easy to win solidarity without taking account of our differential locations and positionalities vis-à-vis one another. We have to have respect for other ways of life—other than those in the West—without succumbing to patriarchal imperatives. A vibrant transnational feminist movement can thrive only if there is mutual respect. I remain positively optimistic.

Lee Maracle offers a unique and important critique of the North-South divide from the location of Indigenous communities: "There is no North-South divide if you are indigenous. Canada's north is essentially indigenous, as is Russia's and America's. The middle is where privilege is. There is a mid–North American and South-North divide with the South and the North being equal and the mid-area of southern Canada and the United States being areas of privilege. The North-South divide of Europe, China, and the South is shifting as well."

Maracle's claim shows the profound connections between geopolitical location, historical and cultural lifeways, and the epistemological privilege of Indigenous scholars engaging in a critique of power and inequity. It illustrates the politics of knowledge embedded within geographies of power relations and challenges many of us to think carefully about the privilege of the middle. Maracle goes on to talk about the environmental movement as "the first totally global movement in the world, and it is humanizing human thought and changing how people see one another, respect for Earth and women. I'm not sure if this is a new feminist praxis, but it is also a return to indigenous beliefs among 350 million people on the globe that is influencing the beliefs of others."

Himani Bannerji, situated in both India and Canada, defines her socialist feminist politics and site of knowledge production in different, albeit connected, ways to Maracle:

> I've tried to make my feminist politics and ideas by understanding the processes of emergence not only of socially marginalized but also of exploited and excluded "communities" who in actuality form the majority of the people on Earth. This understanding cannot but come from an analytical grasp of capitalist development both in its continuance as capitalism, with the same labor-capital relations, and in the special characteristics that modify it through the role played by finance capital in its present stage and modern capitalism's ability to annex all areas of life, the whole human body and mind, in new forms of slavery and commodity. . . . All socioeconomic and political projects that we undertake for the economically marginalized or exploited must be conceived through a feminism that takes into account race, class, caste, ethnicity, and other powered forms of difference. This calls [sic] for politics makes our project specific and concrete, suitable to the time and space.

Urvashi Butalia reflects on this idea of a feminist politics that impacts marginalized communities: "What I have found over the years is that while it is difficult to name feminism as having a direct influence or impact on praxis among marginalized communities, there is little doubt that its influence and spread is both wide and deep. How wide and how deep is difficult to measure because clearly its progress, its history, is not and can never be linear. For one step forward you take two back so that a constant zigzagging becomes the very stuff of feminism."

Richa Nagar, on the other hand, offers a provocative analysis of working as a feminist with marginalized, economically dispossessed communities, drawing attention to the need for cross-border praxis to be attentive to languages of the vernacular:

> My investment in attaching the term "praxis" with "feminism" has decreased over the years, especially as I have witnessed—and participated in—the processes by which the collective of nine Sangtin writers (who authored *Sangtin Yatra* and *Playing with Fire*) transitioned into a movement of six thousand peasants and laborers in the villages of Sitapur. While we have learned important things in, from, and through feminist understandings, there are two things that often work against feminism in the kind of communities I work with.
>
> First, the violence perpetrated by many mainstream projects that invoke the label of "feminism" or "gender" has made many people distance themselves from things that make claims and articulate project goals and ideas in the name of feminism. Two, the kind of praxis that has inspired me and my grass-roots activist colleagues in rural North India over the years is being lived and created by many people (academics, movement-based intellectuals, artists, peasants) who do not speak the language of feminism. I have therefore found it necessary to grapple with ways ideas that some of us might see as feminist can actually grow in conversation with efforts of nonfeminists who are integrating theoretical and grounded knowledges and practices in creative and committed ways.

Julia Oparah also complicates our understandings of feminist praxis, reflecting on her own activist genealogy and claiming of transnational feminist politics:

> When I entered activism, I, alongside many black women in Britain, rejected the term "feminism" in favor of "womanism" for black women activists, because of our perception that (white) feminists had colonized that term and produced a feminist praxis with little relevance for women of color. This shifted when I entered the academy in the United States and began to work alongside feminist activist scholars. I started to label myself a transnational feminist/transnational black

feminist and to be more critical of the ways that womanism can elide questions of anticapitalism and sexual orientation. I developed the (un)field of transnational feminist antiprison studies as a way of putting feminist questions and a critical analysis of global capital at the center of antiprison praxis here in the United States as well as elsewhere. More recently I have begun to explore the intervention of transfeminisms and to examine critically the places where transnational feminists and antiprison feminist abolitionists have been complicit with the violence and policing of the gender binary.

Alissa Trotz and Andaiye point out some of the challenges they encounter in working through feminist praxis with women in Guyana:

In our part of the region, there is not a lot of experience to draw on of feminists "working through the intersections of race, class, gender and sexuality on the ground." For example, in the ongoing discussions about how other women should relate to the women prime ministers of Jamaica and Trinidad and Tobago, there's an assumption that women, as women, are, or ought to be, on the same side. Our organizing experience is with Red Thread in Guyana. (Andaiye is a founding member and now international coordinator, Alissa as an overseas member.) We share the position of the global women's strike, of which Red Thread is a member: we begin with the needs, interests, and demands of women who are poorest; we recognize that the divides, the power relations, among us (of, e.g., race, sexuality, age, nationality, disability, immigration status) frame our lives and relationships; and we believe that to cross those divides, each sector of women through its autonomous struggle brings its demands to the table, enabling us to work out how collectively we fight to win both their demands and ours. If we don't do this, then the sectors with the least power inevitably lose out, having to fight harder all the sectors with more power. Inside every "democratic" organization—whether of women or men or both—this process is what is happening.

Laila Farah reads up the power structure, drawing attention to power differences among feminists and the need to continually engage in unlearning privilege:

My vision of a transnational feminist movement requires that emissaries from multiple spaces, many of whom do not identify as feminist per se, should have more access to one another to continue the work of undoing privilege, of unlearning the confines of formal knowledges, of shattering completely the differentials and valuation of formal and informal knowledge, and of being willing to share resources more concretely. Focusing on the south and east first in terms of the varied and effective forms of resistance and strategies for creating change should hold primacy in these endeavors. Exchanging or utilizing privilege for solidarity on the ground might stand a much better chance of taking root and having more long-term alliance building leading to a more realistic socially just movement.

Margo Okazawa-Rey asks the same question: Can we create spaces where feminists in the North examine and figure out what to do about the asymmetrical power relations between us and feminists in the South? She goes on to challenge us all when she poses larger questions of values and principles that are attentive to the politics of identity while moving away from a narrow identity politics:

There need to be more complex understandings of North and South including one inside the other and the various kinds of divides. I think one of the questions is who is divided and who is connected, and on what bases is each happening? Another extremely important question I see playing out in various locations I operate in— the United States, East Asia, Palestine, and English-speaking West Africa—what organizing principles besides identity politics should frame our movement? Are there generative principles and values that can lead rather than identity categories, while simultaneously taking full account of the politics of identities?

Teresa Cordova speaks of the need to create an "alternative vision" for feminism, while Himani Bannerji, Avtar Brah, Rhoda Reddock, and Angela Davis speak of the need for an explicitly socialist, internationalist, and anticapitalist feminism. Cordova says, "The movement of capital crosses borders in complex networked systems. So too, must we build transnational networks of resistance, solidarity and alternatives." Beverly Bain agrees, framing her thoughts this way: "I live a life that has always prioritized ending oppression against women in all its forms. I have never viewed feminism as separate from colonialism, racism, imperialism and class oppression. . . . To do away with feminism is to do away with strategies and approaches that can help to make visible how the discourses of race, nationalism, citizenship, colonialism, queerness, economics, culture are invested in whiteness, masculinity, class privilege, and homonormativity."

Given the ubiquity of neoliberal cultures and global capitalist and imperialist/militarist national and transnational adventures globally, what are the prospects for feminist solidarity across borders? A number of the feminist scholar activists we surveyed were wary of assuming solidarity too quickly. Almost everyone pointed to the challenges of acknowledging differences in power and access while building alliances and solidarities across North-South and historical-cultural divides. Judith Wedderburn encapsulates comments from a number of respondents: "The main challenges will lie in addressing the imbalances (in access to resources) not only between feminists of the global North and South but also between feminists of the global South. Quite often the sharing of experiences and lessons learnt (taking account of, e.g., cultural and social differences) can lay the basis for building of solidarity among feminists, but lack of knowledge that this information even exists is a problem. This will call for more use of technology to build personal and organizational relationships—given that travel is often not possible."

Islah Jad echoes this sentiment: "The real challenge is how to rebuild women's solidarity on the basis of deep understanding of our differences and our different locations, our different realities, and our different needs and aspiration. The real challenge is also to show the false promises of neoliberalism." Joan French has a response to Jad's challenge:

> Because of the diversity of the feminist movement, there is divergence and contention and huge differences will exist. . . . The counterstruggle is on everywhere, and it includes the women of the feminist movement in processes that are often complex and riddled with contradictions and ebbs and flows of consensual action, as in Egypt. The parallels in consequence despite the difference in geographical location allow for common cause if the origin of the problem is adequately identified and if the basic principles of an alternative founded in equal rights and equity are clear and the specific insertion of each country or area into the global economy is analyzed from these perspectives and guides the continuing struggle. The differences cannot be avoided—struggle inevitably involves some confrontation and evolution in the interplay of differences.

And Julia Oparah suggests we need "to be explicit about making coalitions between movements—antiprison, no borders, queer and trans—and to recognize that transnational feminists are part of all these movements. We shouldn't limit our conversation to 'women's groups' . . . to generate a complex understanding of the term 'woman' that recognizes the different pathways into and out of that identity and includes trans women and gender-nonconforming folks."

One of our questions asked respondents to comment on the prospects for solidarity and for transnational feminist movements at the present time. Beverly Guy-Sheftall speaks eloquently of the challenges posed to transnational feminist movements but also identifies issues that provide common ground for solidarity:

> The idea of a transnational feminist movement is provocative but may be even more daunting given the deepening North-South divide, wealth disparities around the globe, extreme conservatism and religious fundamentalisms (e.g., Christianity, Islam), antifeminist (including among women) and war on women discourse, race and gender fatigue (lack of urgency about the plight of people of color and women and girls), burnout among feminist activists around the globe, difficulty of reaching consensus about what a transnational feminist movement might look like, especially since the rise of women leaders around the globe may give impression that women are OK, extreme individualism and materialism among a younger generation in the United States (and perhaps elsewhere), impact of popular media with respect to knowledge production, and demise of print culture and reliance on popular media for "information." Having said this, I do think that the issue of violence against women (and hegemonic masculinities) and poverty still resonates with feminists of color (and others) around the globe.

Similarly, Fatima Sadiqi reflects on divides and possibilities: "The divides are real (see the case of Egypt). I think that just as Islamist organizations are getting support from Saudi Arabia and Qatar, liberal forces need to get support from elsewhere. The appropriate channels need to be created. . . . This being said, I am a staunch believer in keeping an eye on the two extremes: the root context and the transnational interaction . . . national movement that leaves ample space for local specificities and also try to 'mainstream' them would be ideal . . . to keep up hope."

Asha Hans identifies "issues that cut across the rich and poor divide (patriarchy), issues that bind women of all classes and races (LGBT, disability), and issues where women's solidarity is visible and working well" as the basis for a renewed transnational feminist movement. A number of feminists identify movements that have global-transnational dimensions as models or potential allies in developing transnational feminist solidarities. Angela Davis points to the transnational organizing in the prison abolition movement (which also has a distinctly feminist bent); Mara Viveros-Vigoya, Aida Hernandez, and Lee Maracle speak of Indigenous movements; Margo Okazawa-Rey, Aida Hernandez, and Julia Oparah discuss the success of human rights movements across national borders; and Linda Alcoff asks how the labor movement could provide a model for feminist organizing: "The labor movement is developing some models here when there is a strike in one country against a company that also operates in other countries. Then in the latter countries workers can have temporary work stoppages in solidarity. And help publicize the conditions. In this case, the multinational corporation provides the structure for transnational labor solidarity. This works better with workers on both sides than workers on one side and consumers on the other. So how could such practices be replicated for feminists?"

And then there are some concrete examples of transnational feminist movements and the politics of solidarity working on the ground. Minnie Bruce Pratt provides the most extended example of this in her analysis of the Free CeCe movement—a movement that began in the United States and succeeded in making important transnational links and alliances:

> Chrishaun "CeCe" McDonald, a twenty-four-year-old African American transgender woman from Minneapolis, was sentenced June 4, 2012, to forty-one months in prison for defending herself against a brutal attack by neofascists who verbally and physically assaulted McDonald and her friends outside a bar in June 2011. McDonald, who courageously defended herself and her friends against antitrans, antiwoman, racist slurs and violence, was the only one arrested, charged, and jailed at the time.[13]

> The campaign to free CeCe began locally in Minneapolis with secondhand sales and dance parties to raise money for her defense. Creative organizing extended the reach of the organizing to political marches, rallies, and events throughout the world, with Free CeCe signs being carried at International Women's Day events, LGBT pride marches, prison-industrial complex protests, Occupy banner drops, May Day protests, and Transgender Day of Remembrance events on the steps of city hall[s] throughout the United States and in France, Scotland, Germany, Italy, and India.

See Leslie Feinberg's photographs in the album "This Is What Solidarity Looks Like" for documentation of the campaign in the United States and internationally.[14]

See my story on the passing of the Syracuse transgender rights bill for an example of a local Free CeCe organizing moment.[15]

What Pratt illustrates is the deep and abiding connection between the analysis of intersecting oppressions, local struggles on the ground (Minneapolis and Syracuse), and transnational struggles around women's and trans liberation; antiracist, antifascist organizing; and the right to self-defense. Pratt further reflects on how "issues of women's health constantly bridge national and regional, race, and class boundaries and how right-wing neoliberal agendas attack women's health at a number of points—through immigrant scapegoating, through antiwomen initiatives, through antiworker attacks." Coalitions and solidarity among a wide range of people and organizations supporting reproductive freedom thus illustrate the possibilities of feminist organizing on the ground. We conclude by providing a narrative of two ongoing social movements that connect to Pratt's narrative of transnational feminist struggles making local and cross-border connections in the present.

Just Futures: Transnational Feminist Engagements in Neoliberal Times

In the collective dialogue based on the reflections of our interlocutors, we have followed some key analytic strands about neoliberalism, the state, and the creativity and urgency of feminist engagements at the present time. We conclude this chapter by offering a brief analysis of and reflection on two specific social movements anchored in each of our home or adopted home spaces: India and Canada. Both movements arose in late 2012 in response to specific injustices, and each ongoing movement illuminates the different and similar struggles by women against neoliberal states and capitalist interests, formulates and frames gender-based struggles in the global South and North in useful and interconnected ways, and illustrates the challenges and possibilities of contemporary feminist engagements on the ground. We have chosen to focus on these movements not only because they are examples of women's place-based organizing that have now grown into social movements with solidarity links with feminists and feminist organizations across the globe but also because they underscore the theoretical and activist dialogues we engage here. The movements we refer to are the extraordinary mobilization against sexual violence and patriarchal and misogynist state and cultural practices in India that occurred after the gang rape and murder of Jyoti Singh Pandey (or Nirbhaya, as she is often referred to) in December 2012; and the Idle No More movement founded in November 2012 by Indigenous women challenging Canada's curtailing of environmental protections, thus infringing on Indigenous sovereignty.[16]

Both struggles indicate the difficulties and the visionary potential of solidarity across communities and nations, leading to widespread consciousness about and mobilization against neoliberal state collusion in patriarchal and misogynist cultures in the case of India and to the recognition of the significance of anticolonial women-led Indigenous struggles for sovereignty and environmental justice in the neoliberal spaces of Canada and the extraction-assimilation system of the global North. Both movements are anchored in notions of freedom from injustice and colonization, and both offer strategies for feminist engagements in social justice struggles in the twenty-first century. While social movements anchored in liberal understandings of equal rights have made inroads into and are perhaps more acceptable to the neoliberal state (e.g., LGBTQ rights and gay marriage struggles in the global North), movements anchored in anticapitalist, anticolonial struggles for "freedom" from patriarchal practices and gender-based violence and Indigenous sovereignty and freedom (not equal rights) pose a fundamental challenge that cannot be easily contained by neoliberal states. These two site-based struggles thus offer new and promising visions for challenging the paternalism of neoliberal states in these times.

India: Bekaouf Azadi (Freedom Without Fear) for Women

The global upswing in gender violence (including sexual violence and domestic violence) and misogynistic rape culture ought then to be traced at least in part to the imperatives of global capitalism and imperialism and their local agents to justify an increased burden of social reproduction for women, the availability of women from the former colonies as pliant labor, and rape as a weapon against people's movements resisting primitive accumulation. . . . It is no coincidence that perpetrators of gender violence find powerful advocates (not just in India but across the world) in the misogynistic and rape culture statements by the custodians of the political, religious, and law-and-order institutions. —KAVITA KRISHNAN, "Capitalism, Sexual Violence, and Sexism"

The horrific gang rape of December 16 sparked off a massive movement that brought us all on the streets to say enough is enough and to demand action to ensure women's freedom from sexual violence and gender discrimination. . . . Instead of implementing the Justice Verma Report, the government has instead chosen to pass an ordinance that completely subverts the substance and spirit of the Verma recommendations! —SHUDDHABRATA SENGUPTA, WHIMSY MIMSY BOROGOVES, "Freedom Without Fear/ Bekhauf Azadi"

These opening quotes encapsulate important responses to the December 16, 2012, gang rape on a Delhi bus, which has been described as the seed of the Arab Spring for South Asian women. The rape and its aftermath tipped the region into unprecedented large-scale protests against sexual violence and forced the Indian state to set up the Justice Verma Commission (JVC) and subsequently enact new violence-against-women laws. As Kavita Krishnan suggests, the rise of gender violence around the world is inextricably linked to the "imperatives of global capitalism and imperialism." And as the Bekhauf Azadi (Freedom Without Fear) campaign says, the state ignored the recommendations of the pathbreaking JVC report to pass an ordinance that was in fact a containment and subversion of people's struggles and nationwide mobilizations against the culture and practices of sexual violence. As feminist and social justice activists around the world recognized, the scale of the protests in India was unprecedented globally. And the fact that women and men, girls and boys, across religions, classes, and regional divides, took to the streets to protest the rape of Jyoti Singh Pandey and that the protests morphed into a larger critique of misogyny, rape culture, and institutionalized patriarchy was a major achievement of feminist, left, antifascist, and peasant grassroots movements in India.[17]

In this particular case, the transformation of the movement into a platform that says, "No: this is what freedom really means," to confront patriarchy, the system, and government more broadly illustrates that the struggle is not just about rape or even violence against women but instead about redefining relations between men and women, people and government, freedom and constraint, safety and culture. While the remarkable mobilization of women and men of all ages, especially the youth around the question of women's *azadi* (freedom) and against the death penalty suggests the success of feminist, youth, and left movements, state responses to the protests indicate the responses of neoliberal, masculinist state managers moving to repress, contain, and rewrite Indian patriarchal practices completely gutted the JVC report of its radical antisexist spirit.[18]

While women's movement activists mobilized street actions, political education teach-ins, and advocacy efforts with various state agencies and tirelessly engaged the media and the state on antiquated and sexist attitudes and policies under the banner of Bekhauf Azadi for women in Indian streets, homes, and workspaces, the government responded in predictable ways to suppress the protests. State responses to the mass protests ran the gamut from violent suppression and lathi charges (pushing back against protesters with sticks and batons) to shutting down ten key metro stations in Delhi the day of the mass protest, thus controlling who could afford to join the protest (clearly limiting the class diversity since many could not afford to make their way to the site of the protest).[19] Eventually, the state gutted and reframed the recommendations of the Verma Commission report, touted as one of the most groundbreaking, radical, progressive documents addressing violence against women and centering the discourse on the integrity and autonomy of women's bodies.[20]

There is much to be said about this mobilization and its ongoing transformative impact on the Indian state and on ideologies of masculinity-femininity, patriarchal practices, and the demand of *bekhauf azadi* for women. Given our task in this chapter, however, we want to focus on the transnational reach of the struggle and on the politics of solidarity it engendered. The movement in India actively took on the Eve Ensler–initiated One Billion Rising campaign, which called for one billion women around the world to rise together to dance in a show of collective strength on February 14, 2013.[21] Protests demanding freedom from fear and violence against women spread around South Asia, as Shuddhabrata Sengupta describes, from Delhi to Djakarta.[22] In the United Kingdom, the Freedom Without Fear Platform emerged in solidarity with the Indian feminist mobilization. Amrit Wilson describes how the solidarity meeting organized by a large number of Black, South Asian, and minority ethnic women's organizations at the London School of Economics led to discussion about the ways neoliberal corporate culture sanctions sexual violence against women since it proliferates sexualized images of women in the cities of Britain and India and also in the villages of India. Wilson describes the genesis of the Freedom Without Fear Platform:

> Out of these discussions a new organization has emerged: the Freedom Without Fear Platform (FWFP), a loose coalition of women's organizations and individual women, unfunded by governments, nongovernmental organizations, or foundations, which takes its name from one of the slogans of the antirape movement in India, *Bekhauf Azadi*. Its aim is to build solidarity not only with the movement against sexual violence in India but also with movements and

grassroots struggles elsewhere in the global South and to give a platform to black, South Asian, and minority ethnic women to discuss
and make visible the violence against women and girls in Britain. It
seeks "to counter the imperialist racist discourse that UK mainstream
media continuously bombards us with and to highlight the cynical
co-opting of violence against women and girls' issues by various
groups in the United Kingdom who are seeking to further their own
racist and anti-immigration Islamophobic agendas."[23]

Canada: Idle No More

The Idle No More (INM) movement seeks to make Canada accountable for
five centuries of abuse and exploitation of First Nations peoples in Canada
and for denial of their nations' sovereignty. Four Indigenous and non-
Indigenous women—Jessica Gordon, Sylvia McAdam, Sheelah McLean,
and Nina Wilson, all from Saskatchewan—founded the grassroots protest
organization in October 2012.[24] It was a response to the Canadian state,
which developed a plan for extracting $650 billion worth of natural re-
sources, primarily oil, water, and natural gas, from First Nations peoples'
lands to sell and trade in the open market without consultation with the
owners of those lands. In short, the organizers mobilized to foster resistance
to the federal Conservative Government's omnibus Bill C-45 (2012). This
"unilateral and paternalistic" piece of legislation seriously threatens Canadian environmental protections and Indigenous control of reserve lands,
in effect a direct violation of Treaty agreements that are the legal and moral
foundation for the Canadian state. By passing Bill C-45, as well as seven
other pieces of legislation, without proper consultation with Indigenous
peoples, the Conservative Party (with a mandate from less than 40 percent
of voters in the last federal election) violated Articles 18, 19, and 20 of the
United Nations Declaration on the Rights of Indigenous Peoples.[25]

By December 2012, with the help of social media, INM was known worldwide and garnered solidarity from many other grassroots organizations
as far away as Australia and New Zealand and across the United States.
The movement is focused on three core issues: First Nations sovereignty;
the state's recognition of the legitimacy of treaties between Canada and
the First Nations; and grassroots democracy, on which it hinges its challenges to the Canadian state. While Canada's initial response was to ignore the movement, after a strong showing of support for it by many national and international social justice organizations, including Lawyers
Rights Watch Canada, the Native Women's Association of Canada, and

Amnesty International, Canadian prime minister Stephen Harper agreed to meet with the organization. In other words, the state was not allowed to continue its idle practice but instead was forced by grassroots organizing pressure to address the social justice issues INM raises.

While First Nations peoples have endured centuries of exploitation by the Canadian state and have historically mounted many objections and protests to this, what is different about Idle No More is its deep grassroots structure, its leadership by women, its affiliation with feminists and feminist-inspired engagements, and the respect and support it has attracted because of these marked differences. Indeed, this has sometimes put the movement at odds with Indigenous organizations that have historically been the voice of the First Nations, such as the primarily male-led and some would argue male-defined Assembly of First Nations.

Similar to the Occupy movement, INM has used social media to keep the question of social justice at the forefront of its struggle. Though the movement is rapidly changing, its core principles and concerns remain the same: Idle No More's call for decolonization puts it in direct conflict with the neoliberal political agenda embodied in Bill C-45 with its prioritization of global resource exploitation, indifference to environmental degradation, willful disregard for founding Treaty relations and denigration of local democracy.

While Bill C-45 passed without amendment, INM has continued to grow. Its leaders acknowledge that it was always about more than Bill C-45: It has been about the First Nations' relationship with Canada. It is a relationship that the former see as historically abusive by the latter. It is a relationship that was born of violence by the colonial state and continues to exist through sustained episodes of violence such as Bill C-45 by the neoliberal state.

The Idle No More movement positions its environmental justice concerns as applicable to all Canadians and the threat to First Nations sovereignty as a danger to Canada as a whole. As such, in the face of INM's calls on the state, it is no longer able to promote itself as a harbinger of social justice now that its continued pattern of institutional practices of injustice against the First Nations peoples has been made public.

Today, in the spirit of and in solidarity with the Occupy movement, which invokes the call for social justice for the 99 percent that neoliberalism exploits, Idle No More identifies as a peaceful revolution. INM calls on all concerned to join the fight against the injustices of neoliberalism on First Nations peoples and, in fact, to craft an alternative to neoliberalism.[26] It is now spreading across North America and has engendered global feminist solidarity. It can safely be said that Idle No More is a new women's movement, that is, a movement organized and led by women.

This may not be in the sense of what non-Indigenous feminists want to define as a women's movement. Yet, as Andrea Smith argues, First Nations women have always mobilized and configured their collective action, thus presenting internal challenges to the patriarchal leadership of both the chiefs of First Nations organizations and that of the Canadian state. While identifying with the feminist label has not been a focus of the movement, there are certainly numerous avowed feminists aligned with the movement.[27] What these women share is an anticapitalist resistance to the state and a commitment to social justice that threatens neoliberalism. As such, this is a force represented by women that calls every action of the neoliberal state into question as it constantly reinvents itself and reinscribes its legitimacy based on the market-driven principles of neoliberalism.

Summary

These two movements are not directly connected, yet we see a somewhat similar strategy by women to speak directly and forcefully to the state. They are sending a message that the violences of neoliberalism—gender, class, or indigeneity—will no longer remain uncontested. In spite of the historical, geopolitical, and contextual differences between the Idle No More and the Bekhauf Azadi movements, we believe that each showcases the different and connected ways that women confront injustice. The inequalities both of these movements address have generated a transnational following and solidarity, driven largely by social media. These movements show that there is a distinct connection across the globe among those who feel the heavy-handedness of the neoliberal state (i.e., the 99 percent) as their perpetual oppressor. Whether it is in the state's refusal to address issues of violence against women or in its relentless attempt to trample a people it has historically disrespected and deems powerless, there is an unspoken understanding of a link between both populations across two nation-states stretching from north to south. These movements' strategies of transnational solidarity therefore can suggest a template for how to successfully move a transnational feminist agenda against the neoliberal state forward. We end with Nawal el Saadawi's words urging us to build transnational feminist movements inspired by the example of Egyptian women's revolutionary struggles: "We need a transnational feminist movement, to fight not only against neoliberalism but also against religious fundamentalisms, which are supported by colonial global powers, capitalism, and imperialism. In fact, we cannot separate the global from the local struggle. We now use the word 'glocal.' The Egyptian revolution inspired other revolutions in Arab countries and even in the United States. The demonstrators in the Occupy Wall Street movement were carrying Egyptian revolution slogans the same as in other countries all over the world."

A luta continua!

Notes

This chapter was originally published as "Mapping Transnational Feminist Engagements: Neoliberalism and the Politics of Solidarity," with Linda Carty, in *The Oxford Handbook of Transnational Feminist Movements* (Oxford University Press, 2015), 82–115. Reprinted with permission of the publisher. The chapter inspired a decade-long video archive project: Feminist Freedom Warriors (see http://feministfreedomwarriors.org).

1   Our heartfelt thanks to the sisters and comrades who responded with great generosity to our persistent emails—we owe them deep gratitude for walking this journey alongside us. Thanks also to our fabulous graduate assistant, Anya Stanger, whose smart and incisive research, thinking, and feedback are woven into and an integral part of this chapter.

2   Alvarez, "Translating the Global"; Brenner, "Transnational Feminism and the Struggle for Global Justice"; Campt and Thomas, "Gendering Diaspora"; Mama, "Demythologising Gender in Development"; McClennen, "Neoliberalism and the Crisis of Intellectual Engagement."

3   In this chapter we draw on responses from the following: Sara Ahmed, Linda Martín Alcoff, Peggy Antrobus, Beverly Bain, Himani Bannerji, Avtar Brah, Urvashi Butalia, Teresa Cordova, Elizabeth Crespo-Kebler and Ana Irma Rivera Lassen, Angela Davis, Zillah Eisenstein, Laila Farah, Joan French, Honor Ford-Smith, Beverly Guy-Sheftall, Asha Hans, Aida Hernandez, Linda Peake, Islah Jad, Lee Maracle, Margo Okazawa-Rey, Richa Nagar, Julia Oparah, Minne Bruce Pratt, Nawal el-Sadaawi, Rhoda Reddock, Fatima Sadiqi, Alissa Trotz and Andaiye, Mara Viveros- Vigoya, Judith Wedderburn, and Gloria Wekker.

4   We did not hear back from a number of feminist scholar-activists, and we especially regret not including more African and transgender feminists in this cartography. We believe there are perhaps important gaps in our dialogue as a result of these absences and want to acknowledge them explicitly.

5   We refer to the state as an institutional apparatus that includes the government, the judiciary, and the bureaucracy (the civil service). The state elite is the body made up of the directorships of all these institutions. We are used to assuming that society is controlled and run by the government, but that role is actually carried out by the state. Much of the state's desires, however, are carried out by the government; thus the government is often seen as the most crucial institution of the state.

6 Needless to say, we quote extensively from our interlocutors because their reflections are theoretical, analytic, and historically specific—not merely descriptive. We have chosen to create a theoretical quilt rather than use their voices to support our own story.

7 Harvey, *Brief History of Neoliberalism*.

8 Sassen, *Globalization and Its Discontents*. Sassen examines the globalization of labor and how capital's search for cheap labor has created the globalized city. She observes the conditions of labor in both the North and the South as being determined by the same neoliberal market principles that have created marked similarities for workers in both regions.

9 See Mohanty, "Transnational Feminist Crossings"; Desai, "Transnational Solidarity"; and Davis, "Race and Criminalization," for insight into how the state appropriates feminist language and struggles, uses prisons to incarcerate radical activists, and severely cuts support of social programs, all of which helps it to successfully curtail feminist organizing to counter its neoliberal strategies of domination and social control.

10 Peake et al., "Feminist Academic and Activist Praxis," 112.

11 See chapter 7, "Transnational Feminist Crossings: On Neoliberalism and Radical Critique," for an extended discussion of the neoliberal appropriation of radical feminist praxis.

12 See discussions of this point in Rao and Rose, "LGBTQ Activists of Color Talk Trump."

13 Hamel, "Leslie Feinberg upon Release from Jail."

14 Leslie Feinberg, "This Is What Solidarity Looks Like," accessed March 4, 2024, https://www.lesliefeinberg.net/solidarity-slideshow/.

15 Pratt, "Syracuse Passes Trans Rights Bill."

16 Our analysis of these movements is based entirely on internet sources that provide the most current and up-to-date analysis and documentation of ongoing struggles.

17 Narrain, "Verma Committee"; whimsy mimsy BoroGoves, "Freedom Without Fear/Bekhauf Azadi."

18 Narrain, "Verma Committee"; Nandita Shah, personal email, July 22, 2013. As Arvind Narrain argues, "The Verma Committee Report most fundamentally alters the public discourse on crimes against women by placing these crimes within the framework of the Indian Constitution and treating these offences as nothing less than an egregious violation of the right to live with dignity of all women. What is particularly moving and inspiring about the Report is that it does so by placing the autonomy and indeed the sexual autonomy of women at the very centre of its discourse."

19 For a sharp critique of how government actions deliberately target collective action, see Vellanki, "Breaking the Collective." Vivek Vellanki argues here that "the closing down of the metro stations had a significant impact on the nature of the protests. It brought with it a collective that was 'cleansed' of divergent voices and identities. I am quite certain that the protest was definitely limited from what could have been a democratic collective of people involved in a democratic process."

20 Zitzewitz, "Timeline of Events in the Delhi Gang-Rape Case." For discussions of the JVC report, see Sengupta, "Water Cannons, Tear Gas, Ordinance."

21 See Akshara Centre, "One Billion Rising Campaign," February 14, 2014, https://aksharacentre.org/#press.

22 See Husain, "From Delhi to Djakarta."

23 Wilson, "India's Anti-Rape Movement." See also Freedom Without Fear, accessed November 6, 2013, http://freedomwithoutfearplatform.blogspot.com.

24 See detailed information on the Idle No More movement at https://idlenomore.ca.

25 See Pembina Institute, "Environmental Groups, First Nations Join in Opposition to Omnibus Bill C-45."

26 See Naomi Klein's interview with Leanne Simpson, one of the founders of Idle No More: Simpson, "Dancing the World into Being."

27 See Andrea Smith's "Indigenous Feminism Without Apology," in which she argues that First Nations women have always been feminists but resist the label due to its imperial import and inability to capture their reality.

4

BORDERS AND BRIDGES

Securitized Regimes, Racialized Citizenship,
and Insurgent Feminist Praxis

Voyager, there are no bridges, one builds them as one walks.
—GLORIA ANZALDÚA, *This Bridge Called My Back*

It is July 2020 and we are in the midst of an unprecedented global health pandemic that has laid all social inequities bare, an ongoing antiracist revolution in the streets of US cities and around the world proclaiming *Black Lives Matter* following the violent death of George Floyd (and Breonna Taylor, Ahmaud Arbery, Tony McDade, among others), an acute economic crisis, and the "failure of the social experiment that is America," as Cornell West named it. So what does a radical, antiracist, anti-imperialist feminist struggle entail in these violently racist, misogynist, neoliberal times?[1] What do antiracist feminist scholars, activists, and cultural workers need to know, analyze, and learn about so we can forge ethical solidarities across material and virtual borders, and build the landscapes of racial and gender justice that we dream about and struggle for? What does it mean to craft insurgent knowldges through our writing, our art, our cultural productions, our activism, and our pedagogies?

In 2020 our understandings of feminism, decolonization, and transnationalism are in flux, contested in social movements, state policy, and social and political theory. In 2020, the transnational necessitates acknowledging explicitly carceral regimes; geopolitical climate destruction; militarized national borders; massive displacement of peoples (war, climate, and economic refugees); the proliferation of corporatist, racist, misogynist cultures; lean-in and glass ceiling (liberal) feminisms; the decimation of labor movements; and the rise of right-wing, proto-fascist governments around the world (Modi in India, Erdoğan in Turkey, Bolsonaro in Brazil, Trump in the United States). All these phenomena are of course connected to global economic crises (the oil crisis in the 1970s and the stock market crash in 2008 and now 2020), neoliberal governmentalities, global racialities, and mass unemployment, displacement, and dispossession of particular groups of people worldwide.

Undergirding all my scholarly work are my activist commitments to building radical, antiracist, transnational feminist communities in all the spaces I have lived in over four-plus decades of living in the United States. None of this work would be possible without these dissident communities. And this I think is the key to living an insurgent life as an antiracist, anti-imperialist feminist in these times. Building and sustaining the "intellectual neighborhoods" (Toni Morrison) and communities of dissent that inspire and can sustain an insurgent feminist life. The very first "intellectual neighborhood" I collaborated in building, and which set me on my journey over four decades ago, was as a graduate student at the University of Illinois, Urbana-Champaign. I co-organized, with Ann Russo, the "Common Differences: Third World Women and Feminist Perspectives" conference in 1983—I believe this was the first or one of the first conferences of this scale to bring US women of color and feminists from the "third world" into conversation about the "common differences" in our feminist praxis. It was the beginning of my intellectual journey in the company of feminists of color. Historically, the conference emerged from decades of anticolonial, anticapitalist, and national liberation movements that women in the global South (we called ourselves third world women then) had waged since the 1940s, and the revolutionary freedom and civil rights movements that women of color had waged in the global North. Questions of intersectionality and relationality of structures of power and women's place-based resistance; the complexities of working across race, class, sexuality, and nationality in the context of multiple colonial legacies and imperial adventures of the United States; the centrality of economic issues, poverty, and class in envisioning and enacting gender justice; the significance of identity and community (who are the "we"?); and the theoretical and epistemological contributions of a decolonial feminist engagement were all issues that emerged from this collective space—and that have stayed with me through all the work I have done since then.[2]

I have always believed that the intellectual work we are passionate about is in some way connected to (but not identical to) our biographies. My experience of a radical community of third world and women of color thinkers at the "Common Differences" conference made it clear that an antiracist, anticapitalist, and anti-imperialist feminist community was possible, indeed necessary, in and outside the academy. My definition of transnational feminist praxis is anchored in these very particular intellectual and political genealogies—in studies of race, colonialism, and empire in the global North and South; in the critiques of feminists of color in the United States; and in studies of decolonization, anticapitalist critique, and LGBTQ/queer studies in the North and the South. My use of this category is thus anchored in my location in the global North, and in the commitment to work systematically and overtly against racialized, heterosexist, imperial, corporatist projects that characterize North American global adventures. My interest lies in the connections between the politics of knowledge and the spaces, places, and locations that we occupy. This chapter is an attempt to think through the political and epistemological struggles that are embedded in radical critical, antiracist, anticapitalist feminist praxis at this time.[3]

Neoliberal Regimes: Capitalist Dispossession, Securitized States, Imperial Democracies

I began thinking about borders and bridges—specifically about neoliberal/securitized regimes, antiracist struggles, and anatomies of violence—after hearing about the building of a US "mega-security wall" along the South Texas/Mexico border, and the struggles of immigrant activists and the Lipan Apache Women's Defense (LAW Defense) organization to halt this explicitly imperialist partition project. What seemed obvious was the use of unjust, militarized state practices similar to those used in the war zones of Iraq and Afghanistan, using the pretext of the "war on terror" and its earlier iteration, the "war on drugs," to mobilize simultaneous discourses of Islamophobia and nativism. And yet, at that time, a decade ago, the struggles of LAW Defense, even the building of the mega-security wall in East Texas, were almost completely absent from public discussion, in the media, and in left/feminist circles. Now of course the family separation of migrants has its epicenter in Texas, especially in the Rio Grande Valley. It is home to the largest center for "undocumented migrants and asylum seekers" and the "Casa Padre" shelter for minors, which has a capacity to hold fourteen hundred children. While US imperial projects are not new, the post-9/11 global formation and operation of securitized states, anchored within the rhetoric of protectionism and the war on terror and accompanied by militarized, neoliberal corporate ambitions, is a phenomenon that deserves our ongoing attention.[4]

In this essay I examine three neoliberal, securitized regimes and three specific geopolitical sites—the US-Mexico border struggles around immigration, and cross-border Indigenous rights in the Lower Rio Grande Valley in Texas; Israel's rule over the occupied Palestinian territories of the West Bank/Gaza; and India's military rule and occupation of the Kashmir Valley (Jammu and Kashmir) as zones of normalized violence. Needless to say, each site is precisely about racialized citizenship projects that are constitutive of each of the three nation-states. At these sites, neoliberal and militarized state and imperial practices are often sustained by development/peacekeeping/humanitarian projects, thus illuminating the old/new contours of securitized states that function as neoliberal, imperial democracies.

Each site encodes genealogies, memories, and traumas of colonial occupation, partition, and violence in the building of the nation—what the novelist Bapsi Sidhwa calls the "demand for blood" when the earth is divided.[5] And in each of these geopolitical sites at the territorial borders of the nation, civilians are subjected to militarized violence anchored in the production of reactionary gender identities and dominant and subordinate (often racialized) masculinities. These three sites constitute occupied, disputed territories with violent colonial histories, and together they illustrate a new/old global order of militarized, racist violence engendered by neoliberal economic priorities.

Since the early 1990s, with India's shift to neoliberal economic and political policies, the ties between the United States, Israel, and India have been forged through the vision of the regimes in power at that time: Bush and the neoconservatives, Sharon and Likud, and the Bharatiya Janata Party (BJP)/Hindu Right. As Rupal Oza suggests, since the early 1990s, the geopolitical triad of the United States, Israel, and India have shared a vision of threat and security based on Islam and Muslims as the common enemy, cemented through close and ongoing economic and military alliances.[6]

The same anti-Muslim rhetoric is evident in the current refugee crisis in Europe, where Hungarian prime minister Viktor Orbán says Muslims must be "blocked" to "keep Europe Christian. . . . Europe and European identity is rooted in Christianity."[7] We witness neo-Nazi attacks on asylum seekers in Germany (remember the majority of the refugees from Syria, Iraq, and Afghanistan are Muslims) and the growth of detention centers, "reception centers," or "camps" in Hungary and Turkey.

And we cannot forget Trump and his deployment of an "us and them" language of a securitized state, talking about refusing Muslims entry to the United States and holding the government hostage to the building of a wall at the US-Mexico border. As Naomi Paik argues, Trump signed three executive orders immediately after taking office in January 2017: the so-called Muslim ban, an order focused on border security (building the wall), and a third order that bolstered immigration enforcement (giving Immigration and Customs Enforcement a sweeping mandate to remove all "illegal immigrants").[8] Taken together these executive orders are in fact an explicit legacy of the building of a historical US citizenship project anchored in governance practices of exclusion and exploitation anchored in race, gender, and labor. Since 2015, a new federal government initiative called Countering Violent Extremism (CVE), a pilot project in Los Angeles, Boston, and Minneapolis, has been underway. CVE is described as a program that aims to deter US citizens from joining "violent extremist" groups by bringing community and religious leaders together with law enforcement, health professionals, teachers, and social service employees. In Los Angeles, CVE, the American Muslim Women's Empowerment Council (AMWEC), the LAPD, CIA, and FBI are partners in the creation of "patriotic Muslim women" who take on the task of countering violent extremism in their communities—thus producing empowered, loyal, Muslim women citizens. Azza Basarudin and Khanum Shaikh suggest that it is liberal feminist discourses of motherhood and empowerment that are appropriated in the service of national security and "motherwork" deployed so that gender appears and disappears in the war on terror. In moments that the US policies of rendition and/or torture impose violence on their bodies they become invisible, but in moments when there is a productive convergence between the empowered Muslim woman and state policies, she becomes hypervisible.[9]

However, while the "us versus them" ideologies of securitized states justify borders, walls, and regimes of incarceration and, more recently, regimes of mass deportation in the name of protection of the homeland, it is the connectivity and commonality of analysis and vision of justice (the bridges) between peoples across borders that feminists and antipartition activists have in common that inspires my reflections. I argue that we have much to learn from analyzing the resistance politics and collective aspirations of freedom and self-determination across these sites and that developing these transnational feminist frameworks is in fact key to envisioning solidarities and building bridges across borders. A comparative analysis of the wars and walls (symbolic and material) that constitute the securitized regimes and colonial/imperial ventures of the United States, India, and Israel reveals the ideological operation of discourses of "democracy" within the overtly militarized, securitized nation-states of India, Israel, and the United States and suggests that the militarization of cultures is deeply linked to neoliberal capitalist values and the normalization of what Zillah Eisensteinand Arundhati Roy have called "imperial democracy."[10] Needless to say, militarization always involves masculinization and heterosexualization as linked state projects, and neoliberal economic arrangements are predicated on gendered and racialized divisions of labor and constructions of subjectivities, thus necessitating *feminist* critique.

National security states or neoliberal securitized regimes typically use connected strategies of militarization, criminalization, and incarceration to exercise control over particular populations, thus remaking individual subjectivities and public cultures. Tanya Golash-Boza adds another layer— she argues that mass incarceration is the other side of the coin of mass deportation and that mass deportation is a gendered and racialized tool of state repression implemented in a time of crisis.[11] So, for instance, while Black men are the largest group incarcerated in the United States, Latino men are the largest group facing mass deportation. This understanding of mass incarceration and state violence is now in the public domain after Ferguson and the Black Lives Matter movement (not to mention George Floyd and the call for defunding the police). The now visible history of mass deportations since Obama (today nearly 90 percent of deportees are Latino and Caribbean men) and its link to the gendered and racialized immigration history in the United States is also no longer obfuscated by state managers. In addition, in terms of the so-called European refugee crisis, Greece built a barbed wire fence along the Greece-Turkey border in 2013; Hungarian prison inmates worked on preparing materials for nine hundred military personnel to begin construction of the 109-mile-long razor wire fence along the border with Serbia to "protect" Europe from migrants, and they are ready to build a fence along the border with Romania; and Austria, Slovakia, and the Netherlands all introduced border controls to "manage" the refugee crisis. These are all connected sites of neoliberal citizenship projects that are deeply raced and gendered, anchored in colonial and neocolonial histories and economic priorities.

As the feminist philosopher Iris Young argues, security states mobilize a particular gendered logic of masculinist protection in relation to women and children—a logic that underwrites the appeal to "protection and security" of the nation and expects obedience and loyalty at home (patriotism).[12] At the same time, the state wages war against internal and external enemies. In the context of the United States, it is this logic that Young claims legitimates authoritarian power in the domestic arena and justifies aggression outside its borders. Here again, the AMWEC and CVE example is instructive. As Basarudin and Shaikh argue: "Partnering with law enforcement in celebrating American multiculturalism and women's empowerment is problematic when nestled firmly within a logic of securitization, surveillance, and vitriolic xenophobia against immigrants and people of color. Mining motherhood for soft counterterrorism becomes a productive convergence between state agencies and AMWEC members."[13]

Militarized, neoliberal state projects in the United States, Israel, and India create and sustain endless wars and border zones of violence while normalizing incarceration regimes within their respective domestic landscapes. The United States invests in a fast-growing, privatized prison-industrial complex within its borders, while consolidating postinvasion regimes of torture and collective punishment in Iraq and Afghanistan. Similar questions need to be posed in relation to the "democracies" of Israel and India. In all three geopolitical contexts, the state mobilizes a masculinist securitized ideology based not on the defense of the nation but on coercion that requires neither participation nor consent from its citizens.[14] This gendered ideology is anchored in militarized masculinities (or muscular militarism) and in patriarchal ideologies of protection and security that require obedience and consent from citizens.

In the Texas-Mexico borderlands, the West Bank and Gaza, and the Kashmir Valley, dispossession of particular subjects (women, poor, Indigenous, migrant, Muslim, etc.) involves the social control and legal dispossession (or social death) through "justified" forms of surveillance and violence at multiple levels. The political economy of securitized states is focused fundamentally on the permanent abandonment of certain "captive populations" that are marked as threats to the neoliberal order.[15] After all, surveillance and secuity have always been conjoined techniques of colonial control of so-called dangerous populations. Here militarized capitalism enshrined within securitized states works in concert with fundamentalist Hindu, Muslim, Zionist, and Christian social movements to produce a surge of reactionary neoliberal gender identities. Kalpana Wilson and colleagues suggest that "within contemporary Hindutva, virulent Islamophobia, caste supremacism, and patriarchal values are intertwined with a commitment to supporting the interests of neoliberal corporate capital through the intensification of gendered processes of exploitation, displacement and dispossession."[16] Thus, in this context, statecraft, economic imperatives, and gendered narratives of patriotism are profoundly intertwined.

Securitized Regimes and Cultures of Impunity

Speaking of Argentina in the twentieth century, Rita Arditti refers to the exercise of state violence within a culture of impunity.[17] A culture of impunity occurs when the state operates without fear of punishment, and impunity is normalized as a routine procedure across political and legal domains, producing a kind of disordered order or state of exception necessary for the process of domination.[18] This is a form of governmentality where the state regimes of surveillance, criminalization, and the legal suspension of rights in the name of protecting the nation from so-called insurgents and illegals operate with impunity—disappearing citizens, imprisoning others, and denying basic civil and economic rights to particular marginalized communities. Migrant detainees form one of the fastest-growing prison populations around the Western world. Three countries including the United States and Israel have built thirty-five hundred miles of walls on their borders, and over forty thousand deaths since 2000 are linked to migration. A very brief snapshot of the operation of securitized regimes in each of the sites follows.

Democracy and Security in Israel and Palestine

In an incisive analysis of gendered violence in occupied Gaza, Hagar Kotef argues that the framework of democracy in Israel is now the framework of security—a radically inequitable frame where the security of some groups means the insecurity of others, where Israel's security constitutes so-called democracy for Palestinians.[19] The State of Israel bases its democracy entirely on an ethnic, demographic notion of citizenship with the "right of return" for Jews only. Israel is a capitalist, class-divided, securitized state that excludes non-Jews and Arabs from citizenship—noncitizens have very few rights and no claim on the Israeli state.[20] Since 1948, the "partition" of the Palestinian territory has meant the establishment of the State of Israel and the simultaneous uprooting of and mass dispersal of Palestinians from their homeland. Thus, while 1948 represents the building of a homeland for Israel, it represents Al-Nakba, the "catastrophe," for Palestinians—defeat, displacement, trauma, dispossession, and the beginning of a liberation movement.[21]

Kotef suggests that the contemporary discourse of terror collapses the distinction between civilians and soldiers in national security states and that "humanitarian" actions thus become accessories to state violence against Palestinians. She argues that humanitarianism provides, alongside terror, the logic of security.[22] It is in fact Israel's closing off of the Gaza Strip that has led to a "humanitarian" crisis of vast proportions, and it is in the name of humanitarian missions that Israel controls access to Gaza. While humanitarianism offers a framework of rights and redress for multiple communities around the world, it also potentially entrenches power for occupying regimes by creating and sanctioning categories of "natives" and "refugees." Under occupation, as Bhan and Duschinski suggest, "humanitarianism can be used to whitewash crimes against humanity in occupied contexts and further empire building through discourses of 'participatory militarism.'"[23] What is a "separation fence" to Israelis in the West Bank is, after all, an "apartheid wall" to Palestinians. What is a mega-security wall for elite landowners in Texas is in fact containment and imprisonment for the Indigenous nations that cross the US-Mexico borderlands.

Militarized Regimes and the Politics of Violence in Jammu and Kashmir

The Kashmir Valley (i.e., Jammu and Kashmir) is one of the most highly militarized zones in the world. The Indian government has deployed over six hundred thousand border security and over a quarter of a million paramilitary forces in the valley, which has a population of thirteen million. This is one of the highest soldier-to-civilian population ratios anywhere in the world.[24] While much has been written about the history of Indian occupation of Kashmir, and about the way the 1947 partition of India and Pakistan creates and re-creates this trauma in Jammu and Kashmir, I am most interested here in the functioning of the Indian militarized state apparatus in the Kashmir Valley and the way in which it controls and defines identity, community, and subjectivity, especially since 2014 and the rise of a Hindutva state that actively victimizes and dehumanizes Kashmir and domesticates and punishes all forms of dissent.

The object of three wars, an arms race, and a nuclear race between India and Pakistan, Kashmir has been disputed territory since 1947. It has witnessed the increasingly political role of the military and of Islamist movements in Pakistan, as well as the rise of Hindu fundamentalism in India. The Kashmir Valley has been treated by India as a state of emergency since 1947. In fact, postcolonial India can be analyzed in terms of two contradictory narratives—that of a progressive, anticolonial, democratic, socialist nation post-Bandung (1955), and that of a nation that has always exercised violence toward Dalits, Adivasi, women, religious and sexual minorities, Kashmir, the Northeast, and so on, in the name of democracy. Since the 1960s, there has been a growing movement against Indian occupation, leading to escalating tensions in the 1980s with the formation of the Jammu and Kashmir Liberation Front, an underground seccesionist movement engaged in an armed struggle for self determination.

The nature of the rebellion in the early 1990s changed with the emergence of over one hundred separatist organizations, some with explicitly religious and pro-Pakistani politics.[25] In response, India passed the Armed Forces Special Powers Act (AFSPA) in 1990, granting the military state impunity to enforce a regime of surveillance and incarceration in Kashmir. AFSPA underwrote the ideological framing of the Kashmir Valley in terms of fear and threat, mobilizing the rhetoric of insurgency/counterinsurgency and justifying the suspension of constitutional rights and freedoms. The AFSPA in the Kashmir Valley allows the legal suspension of the distinction between legality and illegality. State agents are thus allowed to act with impunity and are "protected" by AFSPA. Custodial killings, torture, detention without trial or charge, disappearances, mass rape (as in the villages of Kunan Poshpora), and use of human shields are "protected" by the AFSPA. Nitasha Kaul claims that in Kashmir, "the funeral and the demonstration do not just look indistinguishable, but are necessarily continuous and the same. The funeral is an act of grief that unfolds into protest, and the demonstration is fired upon and results in funerals."[26] Similarly, Inshah Malik suggests that public mourning rituals are sites of gendered resistance where grieving mothers embody defiance, not passive victimization.[27] Kashmir then functions as what activists have called a "constitution-free" zone similar to the Texas-Mexico border and the West Bank and Gaza.

To summarize, despite the different histories of colonialism and imperialism, there is a remarkable similarity in the forms of governmentality exercised by the securitized states of India, Israel, and the United States (and now the European Union). Recall that the EU response to the migrant/refugee crisis is framed in humanitarian and religious terms, not in terms of justice or democracy or equality of all human beings—and that similar securitized regimes, militarization, and forms of governmentality are being enacted at border crossings in Europe. The historical responsibility and the role of European governments in causing, precipitating, or helping to find solutions to the conflicts are largely absent.

Comparing these geopolitical sites allows us to understand the way the "war on terror" and militarized cultures, state violence, and the transformation of civilians into insurgents and illegals through the legal suspension of civil rights are symptomatic of imperial democracies at this present moment. In each context, the sovereignty of the state is predicated on the operation of "constitution-free" zones at the borders of the nation.[28] The normalized violence against particular bodies—Muslim, female, immigrant, native, and Arab—buttresses the discourses of protectionism and citizenship in each country. In each case, we can identify states of exception whereby the suspension of law is required for the practice of empire. In each context, citizenship remains elusive for the inhabitants of these borderlands, and identity is always in question given the existence of checkpoints, and "I" cards. In these securitized landscapes identity documents become a form of governance and a part of the state apparatus of surveillance. The process of verifying identity produces what Tobias Kelly calls "documented lives"—particular forms of subjectivity that are marked by anxiety, uncertainty, and fear.[29] Kelly's work focuses on Palestinians, but a similar argument can be made in the other contexts as well.[30]

A bio-militarized gendered body project is evident in each site, and women are impacted in different, albeit similar, ways since violence is a part of daily life—as is the presence of paramilitary and police forces. In the Kashmir Valley, women are victims of sexual violence, domestic violence, and rape, and live with increasing trauma, stress, depression, miscarriages, and spontaneous abortions.[31] There are increasing numbers of widows and so-called half widows (women whose husbands have disappeared). In 1947, women's militias were an integral part of the Quit Kashmir movement, while many women in recent years have organized under the banner of the Association of Parents of Disappeared Persons (APDP) and under the Kashmiri Women's Initiative for Peace and Disarmament.[32] The impact of Israeli occupation on Palestinian women is profound as well. The erasure of the difference between home and battlefield and between civilians and soldiers means that neighborhoods and homes become the battlefield in Gaza. In Israeli official death counts in Gaza, the men are counted as militants, while women and children are counted as "collateral damage."[33] The occupation shrinks public space, confining women to the household, while long-term unemployment for men in Gaza was at 40 percent before the Israeli invasion in June 2014. Such instabilities translate into changed family dynamics and often a rise in domestic violence in the home.

When the very identities of people come under question, when sexual, ethnic/racial, and political violence becomes normative, as it does in these landscapes, the structure of imperial democracies is laid bare. In fact, the governance practices of securitized regimes are such that security is deeply entangled with citizenship or subjectivation processes. While democratic state projects focus on producing national citizens, in securitized regimes what is at stake is the opposite—the undoing of the very possibility of citizenship for targeted populations like Indigenous and Mexican peasant migrant workers, Palestinians in the Occupied Palestine Territory, civilians in the Kashmir Valley, and so on.[34] These borderlands constitute "shadow" communities at the social and territorial margins of the state—places that exist as part of the formal state, but excluded from it so that the violent realities of everyday life, and the legal and extralegal networks that support them are caught up in layers of invisibility.

Thus, this logic of violence, containment, and expulsion produces patterns of social abandonment and death with consequences both for communities targeted as enemies and outsiders, and also for the entire political body of rights-bearing citizens because it draws them/us into the field of state violence.[35] These forms of truncated subjectivity and noncitizenship are a profound marker of neoliberal global security landscapes at this time.

Walls, Borders, and Connectivities: Enacting Solidarities

The first colonization of the "Americas" by Europe dismembered the land and put in motion a process that wiped out Indigenous peoples and their civilizations. Zionist colonization of Palestine has also dismembered the land and attempted to eradicate the Indigenous people's cultural identity and destroy any sign of their previous presence in the land. It wiped over 400 Palestinian villages and dispossessed their residents turning them into stateless refugees in the lands of exile and outsiders and strangers in their own land. The Southwest was subjected to another wave of colonization by American settlers. This act of imperialism divided the Mexican people between two sides of an artificial border.
—NADINE SALIBA, 2006, quoted in Kamala Platt, "Women on Wars and Walls"

The above quote illustrates the historical and contemporary connectivities forged by feminist and antipartition activists at the Esperanza Center in San Antonio, Texas. The US Secure Fence Act of 2006 gave the Department of Homeland Security (DHS) unilateral power to waive thirty-six federal laws at the Texas-Mexico international border and, in collaboration with NAFTA partners, begin building a Berlin-style, concrete mega-security wall. This waiver of laws led to the militarization of the entire region of the Lower Rio Grande, voiding legal rights and protections of Indigenous peoples to culture, environment, biodiversity and sacred sites—a clear example of US imperial policy seen as "rational" through the frame of the war on terror, and an incarceration regime that targets immigrants. The 2006 act authorized hundreds of miles and $1.4 billion worth of additional barriers, checkpoints, border agents, and surveillance technology like drones. In this case, laws (and their suspension) are used as weapons to destabilize, fragment, assimilate, and disappear communities historically residing along the Lower Rio Grande. LAW Defense (founded by mother and daughter Eloisa García Támez and Margo Támez in 2007) focuses on community organization and documentation, and research and education, thus strengthening Indigenous people's struggles against US colonial violence, as well as in relation to legal struggles in tribal, US, and international law courts. The Secure Fence Act also led to the building of a seventy-five-mile border wall on the Tohono O'odham territory in Arizona and the O'odham resistance and organizing against Trump's "new" border wall that led in 2018 to the longest government shutdown in US history!

Capitalist profit-making and corporate agendas (instigated by the United States, NAFTA partners, and corporations with mining interests) operate in full force in Texas and Arizona as waivers work differently for rich landowners and industrialists and for poor Indigenous and Mexican border communities. Rich landowners have waivers from the building of the wall, while Indigenous communities have walls built on their land (what activists have labeled a "constitution-free zone"). Thus, Indigenous peoples and illegal immigrants (poor Mexican peasants) are constructed in similar ways: criminalized and defined as drug lords, terrorists, labor migrants, and civic resisters. It is therefore imperative to disaggregate *both* categories—immigrant *and* Indigenous—since at this historical juncture, both are produced by a securitized state engaged in a "war on terror."[36] The continued reinvention of the immigrant and the Indigenous and the way in which immigration laws, especially laws against the "illegal immigrant," have profound impact in Indigenous communities is new. The O'odham and Lipan Apache territory crosses the US-Mexico border. Mexico now requires US passports for the O'odham who travel beyond twelve miles into Mexican territory.

Arizona Law SB 1070 justifies the presence of Border Patrol on reservation lands. Checkpoints have been established throughout the territory, thus controlling free movement of the Akimel and Tohono O'odham peoples, especially elders who do not have birth certificates but need to travel across the US-Mexico border to Malina/Magdelena in Mexico for religious pilgrimage.[37] Reports by National Public Radio and community organizations like Grassroots Leadership revealed that SB 1070 was funded by the for-profit prison complex.[38] While SB 1070 talks specifically about "enforcement through attrition" of illegal immigrants, it has morphed into the policing of Indigenous lands and communities. The checkpoints on the reservation resemble checkpoints in Palestinian territory. People who live on the Tohono O'odham reservation have their everyday lives profoundly shaped by the surveillance and militarization enforced by SB 1070. Along with authorizing the construction of fencing, the 2006 bill also authorized added vehicle barriers, checkpoints, and lighting along the southern border as well as an increased use of advanced technology like cameras, satellites, and unmanned aerial vehicles. Thus militarization is fundamental to the construction of community and identity.[39] The combination of checkpoints, identity verification, and surveillance suggests a specific form of the production of "documented subjectivities." As Naomi Paik describes, for most of US history borders were both porous and movable.[40] It was only with the nineteenth-century Chinese Exclusion Act that the United States began to police its borders. Thus, the building of walls, fences, and resulting documented lives as governance strategies for the creation of white, male citizenship projects has a long history in the United States.

Since 2013 there have been two important megaprojects underway across the Texas-Mexico border: (1) a large rail transport system that will traverse the border wall in the Lower Rio Grande Valley, and (2) the building of a trans-Texas corridor that connects Alberta, Canada, to South Texas, to Mexico that is part of a transhemispheric "security prosperity partnership" that entails "priority matters of national security" being transported by a mega-heavy rail freight bridge over the Lipan Apache territory. And, as mentioned earlier, given the fact that Texas and the Rio Grande Valley are home to the largest immigration detention centers, since May 2018 more than twenty-three hundred children have been separated from their parents or guardians while crossing the border illegally or seeking asylum. Since June 20, 2018, when Trump ordered an end to family separations, two thousand children remain alone in these "processing centers." What this spectacle at the border hides is the US reliance on and exploitation of particularly undocumented migrant labor.

As Nadine Saliba suggests above, there are clear confluences between the impact of US colonial and imperial projects and Israel's colonization and occupation of the West Bank and Gaza.[41] The organizing work of the Esperanza Center brings these connections home in terms of the impact of walls, borders, and dispossession in the lives of women in Palestine and the borderlands of South Texas and offers a moving and illuminating look at the amazing cross-border, transnational feminist organizing and community building that has occurred over the last five years.[42] While the profiteers and state managers in each of these sites share resources and technologies of surveillance and violence, it is the people in the impacted communities who share forms of survival and resistance to the normalized violence of the securitized regimes in the United States and Israel.

In both contexts, social movements focus on environmental justice and land struggles. The militarization of the US-Mexico border and the building of the mega-security wall destroy agriculture and livelihoods for peasants and Indigenous communities on both sides of the border. The "apartheid wall" and the endless war in the occupied Palestinian territory has destroyed homes and uprooted olive trees and orchards—a symbol of livelihood and home for Palestinians. These are shared colonial histories of violence and dispossession; they can be mobilized to create connectivities and resistance to partitions and walls in Palestine and South Texas.

What is hopeful here is the way communities organize in resistance. In the US-Mexico borderlands there are new political formations and alliances between organizations of day laborers, migrant workers, radical high school and university students, and queer and transgender Mexican migrants. Indigenous peasants and migrants, anarchists (Native anarchists), antiracist white organizations, neighborhood groups (Barrio Defense groups), antiprivatization organizations (prisons and detention centers), prison abolitionist organizations, edu-activists, and mainstream alliance organizations like the Mexican consulate, legislatures, and unions (Somos Arizona) work in solidarity. Women of color do the majority of on-the-ground organizing in most of these groups. This coalition is constituted as it is because activists have conjoined a number of Arizona laws that have decimated ethnic studies (HB 2281, passed in May 2010, bans Arizona schools from teaching ethnic studies), cast aside affirmative action (Proposition 107, anti–affirmative action legislation passed November 4, 2010), and SB 1070.[43] All of these laws may look like they target separate communities in separate places, which is precisely how the state and hegemonic power want to have it function, but clearly political organizing has done the work of connecting the links, showing the connectivity within the different kinds of violence to which communities are subjected.

Similar cross-border and cross-community coalitions are evident in the Israeli and Palestinian feminist struggles against the Israeli occupation, and in Indian, Pakistani, and Kashmiri women organizing against all forms of state and communal violence across borders, religions, and national loyalties.[44] The insurgent knowledges generated by these forms of activism engender the new political subjectivities and visions of citizenship necessary to confront imperial democracies.

While the anatomies of violence in these borderlands are more overt, imperial democracies militarize all domains of social life and discipline/imprison not just abandoned and criminalized communities but *all* state subjects. The border, after all, is not confined to the edges of the nation—it is not a wall or barrier but a logistical infrastructure with its own architecture of surveillance, documentation, and big data technologies that are constitutive of subjectivity and citizenship in neoliberal times. Perhaps we need to be attentive to the ever-enchroaching spread of the "border" and all the violences that it signifies.

Borders and Bridges: On Solidarity

So, what does it mean to decolonize feminism and to envision ethical transnational feminist futures? How do the frameworks/approaches of decoloniality, anticapitalism, and feminism inform, enhance, contradict, and mutually influence one another? These are urgent and important political and intellectual questions at this time when the rhetoric of "transnational" has been co-opted on a large scale in neoliberal university settings. Administrators are "transnational" since they travel across the globe in search of profitable partnerships with universities in other countries, and for "international" students who can pay for higher education that is no longer available to working-class and poor students in the United States. Academic curricula are also "transnational" since "study abroad" programs now buttress a normative curriculum that supposedly prepares students to compete in a global market. In the US academy, then, "transnational" often becomes a placeholder for business as usual, marked as "progressive" in the face of a conservative, xenophobic backlash. Globalization and transnational knowledge production become the new managerial mantra in neoliberal universities.

In addition, the larger geopolitical landscape poses urgent and significant challenges to those of us committed to an anticapitalist, anti-imperialist, decolonial feminist praxis. While the old/new, constantly shifting political terrain of Trump and company suggests the consolidation of a white supremacist, ableist, heteropatriarchal, carceral regime with billionaire state managers, the multiple, visible, and persistent uprisings of communities in resistance are truly extraordinary. Since the inauguration of Donald Trump, there have been hundreds of documented demonstrations, rallies, boycotts, and strikes across the country, in small and large cities and towns. The latest post–George Floyd uprising has brought pandemic and protest together in new and deeply hopeful ways. New solidarities have been forged, and feminists of all stripes and colors continue to be in leadership in most of these mobilizations. What lies ahead is the hard work of deepening and consolidating the nascent solidarities that have emerged through these mobilizations, to imagine a decolonized public polity anchored in a horizontal feminist solidarity across borders and divides.

I have always believed that solidarity is an achievement, not something that can be gifted or assumed lightly. In these neoliberal times, solidarity has been commodified and repackaged as charity or consumption (buying products made by women in impoverished communities to show solidarity with them). A radical vision of connectivity/solidarity requires building ethical, cross-border feminist solidarities that confront neoliberal racism and militarized gender regimes globally. This framing points toward strategies of resistance that can fundamentally transform economic and social inequalities from the ground up, leading to the creation of new political landscapes and visions of solidarity.

I firmly believe that, like in the BLM, the Black and migrant feminist organizations in Europe, the Indigenous, undocumented, and antiracist feminist organizations in the United States, and Dalit feminists making common cause with Muslims in a Hindu fundamentalist regime in India, it is the everyday experiences of marginalized communities, especially women, queer, and trans Black, brown, Indigenous, and other minoritized folks who so often sustain the networks of daily life, that must inform processes of creating radical, cross-border visions for economic and gender justice. I have always believed that radical scholars are made (not born!) and that we are forged within communities and collectives that teach us how to resist the kind of individualized, neoliberal seductions and erasures that result in colonized mindsets or despair. This to me is the essence of living an insurgent life. I remember Audre Lorde saying to the 1989 graduating class at Oberlin College—"remember that the rumor that you cannot fight city hall is started by city hall." So the way to combat neoliberal and authoritarian cultures and institutions is (1) to always question what appears to be normative within our local sites and connect these spaces to larger geopolitical processes of capitalism, racism, sexism, fascism, and so on (i.e., denaturalize and demystify power); (2) to nurture radical communities of dissent in and outside the institutional spaces we occupy at any given moment (i.e., refuse the isolation that neoliberal, commodified cultures thrive on and actively cultivate mentors, guides, and teachers who inspire us); (3) to seek for what Angela Davis calls "unlikely coalitions" that encourage us to struggle against injustice of all kinds; and (4) to always remember that we are not the first or the last to engage in oppositional social movements or the hard work of resistance—we stand on the shoulders of many others who came before us. Histories of decolonization, resistance, and revolution are crucial reminders that radical scholarship and activism are legacies we inherit and must claim.

Notes

This chapter was originally published as "Borders and Bridges," in *Transnational Feminist Politics, Education, and Social Justice: Post Democracy and Post Truth*, ed. Silvia Edling and Sheila Macrine (BloomsburyAcademic, an imprint of Bloomsbury Publishing Plc, 2021), 23–40. Reprinted with permission from the publisher.

1 For a discussion of neoliberalism and feminist critique, see my essay "Transnational Feminist Crossings."

2 The 1991 book *Third World Women and Feminist Perspectives*, coedited with Ann Russo and Lourdes Torres, emerged from this conference.

3 This essay draws on an earlier essay, "Imperial Democracies, Militarized Zones, Feminist Engagements."

4 For an excellent analysis of the historical and current interweaving of US labor, immigration, and racial regimes see A. N. Paik, *Bans, Walls, Raids, Sanctuary*.

5 Bapsi Sidhwa is the author of numerous compelling novels. See especially *Cracking India* (2006).

6 Oza, "Contrapuntal Geographies of Threat and Security."

7 Mackey, "Hungarian Leader Rebuked."

8 A. N. Paik, *Bans, Walls, Raids, Sanctuary*.

9 See Basarudin and Shaikh, "Contours of Speaking Out." Under the Trump administration, CVE has been revamped to reflect Trump's rhetoric of getting tougher on "Islamic terrorism." Thus, while revamping the funding structure and priorities for CVE, the Trump administration also floated the idea of changing CVE to Countering Jihadist Terrorism or Countering Radical Islamic Extremism.

10 Eisenstein, *Sexual Decoys*, 17; Roy, *Ordinary Person's Guide to Empire*, 42.

11 Golash-Boza, "Parallels Between Mass Incarceration and Mass Deportation."

12 Young, "Logic of Masculinist Protection."
13 Basarudin and Shaikh, "Contours of Speaking Out," 127.
14 Lutz, "Making War at Home in the United States."
15 Gordon, "Abu Ghraib."
16 K. Wilson et al., "Gender, Violence and the Neoliberal State in India," 2.
17 Arditti, *Searching for Life*.
18 Agamben, *State of Exception*.
19 Kotef, "Objects of Security."
20 Bannerji et al., "Of Property and Propriety."
21 Greenberg, "Generations of Memory."
22 Kotef, "Objects of Security."
23 Bhan and Duschinski, "Introduction," 3.
24 Bhatt, "State Terrorism vs. Jihad in Kashmir."
25 Butalia, *Speaking Peace*; Khan, *Islam, Women and Violence in Kashmir*; Duschinski, "Reproducing Regimes of Impunity."
26 Kaul, "India's Obsession with Kashmir," 130.
27 Malik, "Gendered Politics of Funerary Processions."
28 See Nde' North American Newswire, "Indigenous Peoples' Truth and Memory."
29 Kelly, "Documented Lives."
30 See also Berda, "Managing Dangerous Populations," for an analysis of the role of documentation and data management as technologies of civilian population management in the occupied West Bank.
31 Butalia, *Speaking Peace*.
32 Khan, *Islam, Women and Violence in Kashmir*.
33 Johnson, "Displacing Palestine."
34 Kotef, "Objects of Security."
35 Gordon, "Abu Ghraib."
36 This analysis was developed collaboratively with my colleague Jacqui Alexander and first presented at the National Women's Studies Association conference in Denver, November 2010.
37 See the organizing work of the O'odham Solidarity Across Borders Collective in "Movement Demands Autonomy."
38 See Grassroots Leadership's "About" page for more on their organization: https://www.grassrootsleadership.org, accessed January 30, 2024.
39 Border Patrol agents increased from 3,600 in 1986 to 20,000 in 2018.
40 A. N. Paik, *Bans, Walls, Raids, Sanctuary*.
41 Saliba, "Resistance Through Remembering and Speaking Out."
42 Platt, "Women on Wars and Walls."
43 Information about these coalitions and the cross-border organizing is based on personal communication with scholar-organizer Alan Gomez, who has been involved in this struggle for a number of years.
44 Butalia, *Speaking Peace*.

PART II

Neoliberal Academic Landscapes, Transnational Feminisms, Cross-Border Solidarity

5

US EMPIRE AND THE PROJECT
OF WOMEN'S STUDIES

Our strategy should not be only to confront empire, but to lay siege to it. To deprive
it of oxygen. To shame it. To mock it. With our art, our music, our literature, our stubbornness, our joy, our brilliance, our sheer relentlessness—and our ability to tell our own
stories. Stories that are different from the ones we're being brainwashed to believe.

The corporate revolution will collapse if we refuse to buy what they are selling—their
ideas, their version of history, their wars, their weapons, their notion of inevitability. Remember this: We be many and they be few. They need us more than we need them. Another world is not only possible, she is on her way. On a quiet day, I can hear her breathing.
—ARUNDHATI ROY, World Social Forum, Porto Alegre, Brazil, January 2003

I began thinking of questions of empire, anti-imperialist feminism, and citizenship some years ago when the adoption of my daughter Uma necessi-
tated my becoming a US citizen. Given that questions of identity, location,
and accountability have always haunted my work on transnational justice
and solidarity, it was entirely logical that my becoming a US citizen at a

time of militarized war and US empire building meant that my shift from immigrant to citizen could not be an innocent one. I had to examine this "new" status, to ask what it means for an immigrant woman of color turned US citizen to engage in transnational feminist politics at a time when some of "my" peoples are seen as noncitizens and threats to the US nation. This essay constitutes my reflections on these difficult shifts, and the questions and explorations they make possible. My project of transnational feminist solidarity remains central to these new efforts to examine race, empire, and citizenship in US feminist and women's studies projects.

In a May 2003 interview the writer and activist Arundhati Roy identifies the checkbook and the cruise missile as the tools of corporate-led globalization. If the checkbook (read economic control) doesn't work, as in Argentina, then the cruise missile will—as in Iraq, an apt description of unilateral, corporatist US empire.[1] This combination of economic control and physical violence and destruction has a centuries-old legacy of colonialism and imperialism. In 2006, however, it is important to specify how the colonial traffics in the imperial. Post–Cold War, and post-1989, we enter an era of accelerated forms of corporate and militarized rule, with the United States emerging as the lead bully on the block, ably assisted of course by the United Kingdom. If, as a rather incisive 1942 *Fortune* magazine editorial claimed, the representatives of the British Empire were "salesmen and planters," and those of the post–World War II American empire were "brains and bulldozers, technicians and machine tools," the current representatives of US empire may be corporate executives and military and security personnel—those who wield the checkbook and the cruise missile.[2] Each of these groups of imperial actors—the salesmen and planters, the brains and technicians, and the executives and military/security personnel—tell very particular stories not just of political economy and territorial control but also of the gender and color of empire, of racialized patriarchies and heteronormative sexualities of empire at different historical junctures. These stories (and others like them) necessitate mapping a landscape where corporate cultures of power, domination, and surveillance coincide with a politics of complicity in the academy and elsewhere.

One way to address the politics of complicity is to analyze the languages of imperialism and empire deployed explicitly by the US state, and sometimes adopted uncritically by progressive scholars and activists alike. In a provocative essay called "Imperial Language," Marilyn Young argues that the languages of imperialism and empire are distinct, even contradictory. She distinguishes between the language of empire and the language of imperialism whereby the former is "benign, nurturing, polysyllabic," and the latter, the language of "the act of creating and sustaining empire . . . immediate, direct, often monosyllabic." She goes on to claim that at this time both languages dovetail in the re-creation of an Anglo-American "colonizing, warrior past"—a clear instance then of the colonial trafficking in the imperial.[3] What role have US feminists who supported the Bush administration's war in the name of "rescuing" Afghan and Iraqi women played in this narrative of empire and imperialism? This is one of the questions we need to pose to address the politics of complicity and dissent within contemporary feminist projects.

This essay maps my understanding of some of the most urgent challenges feminists confront in relation to imperialism, militarization, and corporate globalization in the United States. It outlines the possibilities for feminist anti-imperialist praxis, specifically in terms of the genealogies of academic and nonacademic projects engendered by US politics and by women's studies. What I am suggesting is not necessarily new. Two recent books by Zillah Eisenstein and Cynthia Enloe offer excellent analyses of the intellectual and political stakes for feminists confronting empire.[4] The argument I am making here is very simple: Imperialism, militarization, and globalization all traffic in women's bodies, women's labor, and ideologies of masculinity/femininity, heteronormativity, racism, and nationalism to consolidate and reproduce power and domination. Thus, it is antiracist, antiimperialist, anticapitalist, multiply gendered feminist praxis that can provide the ground for dismantling empire and reenvisioning just, humane, and secure home spaces for marginalized communities globally.

A number of scholars, including Leo Panitch and Sam Gindin, conclude that since the last decades of the twentieth century, the US has ruled through the mechanisms of "informal empire," managing the flow of corporate capital globally across and through the borders of nation-states, as well as through military interventions in countries that resist this form of capitalist globalization.[5] However, I would argue that these mechanisms of informal and not violently visible empire building are predicated on deeply gendered, sexualized, and racial ideologies that justify and consolidate the hypernationalism, hypermasculinity, and neoliberal discourses of "capitalist democracy" bringing freedom to oppressed third world peoples—especially to third world women. The US war state mobilizes gender and race hierarchies and nationalist xenophobia in its declaration of internal and external enemies, in its construction and consolidation of the "homeland security" regime, and in its use of the checkbook and cruise missile to protect its own economic and territorial interests. It mobilizes languages of both empire and imperialism to consolidate a militarized regime internally as well as outside its territorial borders.

Bringing "democracy" and "freedom" (or more precisely the free market) to Afghanistan and Iraq most recently, then, has involved economic devastation; demasculinization; destruction of cultural, historical, natural, and environmental resources; and, of course, indiscriminate massacres in both countries. Similarly, "making the homeland safe" has involved the militarization of daily life, increased surveillance and detention of immigrants, and a culture of authoritarianism fundamentally at odds with American liberal democratic ideals. If the larger, overarching project of the US capitalist state is the production of citizens for empire, then the citizens-for-democracy narrative no longer holds. Where US liberal democratic discourse posed questions about democracy, equality, and autonomy (the American dream realized), neoliberal, militarist discourse poses questions about the free market, global opportunity, and the protection of the United States' interests inside and outside its national borders. Capitalist imperialism is now militarist imperialism. Capitalist globalization is militarized globalization.

The rest of this essay reviews the form and operation of the US imperial state and develops an anti-imperialist feminist framework, analyzing the Abu Ghraib incidents to illustrate the deeply gendered, racial, and sexual workings of the US military culture and the Bush/Cheney war state. It moves on to an analysis of the genealogies of race, nation, and citizenship in US women's studies as an elaboration of feminist anti-imperialist praxis. Drawing on an insightful analysis of discourses of race, nation, and moral identity in Canadian feminist organizations by Sarita Srivastava, I pose an analogous question in relation to US feminist knowledge projects. Srivastava defines the Canadian national self-image as one of tolerance and nonracism, suggesting that "specific to Western second-wave organizations are the ways that these historical and gendered representations of racial innocence and superiority come together with three other threads: feminist ideals of tolerance, benevolence, and nonracism."[6] If the Canadian self-image is one of tolerance and nonracism, the US self-image is that of a benevolent, "civilized" white paternal nation bringing democracy to the rest of the world. While the United States has always defined itself as a multicultural "nation of immigrants," the race and color of immigrants always mattered. In this context, then, what role do second-wave US white feminist projects play in encoding and reproducing these stories of the nation?

On "Democracy" and Empire: Genealogies of the US State

In an earlier essay charting the colonial legacies and imperial practices of the late twentieth century US state, M. Jacqui Alexander and I argued that the US state facilitates the transnational movement of capital within its own borders as well as internationally.[7] We referred to the US state as an "advanced capitalist" state with an explicit imperial project, engaged in practices of recolonization, prompting the reconfiguration of economic, political, and militarized relationships globally. We argued that postcolonial and advanced capitalist states had specific features in common. They own the means of organized violence, which is often deployed in the service of national security. Thus, for instance, the USA Patriot Act is mirrored by similar post-9/11 laws in Japan and India. Second, the militarization of postcolonial and advanced capitalist states essentially means the remasculinization of the state apparatus, and of daily life. Third, nation-states invent and solidify practices of racialization and sexualization of their peoples, disciplining and mobilizing the bodies of women, especially poor and third world women, as a way of consolidating patriarchal and colonizing processes. Thus the transformation of "private" to "public" patriarchies in multinational factories, and the rise of the international "maid trade," the sex tourism industry, global militarized prostitution, and so on. Finally, nation-states deploy heterosexual citizenship through legal and other means. Witness the US "don't ask, don't tell"/gays in the military debate in the Clinton years, and the decade-long national struggles over the Defense of Marriage Act of 1993, as well as similar debates about sexuality and criminalization in the Bahamas and Trinidad and Tobago.[8] The deployment of race, gender, sexuality, and class in the internal and external disciplining of particular groups evident in the Bush/Cheney war state necessitates understanding these analytic and experiential categories simultaneously, and, since 9/11, the acceleration of the project of US empires developing a feminist anti-imperialist frame. US feminists have always engaged the US nation-state, but it was always the "democratic" nation-state that merited such attention—not the "imperialist" US state. Feminist engagement in the latter context requires making the project of empire visible in the gendered and sexualized state practices of the United States, looking simultaneously at the restructuring of US foreign and domestic policy. It also requires an explicit analysis of the potentially imperialist complicities of US feminism. And it requires examining feminism's own alternative citizenship projects in relation to racialized stories of the nation, of home and belonging, insiders and outsiders.

Both US foreign policy and domestic policy at this time are corporate and military driven. Both have led to the militarization of daily life around the world and in the United States—specifically for immigrants, refugees, and people of color—and militarization inevitably means mobilizing practices of masculinization and heterosexualization.[9] Both can be understood through a critique of the racialized and gendered logic of a civilizational narrative mobilized to create and re-create insiders and outsiders in the project of empire building. Thus, for instance, as Miriam Cooke argues, "saving" brown women in Afghanistan justifies US imperial aggression (the rescue mission of civilizing powers), just as the increased militarization of domestic law enforcement, the border patrol, and the INS (now renamed the Bureau of Citizenship and Immigration) can be justified in the name of a war on drugs, a war on poverty, and now a war on terrorism.[10]

The clearest effects of US empire building in the domestic arena are thus evident in the way citizenship has been restructured, civil rights violated and borders re-policed since the commencement of the war of drugs, and now the war on terrorism and the establishment of the homeland security regime. While the US imperial project calls for civilizing brown and Black (and now Arab) men and rescuing their women outside its borders, the very same state engages in killing, imprisoning, and criminalizing Black and brown and now Muslim and Arab peoples within its own borders. Former political prisoner Linda Evans calls the US a "global police state," one that has adopted a mass incarceration strategy of social control since the Reagan years.[11] Analyzing the militarization of US society, Evans argues that the new definition of "domestic terrorism" heralds the *now legal* return of COINTELPRO, a counterintelligence program that conducted illegal covert operations in the 1960s and 1970s against the Black Panther Party, the American Indian Movement, the Puerto Rican independence movement, and left/socialist organizations. Racial profiling, once illegal, is now legitimated as public policy, including a requirement that Arab and Muslim men from over twenty-five countries register and submit to INS interrogation. Similarly, Julia Sudbury analyzes the global crisis and rise in the mass incarceration of women, suggesting that we must be attentive to "the ways in which punishment regimes are shaped by global capitalism, dominant and subordinate patriarchies and neocolonial, racialized ideologies."[12]

This prison-industrial complex is supported by the militarization of domestic law enforcement. As Anannya Bhattacharjee suggests, there have been dramatic increases in funding, increasing use of advanced military technology, sharing of personnel and equipment with the military, and the general promotion of a war-like culture in domestic law enforcement and also in a range of public agencies (welfare, schools, hospitals—and now universities?) that are subjected to an accelerated culture of surveillance and law enforcement.[13] The effects of these conjoined economic/military policies of the US imperial state represent an alarming increase of violence against women, children, and communities bearing the brunt of US military dominance around the world. In the United States, policies clearly target poor and immigrant communities. In her new work, M. Jacqui Alexander analyzes the primacy of processes of heterosexualization in the consolidation of empire. She suggests that the mobilization of the loyal heterosexual citizen patriot is achieved through the collapse of constructions of the enemy, the terrorists, and the sexual pervert.[14] Similarly, Jasbir Puar and Amit Rai analyze the "terrorism" industry since 9/11, exploring the production of the monster, the fag, and the terrorist as figures of surveillance and criminalization.[15] This clearly gendered, sexualized, and racialized culture of militarism and surveillance is buttressed by a hegemonic culture of consumption and neoliberal conservatism wherein discourses of advancement and technological superiority, anti-immigrant, anti-Muslim sentiments dovetail with ideologies of patriotism and faith-based initiatives and ideologies to justify the war at home and the war abroad. Take Abu Ghraib, for instance.

Zillah Eisenstein claims that Abu Ghraib is "hypermasculinity run amok. Females are present to cover over the misogyny of building empire." Racialized, gendered, and sexualized relations of torture, triumphant power, and voyeurism weave explicitly through the images of Abu Ghraib. White women dominate the rape and abuse of brown men. Brown women are all but invisible. White American women are responsible and accountable—they are collaborators, buttressing the project of racist, masculinist empire. They are also gender decoys in uniform, leaving masculinized/racialized gender in place and furthering the building of empire.[16]

Bob Wing analyzes the color of Abu Ghraib, focusing on the war on terrorism as a racial and religious war, a crusade of the "civilized" against the "uncivilized."[17] He draws on the historical continuities and similarities of the war abroad and the war at home to make his argument. Muslims are demonized as bloodthirsty terrorists just as Native peoples were demonized as savages out to scalp white settlers. Both groups of men need civilizing—and, of course, Christian salvation. The sexual humiliation of Iraqis recalls the rape of Black slaves—the triumphant smiling perpetrators recall the trophy photos of the lynching of Black men. The random jailing of three thousand Iraqis is continuous with the incarceration of Black men in the United States—more

Black men in prison than college graduates. Finally, Wing points to the similarities between the mass roundup and detention of Arabs and Muslims and the internment of Japanese Americans as enemy aliens during World War II.[18] All stories of racialized masculinity and heteronormative imperial power—all stories of the US nation trafficking and recycling colonizing practices. Linda Burnham claims the Abu Ghraib photos reveal as much about the nation as about the particular company of soldiers—the 372nd.[19] They reveal the sexualization of national conquest and the sexual sacrifice of some portion of the population of the conquered nation—usually women and always poor women.

The militarized US state and its imperial projects are thus a crucial site of feminist struggle in terms of the violence and urgency of the struggles themselves but also in terms of the potential interventions feminists could make to unsettle these particular stories and practices of the US nation-state and thus pave the way for transnational anti-imperialist solidarities. In this context there are numerous institutional practices and their effects that feminist scholars could examine. These include detailed analysis of the contradictions of national security/homeland security, the USA Patriot Act of 2001 and 2002, and the corporate/military nexus in the academy. It is to this last site that I turn now to explore stories of the nation and citizenship in the women's studies projects, as a way to engage in feminist anti-imperialist praxis. The question I want to ask concerns the place of women's studies in the academy—an academy that is corporatized, militarized, and deeply contradictory in terms of its citizenship projects. The above discussion suggests that stories of citizenship and belonging are central to the consolidation of empire. Let us now turn to a discussion of the US academy and a provisional cartography of three decades of women's studies in relation to this analysis of the US imperial state and questions of citizenship. For the purposes of this discussion I define citizenship as that particular form of belonging to the nation-state that is based on rights, participation, and obligations and anchored in historical geographies of racial and cultural identities.

On US Feminism and the Project of Women's Studies: Genealogies of Nation and Citizenship

US empire in 2005 works through processes of militarization and economic globalization managed by a hypernationalist state, assisted by multinational corporations, transnational governing bodies like the World Bank and the International Monetary Fund, corporate media, law enforcement/criminal justice policies, the prison-industrial complex, the intelligence and national security apparatus, and last but not least, the US academy.

Over fifteen years ago, Jonathan Feldman, Noam Chomsky, and others analyzed the role of the academy in what was then referred to as the military-industrial complex.[20] In 2005, the academy continues to figure prominently in the consolidation of empire and the operation of the national security state. Most visibly, it aids in the surveillance and policing functions of the state via the USA Patriot Act of 2001, which calls for international students, scholars, and their dependents on F and J visas to be registered on SEVIS, a web-based data collection and monitoring system created to link the academy to the Bureau of Citizenship and Immigration (aka the INS), ports of entry into the United States, and other state agencies. The intimate connections between scientific knowledge, corporate power, and profit have now been examined by many scholars. In earlier work, I analyzed the corporate academy and questions of citizenship.[21] I argued then for an anticapitalist feminist project that examines the political economy of higher education, defining the effects of globalization on the academy as a process that combines market ideology with a set of material practices drawn from the business world. I still believe this is a crucial and urgent project for feminist educators, but now I want to complicate it further by urging us to look at how the corporate academy aids and abets the building of empire—its involvement in the project of US empire, and most particularly I want to reflect on how women's studies and its epistemic and political genealogies figure in this project.

The social organization of knowledge in the academy, its structures of inquiry, and discipline-based pedagogies are inevitably connected to larger state and national projects and engender their own complications as well as practices of dissent. Just as privatized academics engender capitalist, market-based citizenship, they also encode stories of the US nation—a presumably "democratic" nation that is simultaneously involved in the project of empire building. Thus one important aspect of anti-imperialist feminist work is the analysis of stories of the nation and of citizenship in US feminist politics as well as in the project of women's studies.

The strength of women's studies was always that it was "in" and "of" the world and that it envisioned democratic/socialist praxis and addressed questions of social and economic justice. How is US women's studies in and of the world today? How does it conceive of this world? And what challenges lie ahead to make it true to its emancipatory vision? Numerous scholars have analyzed the significance of the category of the political to feminist scholarship and teaching. Mari Jo Buhle's claim that US women's studies emerged out of twentieth-century social movements is echoed by Marilyn Boxer's analysis of the significance of a political and social transformation agenda to the knowledge projects of women's studies.[22] Ellen Messer-Davidow argues that the institutionalization of feminism has led to its domestication in the academy and to a loss of its political edge.[23] Whether we agree with Messer-Davidow's analysis or not, it does point once more to the significance of the category of the political.[24]

Clearly there are multiple women's studies projects in the United States, but it may be possible to identify a potential convergence of effects around questions of nation, nationalism, and citizenship (one important way of addressing the political) in this field. I suggest that the national "subject" of US women's studies remains by and large undertheorized. Normative understandings of citizenship are still domestically bound in an age when the US nation-state is patently imperial. If women's studies and feminist scholars were to ask what it means to be a gendered/racialized citizen of an imperial nation, what kinds of questions of citizenship would need to emerge?

If the racialized, gendered, heterosexual figure of the citizen patriot, the risky immigrant, the sexualized and demasculinized external enemy and potential domestic terrorist are all narrative and state practices mobilized in the service of empire, an appropriate question to ask is whether and how the academy and academic disciplines (specifically women's studies) are involved in contesting or buttressing these practices. For instance, sociology is implicated in the punishment industry and the increased criminalization of daily life, geography has investments in the mapping of "others"(not least through technologies such as GIS), normative economics continues to explain immigration and capitalism in terms that erase the historical inequities and violence involved in both, normative political science has investments in a value-neutral democratic state, and new disciplines like national security studies create the very state managers that an imperial war state needs. And many of us in women's studies have multiple homes in these departments.[25] Let us also not forget the explicit militarized, imperial project of the School of the Americas.

How do we analyze fields like women's studies, LGBT/queer studies, race and ethnic studies, and postcolonial studies in terms of the social organization of knowledge and relation to nation and empire building in the United States? I argue that one way to approach this question is by analyzing the latent or overt citizenship projects (and thus, narratives of nation and nationalism) embedded in these knowledge projects. That these fields have contradictions and have functioned through a simultaneous politics of accommodation and dissent is evident. That they have all experienced a backlash with the growing power of conservatism, neoliberalism and hypernationalism in the academy is also evident. The 1980s demonizing of multiculturalism and feminism via the organized assault by the New Right in the name of political correctness is not very different from the post-9/11 scapegoating of area studies and postcolonial studies as "unpatriotic" and anti-American. There are of course numerous differences as well as parallels between women's studies, LGBT/queer studies, race/ethnic/third world and postcolonial studies and their location in the academy. We can point to histories of activism, theorization of experience and identity from marginalized social locations, commitment to economic and social justice, links to counterhegemonic social movements, contested institutional locations and histories, and so on.

But perhaps another very important commonality is the commitment to a contested (perhaps even counterhegemonic?) citizenship project—a project that lays bare the operation of state power and its effects on gendered/racialized bodies and communities around the world. A project that envisions citizenship in ways that challenge the normative construction of the white, male, heterosexual citizen patriot. And perhaps it is this project that is at stake now as we confront empire. How do we in women's studies and elsewhere craft a citizenship project that does not further the imperatives of empire? In other words, how do we theorize, analyze, and *not* reproduce the "US nation" (and US empire) in the epistemological and political work we undertake in our markedly alternative fields? Failure to critique US empire allows feminist projects to be used and mobilized as handmaidens in the imperial project.[26]

Let us explore this question of a contested citizenship project in women's studies. By a contested citizenship project I refer to a project wherein multiply gendered citizenship becomes one of the vectors that are analyzed and engaged as a primary site of struggle. An analytic question then might be: What does it mean to be a fully empowered differentiated citizen in the academy, community, nation, and world? Women's studies and feminist literacy consists of research, teaching, and organizing around this project. We theorize, think through, and work with people who will be the kind of citizen we want to engender. This suggests theorizing transnational and anticapitalist citizenship for women across class, race, sexualities, and nations, and it means rethinking the many truncated forms of American citizenship, especially the collapsing of consumerism into citizenship. It also means taking on the genealogy of second-wave white feminism not just in terms of its history of race and racism but also in terms of its genealogies of nationalism.

The question of nation and the place of North America has been central to women's studies in the United States since its inception and institutionalized formation in the early 1970s. While feminist scholarship has been attentive to questions of the intersectionality of gender, race, class, and sexuality, the category of the nation has been relatively undertheorized in feminist work on the United States. However, just as US feminist scholarship and praxis has always been racialized and gendered, it has also always encoded stories of North America as central to its knowledge production. In fact it is in times of crisis—in times of war—that these stories of the nation get mobilized and are therefore patently visible for all to see. The most recent debates in women's studies around feminism and war suggest feminist complicities as well as dissent in relation to the project of empire. Similarly, feminist antiglobalization work also poses questions of nation and citizenship.

Second-wave US feminism has encoded and appealed to the US nation-state in various ways. The question of subjectivity and agency (moral and otherwise) suggests ways to understand this. Identifying which groups of women occupy center stage over the decades in relation to the question of agency provides one way of understanding citizenship in women's studies. What subjects can call on the nation for recognition and participation? And what entitlements can be drawn on in terms of this hailing of the nation? The entire racist history of white women's enfranchisement since the first wave of US feminism testifies to yet another way in which the colonial traffics in the imperial. Thus, for instance, following Srivastava's analysis, are white women defined not just as racially superior in the colonial history of the United States, but also as innocent and morally superior markers of the "multicultural" and "civilized" American nation/state?[27] And how are gendered stories of the race and nation encoded and reproduced in genealogies of US white feminism?[28] The benevolent maternalism of early twentieth-century white feminists is echoed in the paternalism of the Feminist Majority in their rescue mission to save women in Afghanistan.[29] Some important questions in this regard include asking in whose name feminist movements have been mobilized, and the field of women's studies established; who occupies the moral center in projects of social transformation and what kinds of feminist moral identities get mobilized, and how all this relates to citizenship defined in terms of the ethics of participation and redistribution.

The genealogy sketched above is a very partial one—but it brings the analytic and political strands regarding citizenship within the discipline into sharper focus.[30] The 1970s epistemic and political project of women's studies was anchored in social movements and activism—the first academic courses and programs emerged as a result of struggle inside and outside the academy. Women's studies was in and of the world in potentially insurgent ways at the time, centralizing a narrative of Euro-American challenges to masculinist heterosexist constructions of knowledge. The "nation" for the most part was an unproblematized democratic, domestically bounded United States, and citizenship was assumed to be the purview of white, privileged males. Thus the largely unstated citizenship project of women's studies then was on behalf of Euro-American, middle-class women. Since the 1970s, feminists have been aware of the contradiction of critiquing the state while simultaneously calling on it for rights and gender justice. Conceptions of rights, subjectivity, and justice all entail notions of protectionism (often in the name of security). Any ideas of protection by the nation-state can involve feminist collusion in the imperial project of the nation.

The 1980s saw the rise of epistemic challenges to hegemonic discourses of Euro-American womanhood from US women of color, poor women, and lesbians. Critiques of racism and heterosexism in women's studies took center stage. This was the time of the consolidation of race and ethnic studies and of women's studies in the academy—a period of building as well as backlash. The citizenship project and stories of the nation became more complicated along race, class, and sexual dimensions. The narrative of a democratic US nation no longer held since the visibility of poor white women, women of color, and lesbians destabilized the image of democratic citizenship. After all, we the people have always had multiply raced, gendered, and sexualized bodies. Using Ruth Lister's analysis, the 1970s and 1980s marked the transition in feminist understandings of citizenship from gender-neutral (nonrevelance of gender to equal rights and obligations) and gender-differentiated (transforming conceptions of citizenship to accommodate the experience of women) paradigms to gender-pluralist (citizenship based on multiple identities and subject positions) ones.[31]

The 1990s marked the entry of antiglobalization and transnational feminisms via the history of the UN conferences on women, the rise of NGOs, the entry of a generation of postcolonial/third world, immigrant scholars into US women's studies, feminist disability studies, the rise of transgendered movements, and the questioning of sex and gender as stable organizing categories for feminist praxis. Now the question of the gendered, racialized nation and of citizenship is recentered. Histories of US imperial-ism, colonization, and of women's complicity begin to surface, as women's studies moves to "internationalize" the curriculum. In earlier work I marked the rise of the feminist-as-tourist, and feminist-as-explorer curricular models of internationalizing women's studies—and advocated what I call a feminist solidarity model. This model focuses on mutuality and common interests across borders, on understanding the historical and experiential particulari-ties and differences as well as the connections between women's lives around the world, and on the connection and division between forms of women's activism and organizing across racial, national, and sexual borders.[32]

However, the narrative above is partial since an aspect of each of these nation/citizenship projects was present throughout these decades of women's studies, just as *all* of us, white, brown, Black, LGBT, immigrant, poor, disabled women were present and active throughout the 1970s, 1980s, and 1990s. This is a landscape of hegemonic (albeit contested) citizenship narratives in women's studies. So where does that leave us in 2005? What are the challenges for women's studies in terms of nation, empire, and gender now? If the 1970s women's studies signaled Euro-American citizenship, and the 1990s drew attention to the nationalist and heterosexist constructs of citizenship, albeit in often problematic ways, in 2005 the citizenship project remains contested for women's studies, if we are to see ourselves once again as in and of the world in nonimperialist ways. And it is the hypernationalist, racist, heteronormative corporate US empire that needs to be confronted. Given the trafficking in women's bodies and the use of women to humanize the war, challenging empire and its racist, heterosexist ideologies must be-come a part of the future of women's studies and of feminist praxis. Gender-pluralist understandings of citizenship only take us so far—at this time it is anti-imperialist forms of citizenship that are needed to construct solidari-ties across the borders of the US nation-state. It is this cross-border, transna-tional feminist understanding that makes alliances and solidarities possible. Thus, drawing on the earlier discussion of the need for an anti-imperialist feminist framework that theorizes the connections between domestic and foreign policy, between inside and outside the borders of the United States, I suggest that similar transnational understandings of citizenship become necessary if US women's studies is to take its own political and epistemic genealogies seriously. Theorizing the place of immigrant, poor women of color in the citizenship narrative of women's studies and challenging the rescue narrative of privileged US feminists wherever it appears is a critical aspect of feminist solidarity praxis at this time.

This counterhegemonic project entails asking questions like: Who or what is women's studies loyal to? How are questions of patriotism and dissent experienced, theorized, and taught in women's studies? How do the culture of racist hypernationalism and the corporatized academic location of women's studies influence our epistemic and political projects? Envisioning and enacting an emancipatory decolonized citizenship project based on creating democratic cultures of dissent is a difficult task at a time when the imperatives of a war economy override the most basic democratic freedoms. So feminists have some profound challenges ahead, not just in terms of mapping the relations of rule of empire and capitalist globalization—wherever we are located—but also in terms of generating adequate responses that disrupt business as usual and transform the hypermasculine, militarist cultures women now inhabit in many corners of the globe. Feminist practice at many levels (daily life, collective movements and organizing, knowledge production, etc.) needs to do the necessary work that disrupts and does *not* reproduce the terms of domination.

Some practical suggestions include acknowledging the centrality of empire in our lives and communities; analyzing the operation and effects of empire using antiracist, anticapitalist nonheteronormative feminist lenses, specifically in terms of the convergence of race and nation in the citizenship projects of women's studies; looking at particular institutions of imperial rule, communities at risk, and sites of resistance and understanding their role in contesting or bolstering empire; connecting our analysis to the politics of movements—making feminist analysis dangerous to empire— engaging in dissent based on careful analysis; being present and visible as feminists in antiwar, antiglobalization, prison abolitionist, pro-worker, immigrant, queer, and disability rights movements; distinguishing between imperial or colonizing feminisms and anti-imperialist feminisms. Finally, it means believing another world is possible and acting on it!

To conclude, this analysis of contested citizenship and stories of the nation in US feminism engages the project of US empire by identifying the racist and nationalist traces within genealogies of women's studies. It facilitates the possibilities of transnational solidarities across borders in specifically academic spaces. Clearly such solidarities have always been part of transnational feminist praxis—however, they have not always been centralized in US feminist academic contexts. Examining the narratives of the US nation and genealogies of citizenship as the landscape for anticapitalist, anti-imperialist work is a project that women's studies and academic feminism needs to undertake.

Notes

This chapter was originally published as "U.S. Empire and the Project of Women's Studies: Stories of Citizenship, Complicity, and Dissent," in *Gender, Place and Culture: A Journal of Feminist Geography* (Winter 2006): 7–20. Reprinted with permission of the publisher.

I thank Leslie Hill for a careful and thorough critique of this essay—and for invaluable suggestions for revision. Thanks also to various audiences at MIT, University College, Dublin, and the University of Oregon as well as the anonymous reviewers of GPC for feedback and engagement with these ideas. Last but not least, thanks to Linda Peake for her patience and gentle persistence.

1 Barsamian, *The Checkbook and the Cruise Missile.*
2 "An American Proposal," *Fortune,* May 1942, 59–63.
3 Young, "Imperial Language," 40.
4 Eisenstein, *Against Empire*; Enloe, *Curious Feminist.*
5 Leo Panitch and Sam Gindin argue that "the dynamism of American capitalism is its worldwide appeal combined with the universalistic language of American liberal democratic ideology to underpin a capacity for informal empire far beyond that of nineteenth century Britain's. Moreover, by spawning the modern multinational corporation, with foreign direct investment in production and services, the American informal empire was to prove much more penetrative of other social formations" ("Global Capitalism and American Empire," 10).
6 Srivastava, "'You're Calling Me a Racist?,'" 34.
7 Alexander and Mohanty, *Feminist Genealogies, Colonial Legacies, Democratic Futures.*
8 See M. Jacqui Alexander's work, especially *Pedagogies of Crossing.*
9 Some of this analysis was published in my earlier essay "Towards an Anti-Imperialist Politics."
10 Cooke, "Saving Brown Women."
11 Evans, "Playing Global Cop."
12 Sudbury, "Introduction," xiii.
13 See Bhattacharjee, "Private Fists and Public Force."
14 Alexander, *Pedagogies of Crossing.*
15 Puar and Rai, "Monster, Terrorist, Fag."
16 Eisenstein, *Sexual Decoys.*
17 Wing, "The Color of Abu Ghraib."
18 Wing, "The Color of Abu Ghraib."
19 Burnham, "Sexual Domination in Uniform."
20 See Burnham, "Sexual Domination in Uniform."
21 Mohanty, *Feminism Without Borders.*
22 Buhle, "Introduction"; Boxer, *When Women Ask the Questions.*
23 Messer-Davidow, *Disciplining Feminism.*
24 For an insightful discussion of the category of the political, see Rubin, "Women's Studies."
25 I am indebted to Jacqui Alexander for this discussion.

26 See, for instance, the role played by the Feminist Majority in supporting the Bush administration's war in Afghanistan, all in the name of rescuing Afghani women from the Taliban.

27 Srivastava, "'You're Calling Me a Racist?'"

28 Srivastava, in "'You're Calling Me a Racist?,'" claims that "even as they produce distinct ethical practices and moral communities, second-wave feminist efforts are also overlaid with the contemporary national discourses of tolerance, multiculturalism, or nonracism common to Western nations such as Canada, the Netherlands, New Zealand, and the United States" (35).

29 See Miller, "Open Letter to the Editors of Ms. Magazine."

30 There are now numerous books examining the past, present, and future of women's studies. However, there is little if any discussion of the underlying nationalist and citizenship projects in the field. See especially Weigman, *Women's Studies on Its Own*; and Kennedy and Beins, *Women's Studies for the Future*.

31 Lister, "Feminist Theory and Practice of Citizenship."

32 Mohanty, "Privatized Citizenship, Corporate Academies, and Feminist Projects."

6

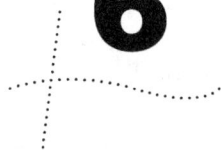

CARTOGRAPHIES OF KNOWLEDGE AND POWER

Transnational Feminism as Radical Praxis

with M. Jacqui Alexander

This chapter is one moment in the process of almost two decades of thinking, struggling, writing, and working together in friendship and solidarity
as immigrant women of color living in North America. Each of us has been
involved in collaborative work in and outside the academy in different racial, cultural, and national sites—and we have worked together in scholarly,
curricular, institutional, and organizing contexts. For us, this collaboration,
over many years and in these many sites, has been marked by struggle, joy,
and the ongoing possibility of new understandings and illumination that
only collective work makes possible.[1]

More than a decade ago, we embarked on a feminist collaborative project that resulted in the collection *Feminist Genealogies, Colonial Legacies,
Democratic Futures* (1997). Its main purpose was to take account of some of
the most egregious effects of the political economic impact of globalization,

what we called then capitalist recolonization—the racialized and gendered relations of rule of the state—both its neocolonial and advanced capitalist incarnations, and to foreground a set of collective political practices that women in different parts of the world had undertaken as a way of understanding genealogies of feminist political struggles and organizing. Our methodological task here was quite steep for the inheritance of the "international" within women's studies, particularly its US variant, and provided little analytic room to map the specific deployment of transnational that we intended *Feminist Genealogies* to encapsulate, especially since we saw that the term *international* had come to be collapsed into the cultures and values of capitalism and into notions of global sisterhood. How, then, could we conceptualize transnational to take globalization seriously while at the same time not succumb to the pitfalls of either free-market capitalism or free-market feminism?

Feminist Genealogies drew attention to three important elements in our definition of the transnational: (1) a way of thinking about women in similar contexts across the world, in different geographic spaces, rather than as all women across the world; (2) an understanding of a set of unequal relationships among and between peoples, rather than as a set of traits embodied in all non-US citizens (particularly because US citizenship continues to be premised within a white, Eurocentric, masculinist, heterosexist regime); and (3) a consideration of the term *international* in relation to an analysis of economic, political, and ideological processes that would therefore require taking critical antiracist, anticapitalist positions that would make feminist solidarity work possible.[2]

In the decade since the publication of *Feminist Genealogies*, there has been a proliferation of discourses about transnational feminism, as well as the rise of transnational feminist networks.[3] Within the academy, particular imperatives like study abroad programs in different countries, the effects of Structural Adjustment Programs on public education globally, the (now lopsided) focus on area studies in geographic spaces seen as crucial to knowledge production post-9/11, and the rise of new disciplines like terrorism studies and security studies can all be read as responses to globalization that have concrete transnational contours. Transnational studies in the academy often dovetail with more radical impulses in social movements, and given the place of transnational feminist studies in the academy at this moment, we have embarked on another large collaborative project, this time seeking to map a genealogy or archaeology of the transnational in feminist and LGBT/queer studies in the United States and Canada.

To this end we pose a set of questions that can probe the definitions of transnational feminism in relation to globalization (local/global/regional) and the operation of the categories of gender, race, nation, sexuality, and capitalism. We want to explore what the category of the transnational illuminates—the work it does in particular feminist contexts—the relation of the transnational to colonial, neocolonial, and imperial histories and practices on different geographic scales, and finally we want to analyze the specific material and ideological practices that constitute the transnational at this historical juncture and in the US and Canadian sites we ourselves occupy. When is the transnational a normativizing gesture—and when does it perform a radical, decolonizing function? Are cultural relativist claims smuggled into the transnational in ways that reinforce binary notions of tradition and modernity?

A number of feminist scholars have distinguished between the categories of global, international, and transnational. Suzanne Bergeron, for instance, argues that globalization is the condition under which transnational analysis is made possible.[4] The transnational is connected to neoliberal economics and theories of globalization—it is used to distinguish between the global as a universal system and the cross-national, as a way to engage the interconnections between particular nations. Feminist scholars have also defined the transnational in relation to women's cross-border organizing, and as a spatialized analytic frame that can account for varying scales of representation, ideology, economics, and politics while maintaining a commitment to difference and asymmetrical power.[5] Radcliffe and colleagues, for instance, connect the transnational to the neoliberal through exchanges of power that impact Indigenous communities across the globe.[6] Felicity Schaeffer-Grabiel defines the current form of economics in relation to ideologies of masculinity, examining what she refers to as the "transnational routes of U.S. masculinity."[7]

Our own definitions of transnational feminist praxis are anchored in very particular intellectual and political genealogies—in studies of race, colonialism, and empire in the global North, in the critiques of feminists of color in the United States, and in studies of decolonization, anticapitalist critique, and LGBT/queer studies in the North and the South. Our use of this category is thus anchored in our own locations in the global North and in the commitment to work systematically and overtly against racialized, heterosexist, imperial, corporatist projects that characterize North American global adventures. We are aware that this particular genealogy of the transnational is specific to our locations and the materiality of our everyday lives in North America. Here our interest lies in the connections between the politics of knowledge and the spaces, places, and locations that we occupy. Our larger project, then, is an attempt to think through the political and epistemological struggles that are embedded in radical transnational feminist praxis at this time.

For this chapter, however, we focus on a particular part of this larger project. Drawing on an analysis of the contemporary US academy and on core women's and gender studies and LGBTQ/queer studies syllabi, we attempt a preliminary map of the institutional struggles over transnational feminist praxis, specifically, the politics of knowledge construction in women's studies and LGBTQ/queer studies in the US academy. Given the privatization and restructuring of the US academy, the hegemony of neoliberalism and corporate/capitalist values and free-market ideologies, and the increasingly close alignment of the academy with the "war on terror" and the US imperial project, we ask questions about the objects of knowledge involved in women's and gender studies and LGBTQ/queer studies. Beginning with a broad mapping of the US academy as a major site in the production of knowledge about globalization and the transnational, we move on to an analysis of the ethics and politics of knowledge in the teaching of transnational feminism. The two fundamental questions that preoccupy us are: What are the specific challenges for collaborative transnational feminist praxis given the material and ideological sites that many of us occupy? And, what forms of struggle engender cultures of dissent and decolonized knowledge practices in the context of radical transnational feminist projects? We believe that at this historical moment, it is necessary to move away from the academic/activist divides that are central to much work on globalization, to think specifically about destabilizing such binaries through formulations of the spatialization of power and to recall the genealogy of public intellectuals, radical political education movements, and public scholarship that is anchored in cultures of dissent. Such work also requires acute ethical attentiveness. In addressing herself to the African Studies Association in 2006, Amina Mama speaks of the need for developing scholarship as a "critical tradition premised on an ethic of freedom." She goes on to define this: "Such scholarship regards itself as integral to the struggle for freedom and holds itself accountable, not to a particular institution, regime, class, or gender, but to the imagination, aspirations, and interests of ordinary people. It is a tradition some would call radical, as it seeks to be socially and politically responsible in more than a neutral or liberal sense."[8] Thus, one of the major points of our analysis is to understand the relationship between a politics of location and accountability and the politics of knowledge production by examining the academy as one site in which transnational feminist knowledge is produced, while examining those knowledges that derive from political mobilizations that push up, in, and against the academy, ultimately foregrounding the existence of multiple genealogies of radical transnational feminist practice.

The US Academy: Mapping Location and Power

The US academy is a very particular location for the production of knowledge. Within a hegemonic culture of conformity and surveillance, many of us experience the perils of being in the US academy. At a time when women's and gender studies, race and ethnic studies, queer studies, and critical area studies run the risk of co-optation within the neoliberal, multiculturalist, corporatist frame of the academy, we bear a deep responsibility to think carefully and ethically about our place in this academy where we are paid to produce knowledge, and where we have come to know that the spatiality of power needs to be made visible and to be challenged. One of the questions we want to raise, then, is whether it is *possible to undo* the convergence between location and knowledge production. Put differently, can transnational feminist lenses push us to ask questions that are location specific but not necessarily location bound? If we take seriously the mandate to do collaborative work in and outside the academy, the kind of work that would demystify the borders between inside and outside and thereby render them porous rather than mythically fixed, it is imperative that the academy *not* be the only location that determines our research and pedagogical work; that we recognize those hierarchies of place within the multiple sites and locations in which knowledge is produced, and we maintain clarity about the origin of the production of knowledge and the spaces where this knowledge travels. And this mandate in turn requires the recognition that knowledge is produced by activist and community-based political work—that some knowledges can only emerge within these contexts and locations. Thus, in not understanding the intricate and complex links between the politics of location, the geographies and spatialities of power, and the politics of knowledge production, we risk masking the limits of the work we do within the academy and more specifically their effects on the kinds of pedagogical projects we are able to undertake in the classroom. We attempt to clarify and address some of these links in the second half of this chapter. Our intention here is not to reinforce or solidify an academic/activist divide, although we are well aware that these divides exist. It is rather to draw attention to different academic and activist sites as differentiated geographies of knowledge production. Thus, we want to be attentive to the spatialities of power and the ways in which they operate in and through the academy, as well as within political movements whose identities are not constituted within it.

In North America, the binary that distinguishes the "academy" from the "community" or the academic from the activist, that has also made it necessary to pen the qualification "activist scholar," has assisted in the creation of apparently distinct spaces where the former is privileged over the latter. This process of binary/boundary making is also a fundamental way to (re)configure space and to mask the power relations that constitute that reconfiguration. We can think of this binary as spatial in that it has its own cartographic rules, which, according to Katherine McKittrick, "unjustly organize human hierarchies in place and reify uneven geographies in familiar, seemingly natural ways."[9] Given over two decades of neoliberalism, privatization, and the accompanying commodification of knowledge that marks academies across the globe, the cartographic rules of the academy necessarily produce insiders and outsiders in the geographies of knowledge production. On the one hand, such cartographic rules draw somewhat rigid boundaries around neoliberal academies (the academy/ community divide), and on the other, they normalize the spatial location of the academy as the epitome of knowledge production. So what are these cartographic rules that normalize the position of the academy at the pinnacle of this knowledge-making hierarchy? Among them are the making of white heterosexual masculinity consonant with the identity of the institution against which racialized and sexed others are made, imagined, and positioned as well as the diffusion of ways of knowing that are informed by the fictions of European Enlightenment rationality, which heighten political contestation from those knowledges that are made to bear an oppositional genealogy and are rendered marginal once they travel inside the academy. These rules are reinforced through an ideological apparatus that creates the academy/community divide in the first place and that is itself an element in the deployment of power while attempting to conceal that power through other border patrol strategies such as academic-community partnerships and the creation of various offices of community relations, as well as devising strategies of governance that delimit the kind of scholar and the kind of scholarship deserving legitimation, which are at odds with the very community with which it has established relations.[10] These cartographic rules are crucial since they create a hierarchy of place and permit the binary to operate as a verb, demarcating the spurious divide between academy and community while at the same time masking the creation of the divide. We say spurious here not because the creation of boundaries does not have serious effects in creating insiders and outsiders along lines similar to those created by the state, for instance, but because the practices of power within the academy bear close resemblance to the practices of power deployed by its allies such as the state and global capital that participate both materially and ideologically in its day-to-day operation. Ultimately these rules promote a spatial segregation that constructs the "community" as a hyperracialized homogeneous space, and it is usually not just *any* community but one that has been subject to forced dispossession. This community may or may not be the same as grassroots mobilizations that derive from many sources. To make visible, then, these racialized geographies of dispossession with their own imperatives that do not rely on the academy for self-definition even as the academy summons them, and reifies them in that summoning, in the service of the formation of its own identity is a crucial strategy. This gesture assists us in demystifying the cartographic rules, fragmenting the hierarchy of place that would make them an undifferentiated mass in relation to the academy and thus in identifying the operation of the very idea of the spatialization of power that points to the social formation of multiple uneven spaces, which individually and together make up the power/knowledge matrix. Who resides in which spaces? Who belongs and whom are rendered outsiders? Who is constituted as the knowledgeable and the unknowledgeable? Which knowledges and ways of knowing are legitimized and which are discounted? Settling these questions stands at the core in making hierarchies of place.

This power/knowledge matrix that creates insiders and outsiders, those who know, and those who cannot know, has of course been challenged in multiple spaces by edu-activists. Two examples of political movements that challenge the cartographic rules consolidated by neoliberal, privatized academies include the Committee on Academic Freedom in Africa (CAFA) and the Italian Network for Self-Education, founded in 2005. CAFA, founded in 1991, mobilized North American students and teachers in support of African edu-activists fighting against World Bank–initiated Structural Adjustment Programs (SAPS) aimed at dismantling autonomous African university systems. Arguing that these SAP initiatives were part of a larger attack on African workers, and that they functioned as recolonization projects, CAFA drew attention to the inexorable dismantling of African higher education, resulting in the shift of knowledge production *elsewhere* from international NGOs training technocrats under the Africa Capacity Building initiative to US international and study abroad programs. Similarly, the Italian Network for Self-Education was formed in 2005 as a result of a mass mobilization of over 150,000 people in response to the restructuring of academic labor by the Italian parliament. Challenging the spatialization of knowledge and expertise within disciplines, faculties, and the logic of neoliberal university systems, the network claims to traverse the division between teaching and research, education and metropolitan production, and theory and praxis. The self-education movement deconstructs traditional modes of knowledge production and research, unsettling the taken-for-granted cartographic binary of the university/metropole, potentially serving as a device for social transformation.[11] Thus, the spatialities of power that anoint the academy as the pinnacle of knowledge are demystified and profoundly challenged by CAFA and the Network for Self-Education.

For our purposes, however, and in order to wrestle with the gendered, racialized, and sexualized spatialization of power, we would have to come to terms with what McKittrick calls its material physicality.[12] In the context of this chapter, this pertains to our own formulations of the objects of transnational feminist analysis and the potential cartographic rules of syllabi, the spaces where colonialism and race dovetail with the practices of empire, where the academy consorts with state and corporatist projects and where oppositional practices take hold in ways that bend those cartographic rules or make them situationally irrelevant to the practices of hegemonic power. Those physical spaces include the detention center; the army, the navy, and other institutions of the military-industrial complex; the institutions of state; the corporation, the factory, the export processing zones, the warehouse for secondhand clothing, the home, the brothel; the capsized boat, makeshift homes, the desert; the neighborhood, the street, NGOs, cross-border networks; the university, the boardroom, the classroom.[13] The question we want to ask then is, under what conditions and for what purpose do particular spaces become dominant in the construction of the transnational?

Almost two decades ago, Jonathan Feldman, Noam Chomsky, and others analyzed the role of the academy in what was then referred to as the military-industrial complex.[14] In 2008, the academy continues to figure prominently in the consolidation of empire, the corporatization of knowledge, and the operation of the national security state. Most visibly, it aids in the surveillance and policing functions of the state via the USA Patriot Act of 2001, which calls for international students, scholars, and their dependents on F and J visas to be registered on SEVIS, a web-based data collection and monitoring system created to link the academy to the Department of Homeland Security, consulates, and embassies abroad, ports of entry into the United States, and other state agencies. The intimate connections between scientific knowledge, corporate power, and profit have now been examined by many scholars.[15] And the earlier discussion of CAFA and the Network for Self-Education points to radical educational movements that challenge the corporatization of the academy and its varied geographies of power in different national spaces.

The social organization of knowledge in the academy, its structures of inquiry, and discipline-based pedagogies are inevitably connected to larger state and national projects. And this is nowhere more palpable than in the mobilization of various disciplines, beyond area studies, to assist the state in the consolidation of empire.[16] They engender their own complicities as well as practices of dissent. Just as privatized academies engender capitalist, market-based citizenship, they also encode stories of the US nation—a presumably "democratic" nation that is simultaneously involved in the project of empire building. One important aspect of a radical transnational feminist project then involves looking at the way curricula and pedagogies mark and become sites for the mobilization of knowledge about the transnational. In what follows we examine syllabi in women's and gender studies (WGS), and in LGBTQ/queer studies, in an attempt to understand the deployment of the transnational. Given our focus on the spatialization of power, we look especially at how those WGS and LGBTQ/queer studies syllabi that deploy the transnational organize a set of cartographic rules that define how knowledge production operates in the academy. We look at syllabi in terms of the racial and gendered spatialization of power. This suggests questions like what kinds of hierarchies of place and space get set up; how power gets configured and reiterated; where teachers locate feminism and queer sexuality in relation to these larger processes of colonialism and imperialism; the organization and presence of the academy and grassroots activism, political mobilizations, and so forth. Put differently, in what ways do syllabi bend or reinforce normative cartographic rules?

The Politics of Feminist Knowledge: Curricular Maps and Stories

The ethics and politics of crossing cultural, geographic, and conceptual borders in feminist and LGBTQ/queer pedagogies in the context of the transnational is a crucial element in analyzing the interface of the politics of knowledge and location in the academy. How we teach transnational feminism in women's studies is crucial in analyzing the struggles over knowledge and power both within the US academy and outside its fictive borders. The way we construct curricula and the pedagogies we use to put such curricula into practice tell a story—or tell many stories of gendered, racial, and sexual bodies in work and home spaces, prisons and armed forces, boardrooms and NGOs, local and transnational organizations, and so on. We suggest that these "stories" are also anchored in cartographic rules that encapsulate differentiated and hierarchical spatialities, thus foregrounding the links between sites, location, and the production of knowledge about the transnational. "Stories" are simultaneously "maps" in that they mobilize both histories and geographies of power. Thus, just as we suggested there are cartographic rules that normalize the position of the academy in the knowledge hierarchy earlier, we now explore whether similar rules are encoded and normalized in the curriculum, specifically in the syllabi we analyze.

We analyze thirteen core syllabi from WGS and LGBTQ/queer studies curricula at a variety of colleges and universities in the United States in terms of these stories and maps. The sample syllabi we chose were from large state universities; private, elite universities; small liberal arts colleges; and smaller state schools.[17] Each of the syllabi gestures toward transnational feminist praxis in some form or another, and most seem to anchor the core curriculum in women's and gender and LGBTQ/queer studies. We suggest that an examination of the core curriculum can help us understand the politics of knowledge and the spatialities of power in the cross-cultural construction of feminist and LGBTQ/queer studies in the US academy, and to ask questions about the academy as a site for such knowledge production. This analysis allows us to see what it is students are being asked to know within these disciplines at this historical moment, what knowledge is being generated within introductory and upper-level classrooms—those spaces where explicitly oppositional knowledges are being produced. It also allows us to make preliminary connections between the politics of location, differentiated spatializations, and the production of knowledge.

Some of the larger analytic questions we might then ask include: How precisely is the transnational deployed in the core curriculum in relationship to racial and colonial histories and geographies, and to the relationship of the local and global? And what happens with the transnational when it encounters women of color, for instance, or queer communities of color? What productive tensions and contradictions are visible when the transnational emerges? Also, what cartographic rules pertaining to the transnational can be made visible in this analysis of syllabi? In what ways are curricular stories also curricular maps? And finally, are there convergences and/or divergences in the ways that these transnational maps intersect with the spatialization of power in the academy as a whole?

Specifically, we analyzed six syllabi designated as core introductory courses and seven upper-level courses in the interdisciplinary fields of women's and gender and LGBTQ/queer studies. Examples of these include Introduction to Women's and Gender Studies, Introduction to LGBT/Queer Studies, and Introduction to Feminist Studies. We were interested in understanding what categories (e.g., gender, race, nation, sexuality) animate the transnational, the work it is being called upon to do in the curriculum, the particular histories and spatialities (colonial, neocolonial, imperial) it mobilizes, and the practices that are seen to constitute transnational feminism.

While our selection of these syllabi was intentional, purposive one might say, in that our explicit focus was the transnational, we should also note that there were many upper-level seminars devoted to an exploration of "urgent contemporary issues" of gender or sexuality in which there was a curious elision of the transnational within the United States, pushing it to operate only elsewhere, outside of the geopolitical borders of the US nation-state.[18] This paradoxical duality of marked absence on the one hand and of hyperpresence on the other might leave no way for students to negotiate the circuits of travel between the local and the global, or to intuit the precise ways in which the local is constituted through the global. Still, we have to leave open the possibility that such linkages are indeed made. We might, for instance, talk about this particular curricular strategy as the cartographic rule of the transnational as always "elsewhere." This "elsewhere" rule thus suggests a separation of the spaces of the local/national and the transnational.

Overall, the interweaving of the categories of racialized gender and sexuality as well as the attention to non-US feminist geographies was impressive. In many of these courses, there was a marked shift from the ways in which racialized and cross-cultural knowledges were being produced in WGS courses in the 1970s and 1980s. Unlike in most WGS curricula from the 1970s and 1980s, women of color texts, queer texts by men and women of color from different parts of the world, and texts by "third world" women are central in the syllabi we analyzed. Yet there were many paradoxes. In the case of LGBT/queer studies, one of the most complex of the introductory syllabi exposed students to the lives and experiences of US queer communities of color, linking these with racialized colonial histories of immigrant and native communities and the contemporary effects of globalization. The central actors in this narrative were thus queers of color, and the conceptual movement of the course mapped sexuality studies in relation to colonialism, racial formation, nation-states, and finally to globalization. Paradoxically, however, the central "stories" remained US-centric with the United States being defined as a multicultural, multiracial nation in the most interesting of these syllabi. Here is yet another cartographic rule, then, one that constructs a hierarchy of place within the transnational: the US-centric or Eurocentric organization of the syllabus. However, this is very different from the "elsewhere" rule in that it suggests a connectivity of the spaces of the local/national and the transnational, but always in terms of a hierarchy of place wherein Euro-America constitutes the norm.

Genealogies of sexuality studies remain largely US-centered in otherwise multiply layered courses. Thus, while racial and colonial histories were often threaded through the courses, these histories remained focused on the United States or Europe. In Introduction to LGBT/Queer Studies, designed as an introduction to the academic interdisciplinary field itself, the syllabus drew on the now familiar canon of theorists of sexuality (Foucault, Sedgwick, Butler), yet again mobilizing Euro-American histories of sexuality while referring to the lives and experiences of queer communities of color.

This paradox of foregrounding subjects of color as agents while reproducing a white Eurocentric center has another effect in that the transnational can be deployed in normative rather than critical terms. In one upper-level seminar, the story of the syllabus was to map the impact of globalization on different women in different parts of the world.[19] Marking this difference is clearly important since it moves us away from thinking of globalization as a homogeneous or homogenizing project. Yet the emphasis on democratization and equality as a way to understand feminist mobilizations among Islamic, Latin American, or African feminists seemed to perform an odd theoretical move that wished to export democracy and equality from the United States to these different parts of the world. Ironically, the syllabus carried a great deal of resonance with earlier formulations of a global sisterhood, though it did so in terms that were ostensibly different: the terms of "multiple feminisms." Indeed residing underneath these multiple feminisms was cultural relativism that housed two interrelated elements. One was the creation of a geographic distance through which an absolute alterity was constructed. It was only through greater proximity to the United States and the inherited categories of the West that women's experiences were most intelligible. The other, implied in the first, was the spatial creation of an *us* and *them* so that Islamic, Latin American, or African feminism could neither be understood relationally nor be positioned to interrogate the kinds of feminist mobilizations deployed in the West.[20] The place of Western knowledge was reconsolidated all over again. Here, too, while spatial connectivities are mobilized, there is a clear hierarchy in place.

Our analysis suggests several important trends. First, in spite of its link to racial and colonial histories, the transnational is made to inhabit very different meanings and emerges at different junctures and in different spaces in the overall story of the syllabi we examined. Second, in the introductory courses to gender and sexuality where the writings and theorizations of US women of color and non-Western women's movements were central, the stories these syllabi dealt with were of complex feminisms anchored in different racial communities of women and queers. However, not only were US and Eurocentric histories mobilized, for instance, the linear periodization of first-, second-, and third-wave feminisms, but also very visible were the genealogies of feminist thought that once again foregrounded narratives of European liberal, socialist, and postmodern theory. Cartographically, then, the transnational was either placed elsewhere or positioned Eurocentrically or within the United States as theoretically normative.

Transnational feminism also emerged in all of these courses in relation to singular and often isolated categories and contexts. Thus, for instance, it was made visible only in relation to discussions of work and globalization, or human rights, or gay diasporas, or cross-border mobilizations. The majority of the readings and topics in the syllabi remained US-centric. Thus, transnationalism might emerge, for instance, only in relation to queer diasporas and the effects of globalization, with only two out of fourteen weeks devoted to "gay diasporas and queer transnationalism," rendering it an exceptional or theoretical option. In other words, the "local" remained intact, and somewhat disconnected from cross-border experiences. Transnationalism was then anchored only outside the borders of the nation (the "elsewhere" rule). Thus, it seems that the transnational has now come to occupy the place that "race" and women of color held in women's studies syllabi in the 1990s and earlier. We have now moved from white women's studies to multiracial women's studies (in the best instances), but the methodology for understanding the transnational remains an "add and stir" method, and the maps that are drawn construct the transnational as spatializing power either "elsewhere" or as within the United States and/or Europe.

Thus, a focus on diaspora, globalization, and colonial discourse as well as on feminist and LGBTQ/queer communities in different national contexts often seems to stand in for what the courses describe as a "transnational perspective." Transnationalism, if identified at all, is understood only in the context of contemporary globalization, or in some rare cases, with nationalisms and religious fundamentalisms that fuel cross-border masculinist and heterosexist state practices. Given our interest in the politics of knowledge and the place of transnational feminisms in the academy, we were especially intrigued by the fact that none of these introductory courses raised questions about the ethics of cross-cultural knowledge production, or about the academy at all. This curious absence of the academy as the space many of us occupy every day, given the larger political battles that often shape our curricula and pedagogy, seems all the more problematic from the point of view of understanding the spatiality of power in terms of the academy and its relationship to other institutions of rule like the state and corporate interests. After all, being attentive to the ethics of knowledge production requires bringing questions of identity, epistemology, and method to the forefront of our scholarship and teaching. If the academy as a political space is absent from our syllabi, even as experience remains central to feminist thinking, surely there is a major contradiction here. We may be erasing our own experiences (and the profoundly material effects of our locations) at our own peril. For instance, as Amina Mama argues, "Our intellectual identities—and the ethics that we adopt to guide our scholarly practices— are informed by our identifications with particular communities and the values they uphold."[21] Thus, if we take the connections between the politics of knowledge and the politics of location (identity) and of space seriously, we may need to take on broad institutional ethnography projects that allow a materialist understanding of academic spaces as mobilizing and reproducing hegemonic power. While some courses touched on urgent transnational issues like HIV/AIDS, and war and militarism, there was no mention of the US imperial project or, say, the prison-industrial complex as a site of analysis or feminist debate, thus begging the question of what particular (transnational) issues women's and gender studies and LGBTQ/ queer studies curricula speak to in the world we now occupy. Interestingly, then, syllabi may serve unwittingly to reinforce and even naturalize the university/community divide in terms of hierarchies of location, identity, and sites of knowledge.

One upper-level seminar, however, was notable in terms of its explicit engagement with some of the ethical conundrums associated with cross-cultural comparison, which seemed crucial in light of its attention to the methodological politics of doing cross-cultural work. The story of this syllabus was a complex one, attempting to map the ways in which sex, sexuality, and gender operated within local and global processes that are at once transnational since the rapid dispersal of peoples and reading and interpretive practices operated everywhere. Within the construction of "queer diaspora" and the making of queer historiography, the social actors were specific communities that included cultures of two-spirit, cross-dressing women in the US Civil War; the *fa'afafine* of Samoa; and gay, lesbian, and transgender communities in different geographies, thus resisting the impulse to create a queer universal subject, and engendering a map that was attentive to different spatializations in the construction of sexualities. The syllabus asked explicit questions about when comparisons were useful or when they participated in reproducing the kind of discursive violence that comes with imposing US social categories on cultural configurations that were not US based. It was also interested in having students see themselves as intellectuals with ethical responsibilities: "What is our responsibility," it asked, "as students of gender and sexuality studies to be aware of the politics of making 'queer' travel?" Thus, this particular syllabus also engaged partially with the US academy as a contested site in the production of knowledge. Finally, all of the upper-level seminars we examined signaled the transnational through some political economic pressures of globalization, diaspora, and migration. Importantly, racial and colonial histories marked the transnational in all instances. For example, in one course the story of transnational feminism was one in which the politics of women of color in the United States was linked to feminist movements among "third world" women, attempting to map genealogies of feminism by asking how these feminisms had reshaped mainstream US feminist praxis. While racialization functioned primarily in relationship to women of color, transnational feminist theory seemed hesitant, however, to engage women of color or "third world" women as sexual subjects or interpolated within sexualized projects pertaining to the state and/or global capital. Most often gender and sexuality were positioned either as theoretical strangers or as distant cousins, once again reinforcing a separation of constructs of race and sexuality in the organization of knowledge about transnational feminisms.

This distancing of sexuality from questions of transnational feminism, or rather the practice of deploying an uninterrogated heterosexuality within transnational feminist analyses, both cedes the domain of sexuality to LGBTQ/queer studies and renders an incomplete story of the ways in which the racialized gendered practices of neo-imperial modernity are simultaneously sexualized. Some of the methodological cues for probing these links have been laid out by Jacqui in earlier work, where she stages a political conversation between transnational feminism and sexuality studies by examining the complicity of state and corporate practices in the manufacture of heterosexual citizenship and nation-building structures as seemingly disparate as welfare, structural adjustment, and discursive legal practices such as domestic violence laws in the Caribbean, the Defense of Marriage Act, and the "Don't Ask Don't Tell" policy of the US military.[22]

She suggests one possible analytic strategy by bringing these practices into ideological and geographic proximity to one another and by foregrounding heterosexual regulatory practices as those of violence. Thus, she is able to bring sexuality within the racialized gendered practices of the state and capital both within and across formations that have been separately designated as colonial, neocolonial, and neo-imperial and conceive of the transnational across a wide range of ideological, political, economic, and discursive practices straddling multiple temporalities and multiple interests. This question about the connectivity of multiple though unequally organized geographies, temporalities, and interests bears on the question that is at the heart of our consideration, that is the relationship between the politics of location and the politics of knowledge production and who is able, that is, legitimized, to make sustainable claims about these links. And it raises additional questions about the analytic and political consequences of deploying an either/or framing: either connectivity or separation. Hierarchies of space and place mark what we have called the cartographic rules of the transnational in the syllabi we examined. Thus, while the transnational as elsewhere signals the spatial separation of sites of knowledge, the transnational as US-centric or Eurocentric signals connectivity, but on the basis of a hierarchical spatialization of power.

Multiplying Radical Sites of Knowledge

Let's now consider the antiviolence and political mobilizations to abolish prisons that dovetail with antiglobalization and antimilitarization campaigns. Activists in these global networks have examined how punishment regimes, including the prison, are intimately linked to global capitalism, neoliberal politics, and US economic and military dominance.[23] More specifically, however, it is the incarceration of increasing numbers of impoverished women of color that enables us to track the links between neoliberal privatization, the US export of prison technologies, organized militarization, dominant and subordinate patriarchies, and neocolonial ideologies. As Julia Sudbury argues, "Women's testimonies of survival under neoliberal cutbacks, border crossing, exploitation in the sex and drug industries, and life under occupation and colonial regimes provide a map of the local and global factors that generate prison as a solution to the conflicts and social problems generated by the new world order."[24] One of those social problems is the massive migration of impoverished women and men from the global South instigated by neoliberal globalization, who are now disproportionately criminalized together with Indigenous and Aboriginal women from Canada and the United States to Australia.

Sudbury's collection, *Global Lockdown*, is significant for thinking through these relationships refracted through the transnational spatialization of power for several reasons. First, it is located within critical antiprison and antiviolence projects such as Critical Resistance, the Prison Activist Resource Center, the Arizona Prison Moratorium Coalition, and Social Justice. Second, the contributors to the collection, in Sudbury's words, are "intellectuals both organic and intellectual, former prisoners, political prisoners, activists, women in recovery, former sex workers, immigrants, and indigenous women," who by virtue of their differentiated locations point to the gaps that ensue when political struggle is not attentive to connectivity.[25] Third, to take seriously the insights of differently positioned intellectuals is not to argue that prison intellectuals or sex workers have knowledge too; rather it is to say that their location engenders an epistemic advantage that researchers not similarly positioned have been unable to mobilize. It helps us to explain why scholars "have yet to locate race, citizenship, and national status at the center of the prison boom."[26] And fourth, it enacts different border crossings of geography and the nation-state; of time and the continued, albeit discontinuous, traffic between the colonial, the neocolonial, and the imperial among and between different colonized spaces; of different yet related political mobilizations at the center of whose praxis is the labor of building connectivity not only to upset the cartographic rules that would position the prison and the brothel as separate and unrelated spaces and the women within them only as "objects of scholarly study and state rehabilitation" but to redraw and therefore reiterate through practice the connectivity of those spaces and ultimately of the political struggles that make that connectivity possible.[27] What, then, is the ethical responsibility of the teacher in the university classroom who wishes to teach about globalization and privatization, militarization, and the racialized gendered global lockdown?

If to talk about space is to talk also about geography, then to talk about geography is to talk also about land and the fierce contestation over land that is at the center of both neo-imperial and colonial land appropriation. And if we think the ways in which the colonial traffics in the neo-imperial, then it becomes possible to delineate the many ways in which white settler colonization continues to be an important dimension of the spatialization of power at this very moment in history. It also explains why struggles for sovereignty and the retrieval of stolen lands figure so centrally in Aboriginal, First Nations, and Indigenous politics.

Aboriginal, First Nations, and Indigenous activists and scholars together have written and organized at the fragile border between the master histories of legislated inclusion and the always disappeared, the twin ideological companions of the material practices of genocide. Locating this matrix within the context of white supremacy, Andrea Smith has argued that "[the logic of genocide] holds that indigenous peoples must disappear. In fact they must *always* be disappearing in order to allow non-indigenous peoples' rightful claim over this land."[28] In *Conquest: Sexual Violence and American Indian Genocide*, Smith pulls from the lived experiences of Native women to draw links between this disappearance and the organization of a colonial patriarchy that deployed sexual violence against Native women—and other women of color—who were and continue to be positioned as "rapable" and "violable," in much the same way in which land is appropriated, raped, and violated. In this formulation, it is not so much the elsewhere cartographic rule that is at work—*elsewhere* as in outside the boundaries of modernity—but rather absence, that "present absence," as Kate Shanley calls it, which in this ideological script has presumably no knowledge to possess.[29] Thus, fashioning political struggles in ways that refuse these contradictory divides provides insight into how and why struggles for sovereignty and for land are simultaneously political, physical and spatial, metaphysical and spiritual.[30] Of course one central question that emerges here has to do with the ways in which that disappearance in the colonial and imperial geography travels within the academy and manifests as negligible numbers of Native students, teachers, and administrators and, as significantly, their disappearance in curricular and other pedagogical projects in the classroom.[31]

We noted earlier that the hierarchies of place position a "community" that is racially homogeneous and otherwise undifferentiated. But mapping community from an understanding of the differentiated and heterogeneous colonial spaces of "containment, internment and exile" creates the possibility of a deeper and more nuanced understanding of the subjects who are positioned to stand outside of modernity, presumably outside of citizenship, displaced from land in the same way that, for instance, the "deportable subject," the "admissible subject," "the present absent subject," the suspect subject are positioned by the state against the exalted national subject (the term is Thobani's) within the segregated landscape of transnational modernity.[32] It is the *combined* work of activists and scholars that has brought these meanings to our understanding of occupied territory within white settler states.

Thinking through the outlines of a radical feminist project at a time when US imperialism, genocide, incarceration, militarization, and empire building have significantly deepened is both tough and necessary.[33] While a "multiple feminisms" pedagogical strategy may be more analytically viable than the "Euro-American feminism as the normative subject" of feminist and LGBTQ/queer studies curricula, the specter of cultural relativism remains intact. Transnational feminist solidarities and ethical cross-cultural comparisons attentive to the histories and hierarchies of power and agency cannot be premised on an "us and them" foundation. Our conceptual foci would need to shift, and that might be possible when different cross-border practices, spaces, and temporalities are brought into ideological and geographic proximity with one another in ways that produce connectivity and intersubjectivity (albeit a tense or uneven one) rather than an absolute alterity. We would need to be attentive to how we think the object of our research, for what the antiprison/antiglobalization mobilizations suggest is that solidarity work provokes us to pay close attention to the spaces of confinement that warehouse those who are surplus or resistant to the new world order.[34] "Multiple feminisms" would need to be anchored in ways of reading that foreground the ethics of knowledge production and political practices across multiple borders—both those that are hypervisible and those that are somewhat invisible—within hierarchies of domination and resistance. And questions of responsibility and accountability need to be central to this pedagogy, as do ethnographies of the academy as sites of struggle and contested spaces of knowledge.

What might a map of a radical, nonnormative transnational feminist solidarity pedagogy that is attentive to the genealogies and spatializations of power across multiple borders look like? Clearly, syllabi are crucial spaces for thinking the reconfiguring of knowledge and spatial practices and for respatializing power. So perhaps the first element in this mapmaking is making the underlying epistemological assumptions visible and tracking that visibility throughout the life of the course. This requires making three interrelated moves. The first is to demystify and destabilize the old cartographic binaries set up by the academy and by the pedagogical and spatial practices within our syllabi so that we can think about the transnational, specifically transnational feminism, by looking at the ways cultural borders are crossed and the way hierarchies of place are normalized. The second attends to the hyperracialization and sexualization of the various "elsewheres." Precisely because the academy fetishizes these elsewheres in the service of its own identity formation, race and sex must be central to our thinking about the transnational. And the third would require that we ask very specifically what kinds of border crossings we want and what are their ethical dimensions? This is a tough question, for it has to do not necessarily with the question that there are, according to Richa Nagar, "varying forms of knowledge evolving in specific places," but more crucially, "what we are in a position to do in producing knowledge, namely, constitute ourselves as political actors in institutions and processes both near and far."[35] Fundamentally, then, we are talking about breaking the "epistemological contract" (the term is Sylvia Wynter's) that consigns the hierarchy of space and positions only those at the top as capable of producing and disseminating that knowledge.[36] And breaking that epistemological contract would necessarily entail disinvesting these academic identities from the will to power, moving beyond a liberal "policy-neutral" academic stance to actively developing a radical ethic that challenges power and global hegemonies.

This map requires that we take space and spatialization seriously. To think the transnational in relation to the inherited uneven geographies of place and space would require holding in tension questions of power, gender, race, and space. Who resides where, and what kinds of knowledges do these residencies generate? We would examine those oppositional spatial politics that are not in the first instance invested in reconstituting insides and outsides, the citizen and noncitizen. The spatial links that the transnational makes visible need always to be emphasized so as not to reinscribe the normative cartographic rule of the transnational as elsewhere and therefore recycle colonial cartographies that support the mandate for conquest. It is these politics of spatialization, with their attendant ethical imperatives, that allow us to understand colonial/imperial racial and sexual underpinnings of border crossings "without losing ourselves" or privileging an elsewhere. Location matters in this model of a feminist solidarity transnationalism.[37] And we can learn how to be location specific without being location bound.

Based on this analysis, then, our earlier definitions of the transnational in *Feminist Genealogies* would need to wrestle with the following: (1) the links between the politics of location, the spatiality of power, and that of knowledge production; (2) the physicality and materiality of space in terms of contestation over land; (3) a sharper focus on the ethics of the cross-cultural production of knowledge; and (4) a foregrounding of questions of intersubjectivity, connectivity, collective responsibility, and mutual accountability as fundamental markers of a radical praxis. Indeed, it is the way we live our own lives as scholars, teachers, and organizers, and our relations to labor and practices of consumption in an age of privatization and hegemonic imperial projects that are at stake here.

Clearly, the world has undergone major seismic changes that might have been difficult to imagine almost a decade ago. It may well be that the contradictions between the knowledges generated in the classroom and those generated within grassroots political mobilization have become more sharpened given the increased institutionalization of oppositional knowledges and the increased embeddedness of the academy within the imperial militaristic projects of the state. And yet it's clear to us that without our respective involvement in political work outside (and sometimes in the in-between spaces within) the academy, it would be almost impossible to navigate the still contested spaces we occupy within it, spaces where we are called upon to be consistently attentive to our spiritual and psychic health. And so we continue to do this work across the fictive boundaries of the academy, constantly wrestling with its costs, and knowing that the intellectual, spiritual, and psychic stakes are high but believing that it is imperative to engage in the struggles over the production of liberatory knowledges and subjectivities in the belly of the imperial beast.

Notes

This chapter was originally published as "Cartographies of Knowledge and Power: Transnational Feminism as Radical Praxis," in *Critical Transnational Feminist Praxis*, ed. Amanda Lock Swarr and Richa Nagar (SUNY Press, 2010), 23–45.

Many thanks to Richa Nagar, Amanda Lock Swarr, Linda Peake, Jigna Desai, and Katherine McKittrick for invaluable feedback on this chapter.

1 We are now situated in academic contexts in the United States and Canada, although much of our work emerges from our location in the US academy for over two decades.

2 Alexander and Mohanty, *Feminist Genealogies, Colonial Legacies, Democratic Futures*, xix.

3 See especially Moghadam, *Globalizing Women*. We should also note that the transnational is not always already a radical category or one that speaks to a transformative or liberatory praxis.

4 Bergeron, "Political Economy Discourses of Globalization and Feminist Politics."

5 On cross-border organizing, see Mindry, "Nongovernmental Organizations, 'Grassroots,' and the Politics of Virtue."

6   Radcliffe et al., "Transnationalization of Gender."

7   Schaeffer-Grabiel, "Planet-love.com."

8   Mama, "Is It Ethical to Study Africa?," 3.

9   McKittrick, *Demonic Grounds*, xiv.

10 Witness the struggle of women of color faculty denied tenure at the University of Michigan, Ann Arbor (Conference on Campus Lockdown: Women of Color Negotiating the Academic Industrial Complex, Ann Arbor, April 15, 2008); witness also the struggle over the inclusion of "scholarship in action" as part of tenure and promotion guidelines at Syracuse University (2007–8).

11 Silvia Federici and George Caffentzis, "CAFA and the 'Edu-Factory,'" contribution to the edu-factory online discussion, June 5, 2007; and "Rete per l'Autoformazione, Roma," edu-factory discussion, March 11, 2007. Chandra was part of this discussion in 2007. For more information, contact info@edu-factory.org.

12 McKittrick, *Demonic Grounds*.

13 In this materialist reading, we do not pose the question about whether the sacred cajoles us into thinking space differently. To think about the sacred in relationship to space and to bending these cartographic rules, see McKittrick and Woods's discussion of the Atlantic Ocean as a "geographic region that . . . represents the political histories of the disappeared," and at the same time a place of the unknowable. Coupling this tension between the "mapped" and the "unknown," they suggest that "places, experiences, histories, and people that 'no one knows' do exist, within our present geographic order" (*Black Geographies and the Politics of Place*, 4).

14 Feldman, *Universities in the Business of Repression*.

15 See my earlier work *Feminism Without Borders*, chap. 7, where I argue for an anticapitalist feminist project that examines the political economy of higher education, defining the effects of globalization in the academy as a process that combines market ideology with a set of material practices drawn from the business world. See also Jacqui's examination of the curricular effects of academic downsizing, the failures of normative multiculturalism and liberal pluralism, and the critical imperatives we face at this moment to teach for justice, in *Pedagogies of Crossing*, chaps. 3 and 4.

16 See, among others, Thobani, *Exalted Subjects*.

17 Many thanks to Jennifer Wingard for research assistance for this project. Most of the research for this chapter was conducted in early 2006, and the syllabi we analyze were all accessed electronically. We deliberately chose not to use our own syllabi, or even to discuss the curricula at our own institutions.

18 This was true of all the syllabi, except for an introductory course to LGBTQ/queer studies, in which colonial, immigrant, and native histories of queers of color indicated a recognition of the transnational within the United States without identifying it as such (the terms used here were *diaspora* and *globalization*).

19 Often, globalization was used to signify the transnational, and sometimes the terms were used to signal the same phenomena.

20 See Alexander, *Pedagogies of Crossing*, chap. 5, for a detailed discussion of cultural relativism in the context of the transnational feminist classroom.

21 Mama, "Is It Ethical to Study Africa?," 6.

22 See Alexander, *Pedagogies of Crossing*, chap. 5.

23 Sudbury, *Global Lockdown*.

24 Sudbury, "Introduction," xiii.

25 Sudbury, "Introduction," xi.

26 Sudbury, "Introduction," xviii.

27 Sudbury, "Introduction," xxiv.

28 Smith, "Heteropatriarchy and the Three Pillars of White Supremacy," 68.

29 Cited in Smith, *Conquest*.

30 LaDuke, *Recovering the Sacred*; Pinto, "Lessons of Candomblé."

31 See *Chronicle of Higher Education*, "Diversity in Academe"; Smith, *Conquest*; Churchill and LaDuke, "Native North America"; Deer, "Federal Indian Law and Violent Crime."

32 On "containment, internment and exile," see Burman, "Deportable or Admissible?," 177.

33 In my earlier work *Feminism Without Borders*, chap. 9, describing three pedagogical models used in "internationalizing" women's studies, I suggest that each of these perspectives was grounded in particular conceptions of the local and the global, of women's agency, and of national identity, and that each curricular model mapped different stories and ways of crossing borders and building bridges. I also suggested that a "comparative feminist studies" or "feminist solidarity" model is the most useful and productive pedagogical strategy for feminist cross-cultural work, claiming that it is this particular model that provides a way to theorize a complex relational understanding of experience, location, and history such that feminist cross-cultural work moves through the specific context to construct a real notion of universal *and* of democratization rather than colonization. It is this model that can put into practice the idea of "common differences" as the basis for deeper solidarity across differences and unequal power relations.

34 Sudbury, "Introduction," xii.

35 Nagar, "Postscript," 154.

36 Wynter, "Breaking the Epistemological Contract on Black America."

37 We are indebted to Katherine McKittrick for this formulation.

7

TRANSNATIONAL FEMINIST CROSSINGS

On Neoliberalism and Radical Critique

What happens to feminist scholarship and theory in our neoliberal academic culture? Have global and domestic shifts in social movement activism and feminist scholarly projects depoliticized antiracist feminist, women of color, and transnational feminist intellectual projects? By considering how my own work has traveled, and what has been lost (and found) in translation into various contexts, I offer some thoughts about the effects of neoliberal, national security–driven geopolitical landscapes and postmodern intellectual framings of transnational, intersectional feminist theorizing and solidarity work. Specifically, I suggest that the way my work has been adapted and developed within a few marginalized feminist scholarly and activist communities offers valuable lessons for all of us who are university-based feminists. It highlights the limitations of postmodernist feminist knowledge projects in the neoliberal academy.

Over the years my work has focused on decolonization in general, but especially the decolonization of feminist scholarship and theory. I have argued against a scholarly "view from above" of marginalized communities of women in the global South and North, calling instead for attention to historical and cultural specificity in understanding their complex agency as situated subjects. Since the early 1990s my work has increasingly emphasized the need for *systemic* analyses, for an examination of broader patterns and structures of domination and exploitation. It is in the context of a call for systemic analyses that I have argued for the building of resistance and solidarities across borders. In an earlier essay I responded to the misreading of my work as being against all forms of generalization.[1] Here I address another, related issue—the brusque dismissal of systemic analysis of institutional processes as necessarily reductionist and totalizing (sometimes called "modernist"), together with the claim that systemic analysis cannot acknowledge the internal conflicts that compromise every system, every operation of power. In what follows, I want to argue that this particular postmodernist position converges with the proliferation of depoliticized multiplicities that is a hallmark of neoliberal intellectual landscapes. The danger is that the intellectual culture that is produced by this convergence in effect domesticates power differences, transforming systemic projects of resistance to commodified, private acts of rebellion.

During a recent solidarity visit to the occupied Palestinian territories as part of the Indigenous and Women of Color Solidarity delegation, I confronted the limits and possibilities of feminist critique across borders. Learning about colonial technologies of occupation, intricate gendered and racialized exercises of power by the Israeli state, I was more convinced than ever of the need for theory to address fundamental questions of systemic power and inequities, and to develop feminist, antiracist analyses of neoliberalism, militarism, and heterosexism as nation-state building projects. Yet, back in neoliberal "post-everything" US academic and political culture, I confront discursive shifts that mystify the conditions in Palestine. Postmodernism would suggest a fluidity (and mobility) of identities and subjects of liberation that obviate systemic critiques of oppression. Postfeminist and postracial discourse would imply Israelis (and Palestinians?) have moved beyond discrimination on the basis of gender and race. Postintersectionality and some postcolonial, poststructural theoretical paradigms would suggest the irrelevance of analyzing the systematic interconnections of institutionalized processes of racism, (hetero)sexism, nationalism, and class exploitation in the colonial project of Israeli occupation. None of these "post" frameworks is useful in making sense of the land-scape of violence, oppression, and incarceration that constitutes everyday life for Palestinians in the '48 territories and in the occupied West Bank. An analysis of the gendered, racialized, capitalist colonial project of the Israeli state, ably supported by US economic and military aid, must remain at the heart of any Palestinian feminist struggle and at the center of emancipatory knowledges and the theorizing of feminist solidarity.[2] This recognition of the limits (and dangers) of the "posts" in Palestine *and* the United States is key to the arguments of this essay.

Are we then left with a "modernist" (read outmoded) feminist eman-cipatory project in Palestine? Minoo Moallem's 2006 essay is an example of feminist critique that I find remarkably generative, representative of a postmodernist position that brings feminist critical race, intersectionality theorists, and antiracist, transnational feminist theorists under the same umbrella.[3] Yet, it is also deeply troubling. Moallem reviews several feminist texts, including *Global Critical Race Feminism* (Wing, 2000) and *Feminism Without Borders* (Mohanty, 2003). Moallem suggests that "a modernist fem-inist internationalist agenda" is problematic for two reasons. It assumes an "other"—a unified subject that either has to be rescued or put in the center of analysis. And it assumes that the local and global can be contained in a counternarrative of anticapitalism (or antiglobalization) rather than ap-proached as nonsystemic ruptures and discontinuities.[4]

The critique suggests that methodologies that entail institutional and systemic analyses of power, anchored in the experiences of subordination and resistance of the most marginalized communities of women, can be (are?) essentialist and reductionist (not postmodernist, hence "modern-ist").[5] This particular postmodernist critique falls short in some very ob-vious ways. It cannot address the politics of colonialism and the struggle for national liberation and social and economic justice that constitutes Palestinian feminist organizing and analysis at the present time. Claims concerning modernism and reductionism do not exhaust what can be said about struggles for emancipation and freedom from systematic colonial oppression. Clearly there is a plurality of antiracist, postcolonial, transna-tional feminist theorizing, and abundant feminist scholarship on the gen-dered limits and dangers of nationalism (not the same as national libera-tion), but postmodernist critique that is skeptical of a systematic analysis of institutionalized power, and of decolonizing methodologies that centralize marginalized experience (women of color epistemology) in struggles for justice, is seriously off the mark—as evidenced in the Palestinian context.

After all, an explanatory account of the systemic nature of power does not entail inattentiveness to local contradictions or contexts of struggle. On the contrary, such a sociopolitical explanation enables recognition of those moments of rupture and possibility that counterhegemonic movements can use to build solidarities across borders.

The convergence of such critiques with the normalized neoliberal rationalities of the late twentieth and early twenty-first century bears examination. Is there a "threshold of disappearance" here—as Foucault defines it—a point at which discursive formations are transformed? In an insightful analysis, Kelly Coogan-Gehr suggests that the emergence of the categories "third world women" and "women of color" in the 1980s displaced and marginalized the scholarship of African American women, thus marking a threshold of disappearance in feminist scholarship.[6]

I want to raise a similar question in this essay. Does postmodernism coupled with neoliberal knowledge economies in effect define a threshold of disappearance where one conceptual frame (systemic or intersectional) is quietly subsumed under and supplanted by another emerging frame, one that obscures crucial relations of power? In this essay, I explore a convergence between neoliberalism and postmodernism that depoliticizes radical theory (or insurgent knowledge, as I prefer to call it). Coogan-Gehr's analysis of the tensions between a politics of territoriality (location and identity) and a politics of mobility (Foucault's notion of capillary politics) in US feminist scholarship on race is relevant to the discussion that follows.

Neoliberal Landscapes and the Depoliticization of Antiracist, Feminist Thought

Neoliberalism has transformed material and ideological conditions in ways that have profound implications for radical critique and insurgent knowledges. Neoliberalism in the early twenty-first century is marked by market-based governance practices on the one hand (the privatization, commodification, and proliferation of difference) and authoritarian, national security–driven penal state practices on the other. Thus, while neoliberal states facilitate mobility and cosmopolitanism (travel across borders) for some economically privileged communities, it is at the expense of the criminalization and incarceration (the holding in place) of impoverished communities.[7]

The last decade has witnessed dramatic cuts in public funding for education and increasing privatization of higher education around the world.[8]

Julia Sudbury and Margo Okazawa-Rey argue that radical knowledges are domesticated by the neoliberal restructuring of higher education.[9] As I suggest above, neoliberal intellectual culture constitutes a threshold of disappearance for feminist, antiracist thought anchored in the radical social movements of the twentieth century. Radical theory in fact becomes a commodity to be consumed; no longer seen as a product of activist scholarship or connected to emancipatory knowledge, it circulates as a sign of prestige in an elitist, neoliberal landscape.

To trace this threshold of disappearance of antiracist feminist thought, what is needed is an analysis of neoliberalism and the knowledge economy that, on the one hand, provides a critique of corporate rationality and labor practices in university settings and in the operation of state and transnational governing institutions and, on the other, addresses the impact of neoliberalism on social movements. Neoliberal governmentalities discursively construct a public domain denuded of power and histories of oppression, where market rationalities redefine democracy, and collective responsibility is collapsed into individual characteristics.[10] Such normative understandings of the public domain, where only the personal/individual is recognizable, and the political is no longer a contested domain, are indeed at the heart of "post" (feminist/race) discourses. For instance, what happens to the key feminist construct of the "personal is political" when the political (the collective public domain of politics) is *reduced* to the personal? Questions of oppression and exploitation as collective/systematic processes, and institutions of rule that are gendered and raced, have difficulty being heard when neoliberal narratives disallow the salience of collective experience or redefine this experience as a commodity to be consumed. If all experience is merely individual, and the social is always collapsed into the personal, feminist critique and radical theory appear irrelevant—unless they confront these discursive shifts.

Neoliberal discursive landscapes in the academy and state and transnational governance practices are characterized by the privatization of the social justice commitments of the post-1960s radical social movements and their attendant insurgent knowledges (originally institutionalized in women's and gender studies, race and ethnic studies, and so on). Privatizing commitments to race, class, and gender justice requires removing the social significance of racism, classism, or (hetero)sexism as institutionalized systems of power and inequality from the public domain, substituting individual prejudice and psychological dispositions or expressions of "hate" instead. This is a perfect example of a discursive shift, of a threshold of disappearance whereby critical feminist epistemological claims regarding experience, like "the personal is political," are transformed into privatized notions of individual experience. Here, political agency itself is redefined as an act of consumption, and I would argue, theory—feminist and/or antiracist—is trafficked as a commodity disconnected from its activist moorings and social justice commitments.[11]

The interwoven processes of privatization, consumption, and commodification of theory result in a politics of *representation* or a politics of *presence* disconnected from the power and political economy of rule. The epistemological and methodological claims of feminist and antiracist thought are transformed into a privatized politics of representation, disconnected from systematic critique and materialist histories of colonialism, capitalism, and heteropatriarchy (what Coogan-Gehr calls a politics of territoriality).[12] This representational/discursive politics of gender, race, class, sexuality, and nation, disconnected from its materialist moorings, can thus be consumed more easily in institutional spaces. The complex political economy focus (highlighting power and hierarchy) of much feminist, antiracist theory, for instance, is either reduced to a politics of representation/presence/multiculturalism or seen as irrelevant in the context of a so-called postrace/postfeminist society. Thus, for instance, race and gender justice commitments are recoded as a politics of presence (or benign representation of various differences) in neoliberal universities.

Similarly, the appropriation of feminism in the expansion of the neoliberal project is also visible in the depoliticized politics of difference mobilized by neoliberal state regimes. Diana Murdock shows how the neoliberal state relies on feminist NGOs for a theory of gender minus a feminist critique of power relations.[13] This depoliticization of feminist theory is the basis for rhetorical commitments to gender justice that actively erase corresponding commitments to social transformations. Murdock argues persuasively that gender and development (GAD) discourse is used by neoliberal states to underwrite a retrenchment from radical feminist politics—delegitimating and domesticating such politics. The state is thus made "postfeminist" before feminists achieve gender justice!

The privatization and depoliticization of social justice commitments through representational politics in neoliberal landscapes requires a profound *flattening* of difference. Bronwyn Davies and Peter Bansel argue that neoliberal governmentality produces generic institutions and generic subjects, while systematically dismantling the will to critique. All knowledge projects are detached from their local and historical moorings and reattached to the global market as "this place" becomes "every other place" and "this subject" becomes "every other subject."[14] It is this *flattening* of difference in the neoliberal knowledge economy that should be of interest to all of us. The transformation of gender and racial justice commitments into representational discourses and practices of diversity and multiculturalism in the US academy is a case in point. If feminist scholars are to preserve their social justice commitments to gender, race, and sexual justice (the heart of radical, systemic, intersectional, antiracist feminist projects), they/we must attend closely to notions of diversity that embrace generic conceptions of difference that are flattened, privatized, and shorn of a critique of power.

Katharyne Mitchell explores the connections between state formation, economic organization, and educational systems in countries with large immigrant populations like the United Kingdom, the United States, and Canada by analyzing the shift from multiculturalism and ethical liberalism as key national narratives of unification in the period from the 1960s to the early 1980s to what she calls "strategic cosmopolitanism."[15] As the transnational, neoliberal landscape of global competitiveness restructured citizenship in the 1990s, strategic cosmopolitanism became associated with shrinking welfare states, privatization, and a culture of efficiency and accountability. The radical politics of difference and the social justice movements of the 1960s, 1970s, and early 1980s were domesticated as social contract management and individual patriotism eclipsed robust conceptions of the collective and the public good. When market logic embedded within neoliberal governmentality infiltrates knowledge projects in the university and the will to critique is either absent or penalized, there are dire consequences for radical women of color and for transnational, antiracist feminist projects.[16]

Conservative scholars, media pundits, and popular magazines and newspapers began referring to a postfeminist and postrace society just as the project of the neoliberal restructuring of education gained traction around the globe. This shift in vocabulary from feminism to postfeminism and from race (and racism) to postrace in popular culture was meant to signify a movement beyond "old" forms of domination and inequality like racism, sexism, and (hetero)patriarchy. Thus, in a postrace, postfeminist universe, the very categories of gender and racial difference no longer signify social values or power hierarchies—they are rather "market niches."[17] Similarly, the move to transcend intersectional approaches in favor of a postintersectional stance is analogous to the postrace, postfeminist move. Postmodern skepticism applied to intersectionality converts what originates as a compelling theory of the interwoven structures and inequities of power to an inert theory of identity that emphasizes difference over commonality, coalition, and contestation.

Feminist scholars have examined the ideological refashioning of racial justice as "color blindness" and "neoliberal racism," which results in the normalization of a market democracy and privatized notions of agency. Rachel Luft's analysis of the flattening of difference in discourses of color blindness suggests that the social denial of prejudice is accompanied by a denial of the very history of the structural presence of race and racism in the US political landscape.[18] Brenda Weber notes that the congruence of postfeminism and neoliberalism privileges entrepreneurial success and the ideology of individual agency as the solution to social ills, actively undercutting forms of political solidarity that are the basis for feminist and racial justice struggles. Weber argues that a postfeminist, neoliberal narrative normalizes the view that "every woman is an island" who provides for herself and has no need for tax-funded support or communal solidarities.[19] The result is a privatization of difference, the depoliticization of hierarchy, and a narrow construal of agency incompatible with all collective forms of struggle for social justice.

In her cogent analysis of the legal academy, Margaret Thornton says that neoliberal rationalities accompanied by a managerial discourse of diversity (rather than the discordant realities of gender and racial injustice) have had a major impact on the sustainability of radical feminist and critical race projects in the academy.[20] Similarly, Brenda Weber argues that postfeminism and neoliberalism share a logic of "political neutrality," which leads to the rejection of feminism as a social project in favor of marketing one's identity as congruent with social norms.[21]

To demonstrate how the privatization and management of difference in the context of postfeminist, postrace discourses influence the cross-border travel of radical feminist, antiracist projects, the next section reflects on how my own scholarship has traveled in three discrete geographic/national spaces—Sweden, Mexico, and Palestine. The analysis of my work, and the extended dialogues with feminist scholar-activists at these sites represent place-based struggles for gender justice and demonstrate how ideas are used or misused, developed, expanded, and enriched in relation to particular geopolitical contexts and communities. (I focus on my own work here mainly because it points to some interesting cross-border dialogues, but such an analysis can also be done of radical ideas from many other sources and contexts.)

Feminism Across Borders: Geopolitical Translations and Crossings

Undertaken to promote the objectives of gender, class, and racial justice, my scholarship and activism over the last three decades have been read and understood in multiple ways, varying with the material conditions and contexts of its reception.[22] The uses and translations of my work as it is embodied in particular sites, communities, and feminist projects illustrate both the productive adaptations of decolonizing antiracist feminist thought and the pitfalls of the convergence of postmodernist feminism and neoliberal logics in the academy.

Two essays of mine, in particular, have crossed multiple borders: "Under Western Eyes: Feminist Scholarship and Colonial Discourses" (henceforth UWE), first published in 1988, and "Under Western Eyes Revisited: Feminist Solidarity Through Anticapitalist Struggles" (henceforth UWE-R), the last chapter of *Feminism Without Borders* (2003). Reflecting on place-based reception and critical framing of this work illuminates the "traffic in theory"—the politics (and commodification) of theoretical travel across social/cultural and national borders.

The transition from UWE to UWE-R marks my explicit engagement with the rise of neoliberalism and the normalization of corporate practices in the academy. The circulation of these works in various geopolitical locales reveals feminist complicity in imperial and capitalist/neoliberal projects and points to the limitations of knowledge-making projects in the academy. It also signals the continued relevance of systemic analyses of decolonization and resistance in transnational feminist praxis. UWE was written from my location as a part-time teacher in the US academy, as an immigrant "third world" woman at an elite institution. Written fifteen years later, UWE-R marked a shift in my own location to a full professor of women's and gender studies (WGS) in a less elite but still predominantly white liberal arts college. UWE is an intervention explicitly addressing the colonizing gestures of feminist scholarship about women in the third world. It was written from within the context of a vibrant political and scholarly community of radical antiracist, transnational US women of color and a large and growing body of critical work by feminists from the global South. The essay was anchored in the experience of marginalization (and colonization) of the knowledges and intellectual agency of immigrant women of color in the United States. It was intended both as a critique of the universalizing and colonizing tendencies of feminist theorizing and as a methodological intervention arguing for historicizing and contextualizing feminist scholarship. UWE had a clear political purpose and was written in collective solidarity with antiracist, cross-cultural feminist activist projects in the 1980s.

The publication journey of UWE is instructive. It was first rejected by *Signs*. As one reader put it, "Why did you waste my time on this essay? It says nothing of value!"[23] The essay was subsequently published in 1988 (in an issue dated 1986) by the left literary/cultural studies journal *boundary 2*. It was immediately picked up and reprinted by the British feminist journal *Feminist Review* and simultaneously translated and published in German and Dutch feminist journals. UWE thus made its way into the US feminist academy via Europe. Since its publication in 1988, UWE has been reprinted in numerous anthologies of feminist, postcolonial, area, development, and cultural studies and translated into more than twenty Asian, Latin American, and Western and Eastern European languages. In the last twenty-five years, this essay has traveled widely across disciplinary, national, and linguistic borders. It is used as required reading in numerous disciplines from anthropology and international relations to literary and visual studies.

In contrast to UWE, UWE-R marks not only a shift in my own location in the US academy but also a different intellectual/political moment of knowledge production as neoliberalism transformed material conditions in higher education in the United States and elsewhere in the world. While my status as a professor of WGS with access to some institutional power and an international audience was key to UWE-R's reception and travel across borders (this time, *Signs* solicited the essay), the essay was also written as an intervention into cross-cultural feminist thought. It was written in part to respond to the ways that my previous work (including UWE) had been absorbed within a hegemonic intellectual culture of postmodernism, primarily by rewriting the materialist basis of the discursive analysis of power and the call for attentiveness to specificity, historicity, and difference among women in marginalized communities into what was described, oddly enough, as support for a theoretical and methodological emphasis on "the local" and "the particular"—hence against all forms of generalization. This particular misreading of my work ignored the materialist emphasis on a "common context of struggle" and undermined the possibility of solidarity across differences.[24]

As in earlier work, UWE-R focuses on decolonizing feminism, a politics of difference and commonality, and specifying, historicizing, and connecting feminist struggles. The problematic reading of my earlier work meant that what was "lost in translation" were the material and historical continuities that were important to my argument in UWE—and the deep critique of Western feminist theory that called for a rethinking of how cross-cultural work is done in the context of racist and colonialist legacies. UWE-R was written to address these losses and the depoliticization of my original project and to model a form of feminist theorizing in the early twenty-first century—a feminist anticapitalist critique that constitutes a radical intervention in a neoliberal academic culture and corporate academy, advanced in conjunction with the rise of antiglobalization solidarity movements around the world.

While UWE was written from a personal and institutional space of colonization and marginalization within Western feminism and the US academy, UWE-R was written from the experience of struggling against neoliberal culture and postmodernist hegemony within the feminist theory establishment and women's and gender studies departments. I consider both essays oppositional gestures in feminist knowledge production in the United States. In 2003, UWE-R was also an insurgent knowledge practice that claimed anticapitalist and anti-imperialist feminist space in the center of the corporate academy and contested neoliberal appropriation of gender, sexuality, and race/ethnicity as "disciplined" objects of study. I was not claiming a voice for "third world women" in the academy, since that project was already underway in the larger, antiracist feminist/women of color communities, and it was already being domesticated by a neoliberal intellectual culture.

My intentions as an author, however, cannot control how my works are read. The final section of this essay traces the way my work has been taken up in different sites as it travels across borders. UWE has resonated with readers who encounter the essay as immigrant, third world women and women of color in academic and activist spaces where the experiential politics of knowledge that UWE critiques has significance. UWE-R has been embraced by intellectuals, teachers, and activists in anticapitalist, antiglobalization, materialist feminist communities. Yet both essays have also been misread. In the context of the neoliberal, postmodern/poststructural capillary politics of mobility, both have been read too quickly as essentialist and reductive. In the end, however, these travels also expose the limits of the "posts" as knowledge-making projects.

Mapping Place-Based Knowledges and the Traffic in Feminist Thought

Arturo Escobar suggests that theories of difference travel between place-based meanings and enactments of Eurocentric/colonial globality. Discussing the geopolitics of knowledge, Escobar rightly says that "the dynamic of an imperial globality and its regime of coloniality" is "one of the most salient features of the modern colonial world system in the early twenty first century."[25] Claudia de Lima Costa frames the geopolitics of knowledge in terms of the uneven migration of analytical categories across borders, causing some knowledge to be "lost in translation" as it travels to different hemispheres.[26] Claiming that analytical categories have different rationalities depending on place, de Lima Costa looks at the traffic in theory by examining the ways that foundational feminist concepts like *gender* and *women of color* have traveled between US Latina and Latin-American feminist spaces. Escobar and de Lima Costa both draw attention to North-South historical divides and colonial misappropriations and faulty translations of place-based theories of difference. Both suggest the need to reflect on the traffic in theory in a neoliberal landscape governed by global coloniality/ Eurocentric globality. Writing about "traveling theories," Richa Nagar raises questions about accountability and political commitments in the theoretical languages and frames mobilized by transnational feminist scholars.[27]

Drawing on these ideas about the relation of place-based knowledge practices and cross-border traffic in theory, I explore below the way my ideas are read, understood, and utilized in Sweden, Mexico, and Palestine. In each space, the work is available in English and in translation (Swedish, Spanish, and Arabic). Although my work has traveled to other sites, I have chosen to focus on these locations because I can draw on multiple levels of engagement and collaboration with colleagues in these spaces. Thus I can address questions of translation and travel of concepts as well as my own accountability to the ideas and communities I work with.[28] At each site, I begin with a brief discussion of the impact of neoliberalism and global coloniality on the knowledge economy and gender justice commitments, then explore the way my work is utilized by feminist colleagues engaged in struggles for gender, class, and racial justice in their own local/global contexts. The discussion of my work as it is taken up by activist and academic feminists in these sites suggests the limits of the "posts" (postmodernism, postfeminism, postrace) as knowledge-making projects in the neoliberal academy. It also indicates why systemic analyses of decolonization are so important for feminist communities—across borders.

Sweden, touted as one of the most progressive countries in terms of gender equity policy, is an interesting instance of neoliberal gender entanglements. Swedish gender discourse is an example of close links between the state and grassroots and academic feminists.[29] Since the 1990s, women's and gender studies projects and the equal opportunity policies of the Swedish state have been quite closely linked. Liinason argues that the concept of gender is reproduced to underwrite a progressive success story (gender equality) of the nation. Similarly, Nina Lykke, Christine Michel, and Maria Puig de la Bellacasa have argued that since the 1990s, EU policies have provided political and economic legitimation of gender equality at the national level, thus weaving the institutionalization of women's and gender studies together with national gender equality projects.[30] The impact of neoliberalism on women's and gender studies programs in Europe has entailed a shift from radical feminist critique to an emphasis on policy-oriented work that produces "equal opportunity experts."

In recent decades the development of antiracist and postcolonial feminist thought in Sweden has led to pathbreaking scholarship on the racial and class parameters of Swedish "gender equality."[31] Mulinari and colleagues draw on constructs of intersectionality and postcolonial feminism to anchor studies in the field of postcolonial Nordic feminism.[32] These studies investigate notions of "Nordic whiteness," exploring immigration policies and the centrality of race and ethnicity to the public landscape. The Swedish feminist debate on intersectionality and postcolonial feminism is both vibrant and multidimensional. For this reason, I found it particularly interesting to look at how my work has been engaged and the struggles it seems to have made possible during a period when neoliberalism has gained purchase on the Swedish state, academia, and grassroots feminist movements.

Feminism Without Borders was translated into Swedish in 2007. I can only track citations to the work in English (a major limitation, I admit), so I asked antiracist, postcolonial feminist scholar Diana Mulinari some direct questions about the impact of my work in Sweden.[33] Mulinari's assessment suggests that the constructs and theoretical/methodological aspects of my work, which have been utilized productively, include the critique of a Eurocentric and colonizing discourse of Western feminist theory; the significance of race and class intersectionality; the politics of location in the struggles of women in the global South and women of color in the United States (women of color epistemology); and the anticapitalist feminist analysis and notion of solidarity across borders. According to Mulinari, these themes have resonated in the academy, in art and cultural production, and in antiracist activism.[34]

Yet Mulinari also identified "misreadings" of my work that occur "through processes of appropriation ... after acknowledging Mohanty in terms of a totemic symbol, (despite everything) 'the center,' (white) authors continue the doing of whiteness as usual, seldom analyzing the lack of women of color within the dynamics of knowledge production." Mulinari's astute observation sheds light on the impact of neoliberalism on antiracist feminist projects, illuminating the appropriation of my work through a citational politics ("acknowledging Mohanty in terms of a totemic symbol"), a rhetorical gesture disconnected from the systemic and materialist analysis of power. Thus even as my work has had a significant impact in Swedish intellectual, cultural, and activist circles, Mulinari charts an "appropriation." By "doing of whiteness as usual," hegemonic feminist knowledge production traffics antiracist feminist scholarship across borders, domesticating women of color epistemology in ways that either erase or assimilate it into a Euro-centric feminist globality. This is a powerful example of a representational politics characteristic of neoliberal landscapes that manages to erase the fundamental theoretical and methodological challenge of *decolonization*, which is central to my work.

Feminist scholarship in Latin America reveals different aspects of the limits and possibilities of traveling theories. Brazilian feminist Claudia de Lima Costa's work first introduced me to a discussion of what is "lost and found" in the translation of feminist theory across borders.[35] De Lima Costa argues that the traffic in theory and the global export of feminist concepts across borders must be understood in terms of dominant and subordinate institutional configurations and historiographies across the North-South divide. Although de Lima Costa focuses specifically on US Latina and Latin American feminist translations, the theoretical points she makes about the potential "untranslatability" of certain concepts like "women of color" and the uneven migration of foundational concepts like "gender" are important considerations in understanding how my own work crosses geopolitical intellectual spaces. De Lima Costa's discussion of the way "gender" replaces "feminism" in the Brazilian academy is echoed in Liinason's analysis of how "gender" replaces "women" in the Swedish context.[36] Both indicate the assimilation and domestication of feminism in neoliberal academic contexts. Focusing specifically on Ecuador and Brazil, Phillips and Cole describe two disparate "translations" of feminism in the era of late neoliberalism, one from above and one from below.[37] "UN Orbit" feminism is an approach toward gender equality embedded in systematic proposal-based global agendas. "Another-World" feminism is anchored in a decentralized, collaborative, diverse, antiglobalization movement. Each of these accounts identifies factors that explain contexts in which there is faithful translation of insurgent knowledges and contexts characterized by distorting appropriations.

In the Mexican context, scholars such as Michelle Téllez, Anna Sampaio, and R. Aída Hernández Castillo have deployed my work to foreground the agency of poor and Indigenous women, drawing on notions of oppositional consciousness anchored in the lives of some of the most marginalized communities of women to suggest possibilities of feminist solidarity and alliance across borders.[38] In addition, they have used the notion of "discursive colonialism" to critique hegemonic Mexican feminism from the epistemological space of Indigenous women in Mexico. As Aída Hernández Castillo notes, my work has been particularly useful in developing critiques of hegemonic urban feminism:

> [Mohanty's] critique of the discursive colonialism of feminism has been applied to the strategies of hegemonic urban feminism towards indigenous women. . . .
>
> The concept of discursive colonialism has been used to refer to the power effect that the victimization of indigenous and Afro-Latina women can have in the lives and struggles of these groups. Also the concept of transcultural feminist work and the politics of solidarity has been used to reflect about the need to create links and alliances between different women in this difficult historical moment of militarization (in the name of the anti-drug war) and criminalization of social movements.
>
> Chandra Mohanty's theoretical-political work has contributed to the development of an indigenous women thought that is questioning ethnocentric visions of academic and political feminism in Mexico and its difficulty understanding evidence that subordination and gender inequality are not isolated, but intersect with ethnic exclusion, class, race and religion, etc. We could say that [her work] has de-centered hegemonic conceptions of gender contributing to the re-conceptualization of the concept of gender as a multidimensional category. Maya intellectuals from Guatemala in dialog with Chandra's work are calling for recognition that there are multiple ways to articulate identities and gender projects within the constellation of actors and movements of a diverse and unequal Latin America.[39]

Hernández Castillo (rightly) suggests that an adequate critique of capitalism in the Latin American context must also engage a discussion of the globalization of the penal state. And she pinpoints particular contexts in which misreadings of my work occur. "Some urban Mexican feminists think that the first article generalizes 'white, urban feminism,' repeating the same mistakes that the article criticizes by homogenizing academic feminism."[40] This critique of the "homogenization of academic feminism" is anchored in a familiar postmodernist argument where "differences within" always trump critical analyses of dominant discourses, leading to a refusal to identify the existence of a hegemonic feminism (one that has systematic effects on marginalized communities). Thus, the very aspects of my work that are useful to Indigenous and Maya feminist intellectuals in identifying "discursive colonialism" in Mexican academic and political feminism and in calling for the self-representation of Indigenous women are dismissed by a critique that refuses to acknowledge its own hegemonic will to power in the neoliberal, postmodern culture of Mexican feminism and the Latin American academy. Within spaces of privilege, my critique of the power of hegemonic feminism from the epistemological space of marginalized communities of women is misread as a representational politics focused primarily on differences within academic feminism. While those involved in the analysis of power and the systemic demystification of global capitalist and neocolonial processes from the epistemic location of poor and marginalized communities of women get me right, hegemonic versions of feminism, invested in privilege, tend to misread my work. These patterns are also evident in the Palestinian context, to which I turn now.

Neoliberalism is felt acutely in the context of the Palestinian women's movement. Given colonial occupation and the urgency of a national liberation struggle, many Palestinian feminist scholar-activists like Eileen Kuttab, Islah Jad, and Penny Johnson call attention to the NGOization of the Palestinian women's movement post-Oslo.[41] Since the first Intifada, the impact of neoliberalism and colonial occupation have led to a dependency on donor-driven NGO funding, engendering a professionalization of social movements. Islah Jad argues that this NGOization has led to the cooptation of grassroots social movements that posed a direct challenge to the occupation, opting instead for issue-based policy changes.[42] Eileen Kuttab also explores the post-Oslo shaping of Palestinian feminism by neoliberal global frameworks, suggesting that since the 1990s, professionalized feminist NGOs have shifted the local focus from the intertwining of gender and national liberation to an international gender equity focus.[43] According to Islah Jad, it is in this context of depoliticization and professionalization of grassroots feminist struggles that my work entered the Palestinian intellectual/political feminist community:

Your work came to Palestine in a moment where the discourse of "peace negotiation as the only option" was starting to prevail after the first Palestinian popular uprising in 1987. Your work helped a great deal to deconstruct this hegemonic discourse that was working to marginalize what can be called "a home grown feminism" not driven by new liberal and universal discourse on women's rights. Your work was a cornerstone that helped us to defend our own notion of "militant feminism" that seeks to liberate the country and women in the same time.

I think it deconstructed once and for all the notion of "sisterhood is global." [Instead] you founded "sisterhood" on the basis of solidarity and resistance to empire and to global capital . . . [reversing a tendency to see] contemporary feminism as "apolitical" and narrowly focused on "women" in isolation from their context.[44]

Unlike Mulinari and Hernández Castillo, Jad says categorically that my work "was not misread at all by us here; on the contrary it gave us a huge energy for reclaiming our 'militant feminism' and it helped a great deal to discredit the 'peace negotiation' camp that worked hard with donor funding to 'bring Israeli and Palestinian women' to build peace, assuming that feminism per se is capable to do wonders. Your work brought us back the spirit of resistance as the basis for solidarity." Here again, Jad's assessment of the impact of my work suggests that the migration of concepts like discursive colonization, anticapitalist, anti-imperialist feminism, and solidarity based on mutuality and accountability is most significant in the Palestinian context. Indeed, Jad concurs with Mulinari and Hernández Castillo that the most important contribution of my work lies in the decolonization of knowledge, the politics of differences and commonality, and historicizing and specifying women's struggles and identities in the context of anticolonial, anticapitalist struggles within a neoliberal global culture.

Situating my work in the context of powerful divisions within transnational feminist praxis, Mulinari, Hernández Castillo, and Jad perceive my work as a critical intervention against hegemonic academic/political feminist formations. It creates a discursive space in which to decolonize feminist hegemonies by according epistemic privilege to the most marginalized communities of women. Thus, all three scholar-activists develop, in their own contexts, one of the central theoretical and methodological points of my work—the focus on decolonization of feminist scholarship and theory, and on woman of color epistemology. Thus, this women of color epistemology inserts questions of racialization and the politics pertaining to racial/ethnic immigrant women into Nordic and Swedish feminist discourses, questions of Indigenous women's struggles and agency into Latin American feminist engagements, and questions of Palestinian feminist militancy and agency into discourses of peace and reconciliation in the Israeli/Palestinian feminist context.[45] Each identifies systemic analyses of domination and resistance as key to radical feminist praxis—racism and anticapitalism/labor movements (Sweden), colonialism and racism/Indigenous agency (Mexico), and colonialism/militant Indigenous feminism (Palestine). It is significant that the communities that find my work useful in all three spaces—immigrant, Indigenous, women of color—are mirrored in the United States as well, once again emphasizing the significance of systematic analysis of colonization and resistance while signaling the limits of the "post."[46]

Yet it is precisely the power of decolonizing feminist thought grounded in women of color epistemology and engaging in systemic analysis that global coloniality seeks to suppress. I began this essay with a discussion of neoliberal intellectual landscapes and the privatization and depoliticization of gender and racial justice commitments through the domestication of feminist thought in state and transnational governance practices, in academic/institutional cultures, and in the transformation of social movements into donor-driven social contracts. One of the primary aspects of this discussion was the *privatization* of social divisions and the individualization of experience—the collapse of notions of collectivity into the personal, and the transformation of power and political agency into acts of consumption.

As the brief examination of divergent receptions of my work in hegemonic and counterhegemonic sites makes clear, there is a threshold of disappearance of intersectional, systemic antiracist feminist projects within these neoliberal intellectual landscapes. A too quick extension of postmodernist skepticism to social and political theory often fits quite comfortably with the neoliberal agenda.[47] The neoliberal privatization and domestication of social justice commitments can go hand in hand with the postmodern/poststructuralist dissolution of the systemic critiques of structures and institutions evident in intersectional, transnational materialist feminist engagements. This compromising of our politics reminds us that it is important to always turn the critique of privilege on ourselves. The dissolving of the systemic analyses of women of color and transnational feminist projects into purely discursive (representational) analyses of ruptures, fluidity, and discontinuities symptomatic of poststructural critique contributes to a threshold of disappearance of materialist antiracist feminist projects that target the state and other governing institutions. It is this danger of the appropriation of radical women of color/transnational feminist projects that should be of deep concern to us all.

The discussion of the travel and translation of my own work suggests the continuing importance of systemic analyses in radical antiracist feminist projects. It also points to the limits of knowledge projects in neoliberal academies. What would it mean to be attentive to the politics of activist feminist communities in different sites in the global South and North as they imagine and create cross-border feminist solidarities anchored in struggles on the ground? How would academic feminist projects be changed if we were accountable to activist/academic communities like the ones identified by Mulinari, Hernández Castillo, and Jad? I believe we need to return to the radical feminist politics of the contextual as both local and structural, and to the collectivity that is being defined out of existence by privatization projects. I think we need to recommit to insurgent knowledges and the complex politics of antiracist, anti-imperialist feminisms.

Notes

This chapter was originally published as "Transnational Feminist Crossings: On Neoliberalism and Radical Critique," *Signs: Journal of Women in Culture and Society* 38, no. 4 (2013): 967–91.

Many thanks to Satya Mohanty for lifelong conversations and sustained, critical feedback; to Jacqui Alexander and Zillah Eisenstein for thoughtful critique; and to Anya Stanger for fabulous research assistance. Thanks also to Kimberlé Crenshaw, Leslie McCall, Sumi Cho, and Beth Ribet for valuable critique and feedback.

1 See Mohanty, "'Under Western Eyes' Revisited."
2 The "old" (and enduring) hierarchies of colonialism, racism, classism, and (hetero)sexism are alive and well in Palestine (as they are in the United States). Global processes of domination and subordination are certainly complex in 2012, but the technologies of colonialism are still accompanied by violence and exclusions that are systemic.
3 Moallem, "Feminist Scholarship and the Internationalization of Women's Studies."
4 There have been similar critiques of my work by a number of feminist scholars. See especially critiques by Felski, "The Doxa of Difference"; Trevenen, "Stretching 'the Political'; Thobani, review of *Feminism Without Borders*; and Seidel, review of *Feminism Without Borders*.
5 Kimberlé Crenshaw's work on intersectionality has been read similarly, with critics often reducing the institutional analysis of state power, and women of color epistemology to essentialist and reductive formulations. On the other hand, Chao-Ju Chen (in "The Difference That Differences Make") draws on the systemic, institutional analysis in both Crenshaw and Mohanty to define the politics of difference in Asian feminism in terms of a differentiated universalism in the context of universal moral commitment.

6   Coogan-Gehr, "Politics of Race in US Feminist Scholarship."

7   See Sampaio, "Transnational Feminisms in a New Global Matrix"; Sudbury, *Global Lockdown*; Davis and Mendieta, *Abolition Democracy*; and Harvey, *Brief History of Neoliberalism*, for analyses of the connections between neoliberalism, incarceration, and criminalization.

8   See Ayers and Ayers, "Education Under Fire: Introduction"; and the entire special issue on public education of the journal *Monthly Review* (Ayers and Ayers, "Education Under Fire").

9   Sudbury and Okazawa-Rey, "Introduction."

10 Giroux, "Bare Pedagogy and the Scourge of Neoliberalism."

11 Giroux, "Bare Pedagogy and the Scourge of Neoliberalism."

12 Coogan-Gehr, "Politics of Race in US Feminist Scholarship."

13 Murdock, "Neoliberalism, Gender, and Development."

14 Davies and Bansel, "Governmentality and Academic Work," 14.

15 Mitchell, "Educating the National Citizen in Neoliberal Times."

16 The Occupy Wall Street movement in 2011 is an important counterpoint to this neoliberal domestication of difference, naming as it does the 99 percent versus the 1 percent in terms of political and economic domination and marginalization. For a brief analysis of the ows movement, see Eisenstein and Mohanty, "In Support of Occupy Wall Street."

17 Giroux, "Bare Pedagogy and the Scourge of Neoliberalism."

18 Luft, "Intersectionality and the Risk of Flattening Difference."

19 Weber, "Teaching Popular Culture Through Gender Studies."

20 Thornton, "Feeling Chilly (Again) in the Legal Academy."

21 Weber, "Teaching Popular Culture Through Gender Studies."

22 For a sampling of critiques and responses to my work, see Moallem, "Feminist Scholarship and the Internationalization of Women's Studies"; Saliba, "On the Bodies of Third World Women"; Clark, "Why All the Counting?"; Gupta, "Towards Transnational Feminisms"; Ayotte and Husain, "Securing Afghan Women"; Bradford, "Representing Islam"; Marchand and Parpart, *Feminism/Postmodernism/Development*; Mendoza, "Transnational Feminisms in Question"; McLaughlin, "Feminism and the Political Economy of Transnational Public Space"; Okin, "Feminism, Women's Human Rights, and Cultural Differences"; Mama, "Rethinking African Universities."

23 It is interesting to note that UWE was reviewed by *Signs* during the period described by Coogan-Gehr ("Politics of Race in US Feminist Scholarship") in the early to mid-1980s as representing an example of a "threshold of disappearance" of the epistemological and methodological contributions of US Black feminists within feminist scholarship.

24 Scholars like Gupta ("Towards Transnational Feminisms"); Ayotte and Husain ("Securing Afghan Women"); and Chen ("The Difference That Differences Make"), on the other hand, draw specifically on the connections between specificity and generalization, on the notions of solidarity across difference and the politics of accountability.

25 Escobar, *Territories of Difference*, 4.

26 De Lima Costa, "Lost (and Found?) in Translation."

27 Nagar, "Footloose Researchers."

28 I draw on scholarly texts as well as personal communication with feminist scholars in all three sites, posing a series of questions to a key feminist colleague in each site. These are colleagues located within intellectual/activist communities I hold myself accountable to, communities that in fact are a part of the transnational, antiracist, decolonizing feminist project within which I situate myself. Clearly, responses from single individuals do not constitute systematic research, but they do provide an embodied and horizontal dialogue across borders that is an important site of knowledge. These exchanges also answer a crucial question that can only be asked and answered directly, that is, the struggles my work makes possible in these three sites.

29 Liinason, "Feminism and the Academy"; Liinason, "Institutionalized Knowledge"; Liinason and Holm, "PhDs, Women's/Gender Studies and Interdisciplinarity."

30 Lykke et al., *Women's Studies.*

31 De los Reyes et al., *Maktens olika förklädnader*; Mulinari and Rathzel, "Politicizing Biographies."

32 Mulinari and Rathzel, "Politicizing Biographies."

33 I asked similar questions to feminist colleagues in Mexico (Aída Hernández Castillo) and Palestine (Islah Jad): "Can you describe briefly how you think my work is read in Sweden/Mexico/Palestine? What constructs/formulations/ideas/theories are most useful? What interventions (if any) into hegemonic discourses does my work make possible? What limitations can you identify in terms of how my work gets translated into a Swedish/Mexican/Palestinian context? How is/can it be misread?"

34 I believe it is worth quoting Mulinari at length since her voice represents a particular locus of struggle:

> Mohanty is one of the postcolonial scholars that has had an impressive impact in Sweden (and in Scandinavian) academic, cultural and political life. She is extensively read and quoted in academic works and has been an important source of inspiration for antiracist activists. Her work has been read through three different academic fields of study (the postcolonial, the feminist, the social justice field) and in three different spaces (the academy, the cultural field and activism). . . . In *Intersektionalitet maktbok*, feminist antiracist activists present her as one of the central voices illuminating issues of colonialism, imperialism and racism.
>
> . . . "Under Western Eyes: Feminist Scholarship and Colonial Discourses" . . . is not only acknowledged as a pathbreaking intervention. It has functioned as a basis for the analysis of how Eurocentric representations of "other women" are at play in topics going from social policy to the media in Sweden and in Scandinavia. Nearly all the works that take a critical approach towards the category of "race" frame their analysis in the arguments developed in Mohanty's article. Important to underline is that the article has had an impact that goes beyond feminist academic circles.
>
> . . . Mohanty's work has in different ways made it nearly impossible to discuss gender without engaging in an intersectional analysis of the different axes of power inscribed in gendered identities with special emphasis on the category of "race." . . . *Third World Women and the Politics of Feminism* puts the Global South in general and women in particular at the center of the doing

of (feminist) theory and has broken new ground regarding the location and the position of Southern feminisms.

   Feminism Without Borders has had an impact not only among postcolonial, antiracist scholars but also on scholars exploring issues of social justice and solidarity. These new developments in her scholarship have strongly contributed to creating a bridge between postcolonial theory and labor studies and between critical development studies and ethnic/racial studies. Mohanty's focus and emphasis on labor makes her work unique among postcolonial scholars, and this focus has been fruitful to introduce and to establish feminist postcolonial analysis in labor and organization studies. (Email exchange, November 5, 2011)

35 De Lima Costa, "Being Here and Writing There."
36 Liinason, "Institutionalized Knowledge."
37 Phillips and Cole, "Feminist Flows, Feminist Fault Lines."
38 Téllez, "Community of Struggle"; Sampaio, "Transnational Feminisms in a New Global Matrix"; and Hernández Castillo, "Indigenous Law and Identity Politics in Mexico" and "Indigeneity as a Field of Power." As Hernández Castillo notes about the impact of UWE to Indigenous women's resistance:

   Her texts were translated and started to circulate broadly in a historical context in which indigenous autonomic demands for constitutional reforms opened a debate about how the recognition of collective rights and self-determination for indigenous peoples could endanger indigenous women rights. In this context an important sector of the hegemonic feminist movement opposed the recognition of autonomous indigenous rights in the name of women's rights, using racist discourses against indigenous cultures and representing indigenous women only as victims of their patriarchal traditions. In this debate, indigenous women activists rejected the feminist representation of their cultures and denounced the colonial effect of these political and academic discourses. Some indigenous intellectuals started to use Chandra Mohanty's work to criticize the colonial effect that the victimization of indigenous women could have in their lives and struggles. At the same time the texts were used in several seminars organized by indigenous women in Guatemala, in which the subject of the decolonization of the Guatemalan academia was discussed. Important Maya intellectuals such as Aura Cumes, Emma Chirix, and Gladys Tzul have used Mohanty's texts to write about discursive colonialism and the need for new strategies of self-representation. (Email exchange, November 18, 2011)

39 Email exchange, November 18, 2011.
40 Email exchange, November 18, 2011.
41 Eileen Kuttab, "Empowerment as Resistance" and "Palestinian Women's Organizations"; Jad, "NGOs" and "Politics of Group Weddings in Palestine"; and Johnson and Kuttab, "Where Have All the Women (and Men) Gone?"
42 Jad, "NGOs."
43 Kuttab, "Empowerment as Resistance" and "Palestinian Women's Organizations."

44 Email exchange, November 6, 2011.

45 This is in contrast to Moallem ("Feminist Scholarship and the Internationalization of Women's Studies"), who critiques a modernist feminist internationalist agenda (which my work is subsumed under)—there are no "others" to be rescued or centered here.

46 See especially discussions of my work by Saliba, "On the Bodies of Third World Women"; Clark, "Why All the Counting?"; Gupta, "Towards Transnational Feminisms"; Ayotte and Husain, "Securing Afghan Women"; and Mama, "Is It Ethical to Study Africa?"

47 I have made similar critiques of postmodern skepticism elsewhere. See Alexander and Mohanty, *Feminist Genealogies, Colonial Legacies, Democratic Futures*; Mohanty, "Imperial Democracies, Militarized Zones, Feminist Engagements."

8

THE CHALLENGE OF SOLIDARITY

Notes on Transnational, Insurgent Feminist Praxis

More than three decades ago, in 1991, I coined the term *cartographies of struggle* to address the politics of "third world feminism,"[1] what we would now call postcolonial or transnational feminism, or even women of color epistemology—the terms and our language have shifted and changed, but the conceptual parameters remain the same. I want to go back to this construct of cartographies of struggle to frame this essay on antiracist struggles and transnational feminism as insurgent praxis. As an analytic concept, cartographies of struggle allows us to grasp how power works through interconnected histories of (1) racial capitalism and labor flows, (2) colonial legacies of heteronormative nation-states and projects of citizenship, and (3) transnational/cross border movements and advocacy for economic and social justice. Cartographies of struggle thus foregrounds the mutual histories and interconnected logics of colonialism, racial capitalism, border imperialism, white supremacy, and the rise and consolidation of religious fundamentalist, authoritarian regimes across the globe. An insurgent anti-racist feminist praxis at this time, then, needs to understand these powerful, systemic transnational processes and interconnected histories in order to build radical collectives and movements based on ethical cross-border solidarities.

Transnational in this context does not mean global (as defined by the UN or by corporate NGOS), it does not mean international (as defined by the fields of international relations and political science to refer to exchanges between discrete nation-states), and it does not always reside outside the United States (transnational is not just the opposite of national). As Jacqui Alexander and I suggested some years ago, given the structuring reality of capitalism and imperialism, the transnational must be seen in the here and now, as always present in the local, the specific, and the particular.[2] Transnational feminist work involves thinking historically, comparatively, and relationally, and it involves fundamentally addressing cartographies of power and difference. In addition to the theorization of cartographies of struggle, I find compelling the feminist geographer Cindi Katz's notion of "countertopography" to understand transnational connections that anchor people's everyday experiences and struggles. Katz says: "Not all places affected by capital's global ambition are affected the same way, and not all issues matter equally everywhere. By constructing precise topographies at a range of scales from the local to the regional and beyond, we can analyze a particular issue—say de-skilling—in and across place, mapping sites connected along this contour line."[3] My analysis today is anchored in these specific conceptual frames.

The last few decades have witnessed the global rise of populism, nationalism, and religious fundamentalism, buttressed by the normalization of ideologies of neoliberalism and white supremacy as a central feature of politics. This normalization of legacies of misogynist racial capitalism, and the neoliberal colonization of language and public life, has led not only to the privatization of social justice commitments but also to what scholars like Henry Giroux have called "neoliberal fascism," a culture and governance structure that conjoins the worst excesses of capitalism with authoritarian ideals[4]—and I would add toxic masculinity and a politics of pollution and disposability as central features of neoliberal fascism. Populism, nationalism, and religious fundamentalism conjoined with neoliberal governance practices often create a moral panic calling for national revivals of unity based on traditional family values, muscular masculinity, compulsory heterosexuality, and parenting based on paternal authority and discipline. And so we have Donald Trump's "America First," Viktor Orbán's "Hungary

First," Jarosław Kaczynski's "One Poland," Narendra Modi's "India Rising," and most recently the victory of the Brothers of Italy party—a direct descendant of Benito Mussolini, led by Giorgia Meloni!

And of course we are in the midst of a global pandemic that has exposed all the colonial legacies and accompanying class, race, and gender inequities that liberal Western democracies are built on and try to hide. The national and transnational now necessitate acknowledging explicitly carceral regimes; geopolitical climate destruction; militarized national borders; massive displacement of peoples (war, climate, and economic refugees); proliferation of corporatist, racist, misogynist cultures; lean-in and glass ceiling (liberal) feminisms; decimation of labor movements; and the rise of right-wing, proto-fascist governments around the world. These are all phenomena that activists, NGOS, think tanks, scholars, and policymakers at all levels need to understand and address. All these phenomena are of course connected to global economic crises (the oil crisis in the 1970s and the stock market crashes in 2008 and 2020), neoliberal governmentalities, and mass unemployment, displacement and dispossession of particular groups of people worldwide.

Given this landscape of a world that is networked globally, binaries of domestic/foreign or national/international don't work, since they assume the primacy of the nation. This moment of global pandemic and antiracist protest crosses national and regional borders in acute and poignant ways. Transnational feminist frameworks in fact challenge the national/international division by introducing the question of colonial legacies and gendered-racial globalities as central to scholarship, activism, and policymaking. Thus, developing an antiracist transnational feminist framework entails thinking about power, imperialism, and global racialities rather than racialized gender in domestic or foreign terms since this framework acknowledges legacies of colonial/racial capitalism and economic and ideological priorities that are constitutive of the operation of the neoliberal, militarized world order of the twenty-first century. And after all, the modern nation-state was born of colonialism; racial and gendered hierarchies of empire are crucial to the construction of the nation as we know it, and, as Gurminder Bhambra says, "the nation is imperial as much as it is national."[5]

So what does an antiracist, decolonial, anticapitalist transnational feminist praxis consist of at this time when colonial legacies and global inequities are no longer invisible and building solidarities and movements across borders is more urgent than ever before? What does it mean to craft insurgent knowledges through our writing, our art, our cultural productions, our activism, and our pedagogies? Simply put, an insurgent feminist lens requires understanding that racialized gender is key to mapping borders, histories, and movements and asking the question: How and why do women, queer, and gender nonconforming people matter in understanding and responding to this moment of global pandemic and protest?

This essay argues that we build a transnational feminist praxis by addressing three interwoven conceptual and political cartographies in these times of pandemic and protest: border crossings, interconnected histories, and intersectional social movements/ethical solidarities.

Our commonsense understanding of geopolitical borders (national, regional, local) involves militarized security forces to "protect" insiders and keep out outsiders/invaders. The COVID-19 pandemic illustrates that borders cannot be shut down to keep the virus "out." In fact, national quarantines are not safe for folks in prison, detention centers, and slums, and, in the United States (and Europe), for Black and Brown communities subject to police violence. The pandemic recalls the discourse of disease as invasive—a virus is invasive just as outsiders (immigrants, refugees, so-called potential criminals/terrorists) are invaders. So borders have to be policed and protected (think of India/Pakistan/Kashmir; Israel/Palestine; the US-Mexico border—all heavily militarized spaces). Of course, the pandemic has shown us that these borders are arbitrary (and largely irrelevant).

The question of borders and citizenship is itself a contested one across the globe. National borders no longer represent a finite geographical space at the edge of the nation—they seep into the nation and determine citizenship for everyone. For instance, since 1953, the United States has legally expanded the jurisdiction of border security forces to one hundred miles of all borders of the country—two-thirds of the entire population of the United States (200 million) live in this geographical area.[6] In addition, the EU has virtual borders in countries like Syria and Iraq where refugees have to pass border control before leaving for Europe.

Over the last fifty years of neoliberal capitalism, all investment in social goods and public services has been withdrawn and reinvested in the social control of particular populations in part by policing borders—what Harsha Walia has called border imperialism, "the processes by which the violences and precarities of displacement and migration are structurally created and maintained."[7] At this time, then, governance policies target particular populations globally (inside and outside the borders of nation-states) and create disparate and unequal citizenship projects. In the United States, Trump's

2016 Muslim ban cannot be understood purely as domestic or national policy; similarly immigration, refugee, and asylum policies in Europe and elsewhere don't fall neatly into national divisions if we are attentive to the history of colonialism and imperialism. So in the United States the so-called Muslim ban, the building of the wall at the US-Mexico border, the prison-industrial complex, deportation policies, and so on (primarily in the name of the security of the white nation) are in fact connected to state control/violence against Black, Brown, and Indigenous bodies. And these policies are all linked to histories of systemic and gendered racism and whiteness—to an ideological and political framework anchored in legacies of settler colonialism and empire, of slavery and indentured labor. These are governance practices of white supremacist patriarchy that create insiders and outsiders, citizens and noncitizens, us and them. In India, the analogy would be Brahmanical supremacist patriarchy and Islamophobia that constitute the ruling practices of Modi's government, criminalizing, incarcerating, and killing Dalits, Adivasis, and Muslims in the name of a *Hindu Rashtra*.

This kind of analysis of borders and interconnected histories is key to figuring out how to respond to the global social inequities and violence that the pandemic has laid bare. Histories of colonialism, imperialism, slavery, and migration are interconnected and cross geopolitical borders—indeed, they can lead to building bridges of solidarity across social justice movements in different geographical spaces, just as the most compelling collaborations and solidarities across national borders have been among scientists who share data toward the common purpose of learning about and finding a solution to the spread of COVID-19.

Borders, Bridges, Solidarity

What does it mean to speak about insurgent feminism and to envision ethical antiracist transnational feminist futures? How do the frameworks/approaches of decoloniality, anticapitalism, and feminism inform, enhance, contradict, and mutually influence one another? These are urgent and important political and intellectual questions at this time when the rhetoric of "transnational" has been co-opted on a large scale in neoliberal university settings. Administrators are "transnational" since they travel across the globe in search of profitable partnerships with universities in other countries and for "international" students who can pay for higher education that is no longer available to working-class and poor students in the United States. Academic curricula are also "transnational" since "study abroad" programs now buttress a normative curriculum that supposedly prepares students to compete in a global market. In the US academy, then, "transnational" often becomes a placeholder for business-as-usual, marked as "progressive" in the face of a conservative, xenophobic backlash. Globalization and transnational knowledge production become the new managerial mantra in neoliberal universities.[8]

In addition, the larger geopolitical landscape poses urgent and significant challenges for scholars and activists committed to an anticapitalist, anti-imperialist, decolonial feminist praxis. While the old/new, constantly shifting political terrain of Trump and company suggests the consolidation of a white supremacist, ableist, heteropatriarchal, carceral regime with billionaire state managers, the multiple, visible, and persistent uprisings of communities in resistance is truly extraordinary. During the Trump years there were hundreds of documented demonstrations, rallies, boycotts, and strikes across the country, in small and large cities and towns. New solidarities were forged, and feminists of all stripes and colors continue to be in leadership in most of these mobilizations. What lies ahead is the hard work of deepening and consolidating the nascent solidarities that have emerged through these mobilizations, to imagine a decolonized public polity anchored in a horizontal feminist solidarity across borders and divides. I would argue that we have much to learn from analyzing the resistance politics and collective aspirations of freedom and self-determination across these geopolitical sites and that developing these transnational feminist frameworks is in fact key to envisioning solidarities and building bridges across borders.

Here are three examples of insurgent transnational feminist praxis that focus on forms of organizing, building campaigns, and creating new political horizons for feminism.

1   In a report analyzing feminist activism twenty five years after the Beijing UN conference on women, Maxine Molyneux and her colleagues talk about generational continuities and differences in feminist activism around violence against women and LGBTQ rights in India, Brazil, and Malawi. They quote Brazilian feminist Cecilia Sardenberg, who says, "Back then [the 1980s] we fought to gain rights; now we fight against them being taken away." They describe young feminists engaging in street demonstrations, in viral online campaigns, and in academic spaces making feminist knowledges available for free on online portals like the Free Feminist University. The interface between academic, policy, and public spaces is a form of insurgent feminist

praxis that is slowly replacing the more elite "transnational feminist networks" of a decade ago and suggests important and productive cross-border feminist alliances.[9]

2 Veronica Gago analyzes the international, revolutionary nature of "the feminist strike" in Argentina (2016) showing brilliantly how the strike constructs transversality between different bodies, conflicts, and territories, connecting sexual and financial violence, labor and racist violence, carceral/police and medical violence, et cetera. She describes how the strike redefines a form of struggle at a new historical moment, expanding political capacities, languages, and geographies—in other words, framing insurgent transnational feminist praxis in relation to materialist and imaginative cartographies of struggle. Sexual violence is reconceptualized and pluralized, connected to other forms of violence (domestic violence in homes, new forms of violence rooted in the expansion of illegal economies—replacing the withdrawl of state resources), dispossesion and looting of common lands and resources by multinational corporations, and new forms of exploitation through the financialization of social life and indebtedness.[10]

3 Finally, another inspiring example is the notion of a feminist commons suggested by feminist scholar-activists like Silvia Federici and Miriam Ticktin. Ticktin suggests that the new egalitarian forms of connection and relationalities that have emerged during the pandemic can be understood as experiments in constructing feminist commons. Drawing on Federici's theorization of feminist commons as the "communing of reproductive activities" that produce people's lives—where the commons (collective kitchens, urban gardens, squats, etc.) become the site of reproduction and redistribution, and the site of struggle (so there is no seperation of reproduction from political organization), Ticktin further defines the commons as a struggle against enclosures and the privatization of freedom—against exclusion and private property; and the sharing of wealth and resources based on reciprocity, respect, mutuality, and responsibility.[11] The commons is anchored in an infrastructure of political care—just as feminist scholars like Deva Woodly have suggested that the Movement for Black Lives (MBL) is grounded in a politics of structural care, that is, care that concerns healing social ills through social action and interdependence. In this context, abolitionism itself becomes a form of care.[12] Ticktin argues that forms of radical collective care against forms of paternalism that have emerged in the United States—masked collective movements,

friendly fridges, pods/bubbles—are profoundly feminist. Remember also the fourteen-month-long Shaheen Bagh occupation by women against the Citizenship Amendment Act in India,[13] and the forms of care and relationalities formed through the feminist strike in Latin America. These are forms of collective care that respond politically to the withdrawal of the state or to securitized state violence.

While there is no definitive conclusion possible at a time when we all struggle on multiple fronts and sort through the chaos caused by the Trump/Musk regime in the United States, I want to reiterate that the movements and communities that continue to inspire me are movements that theorize care work as central to feminist futures; immigrant and refugee movements that problematize nation-state borders and questions of citizenship; antiracist and anticaste movements in the global North and South; anti-imperial, anticapitalist movements; Indigenous movements against settler colonialism; Adivasi, tribal, Dalit movements in India; Palestine Justice struggles; and in the United States, No DAPL (fighting the Dakota Access Pipeline) movements, Mijente (Latinx) organizing, Movement for Black Lives (MBL) and Black Youth Collective movements, and Justice for Muslims/Against Islamophobia. These are some of the movements and modes of collaboration and solidarity that I believe are necessary to envision and enact the most equitable, insurgent feminist futures. Many of these movements in the United States came together on April 5, 2025.

Given the relentless march toward an authoritarian, white supremacist, imperial state in 2025, it is now more urgent than ever to map cartographies of struggle and enact new solidarities and political horizons. April 5, 2025, was a day of massive solidarity mobilization in the United States (and in cities across the world) calling for an end to the authoritarian regime of Trump/Musk. Over 1,400 demonstrations across the country also called for immigrant rights, reproductive rights, and a Free Palestine. We chanted, "Hands Off! Hands Off Our Bodies! Hands Off Our Healthcare! Hands Off Our Schools and Universities! Hands Off Social Security and Medicaid! and Hands Off Gaza!" The mobilization was called for by over two hundred local and national organizations like INDIVISIBLE, MOVEON, Women's March, ACLU, and Hands Off! It was a moment of deep solidarity, rage, and hope as diverse communities marched in fifty states under one banner calling for an end to the protofascist, authoritarian rule of the forty-seventh president of the United States. We called for an end to ICE, for trans people's liberation, for an end to genocide and justice for Palestine, for Indigenous rights, for women's rights, for LGBTQ rights, for the freedom of Black and Brown peoples, for freedom to think, create, teach, and organize in and outside our schools and universities, for access to healthcare and reproductive rights, and for an end to gender violence and the violence of war and occupations around the world. This was a moment of solidarity of movements—in fact Trump and company had created this moment of explosive solidarity—a solidarity that would not have happened without the deep and long-term organizing that had been part of all our social justice movements over decades. It was a moment to hope, to dream, to create new relationalities and new horizons of belonging. Perhaps it was the beginning of the imploding of empire!

This is the struggle I hope future generations will take (and have already taken) up. Refaat Alareer reminds us of the urgency of struggle and resilience now in the context of the ongoing genocide in Gaza that has led to the death of over sixty-two thousand Palestinians:

> If I must die,
> you must live
> to tell my story
> . . . .
> If I must die
> let it bring hope
> let it be a tale[14]

Let us continue to bear witness to histories of violence and histories of struggle (silence can never be an option); let us connect the dots across movements, identities, and systems of violence just as 4/5/25 did, and let us continue to curate dissident communities in all the spaces we occupy—to imagine and enact our own collective insurgent feminist futures. Aazadi!

Notes

This chapter also appears in *The Encyclopedia of Political and Social Movements*, edited by Donna Nevel et al. (Bloomsbury, forthcoming).
1 Mohanty, "Cartographies of Struggle."
2 See Alexander and Mohanty, "Cartographies of Knowledge and Power."
3 Katz, "On the Grounds of Globalization."
4 Giroux, "Rethinking Neoliberal Fascism."
5 Bhambra, "'Forget Westphalia.'"
6 See A. N. Paik, *Bans, Walls, Raids, Sanctuary.*

7 Walia, *Undoing Border Imperialism*.
8 See Mohanty, "Borders and Bridges."
9 Molyneux et al., "Feminist Activism 25 Years After Beijing."
10 Gago, *Feminist International*.
11 Ticktin, "Building a Feminist Commons in the Time of COVID-19."
12 Woodly, "Black Lives Matter and the Democratic Necessity of Social Movements."
13 See *Outlook*, "How Shaheen Bagh Became Hub of Anti-CAA Protests"; Kapoor, "Shaheen Bagh."
14 "'If I Must Die,' A Poem by Refaat Alareer," *In These Times*, December 27, 2023, https://inthesetimes.com/article/refaat-alareer-israeli-occupation-palestine.

Bibliography

Abdo, Nahla. "Imperialism, the State, and NGOs: Middle Eastern Contexts and Contestations." *Comparative Studies of South Asia, Africa and the Middle East* 30, no. 2 (2010): 238–49.

Abu-Lughod, Lila. "Do Muslim Women Really Need Saving? Anthropological Reflections on Cultural Relativism and Its Others." *American Anthropologist* 104, no. 3 (2002): 783–90.

Adams, William, Elizabeth Watson, and Samuel Mutiso. "Water, Rules and Gender: Water Rights in an Indigenous Irrigation System, Marakwet, Kenya." *Development and Change* 28, no. 4 (1997): 707–30.

Agamben, Giorgio. *State of Exception*. University of Chicago Press, 2005.

Agarwal, Bina. "Participatory Exclusions, Community Forestry, and Gender: An Analysis for South Asia and a Conceptual Framework." *World Development* 29, no. 10 (2001): 1623–48.

Aguilar, Lorena. "Water as a Source of Equity and Empowerment in Costa Rica." In *Opposing Currents: The Politics of Water and Gender in Latin America*, edited by Vivienne Bennett, Sonia Dávila-Poblete, and María Nieves Rico, 123–34. University of Pittsburgh Press, 2005.

Ahlers, Rhodante, and Margreet Zwarteveen. "The Water Question in Feminism: Water Control and Gender Inequities in a Neo-Liberal Era." *Gender, Place and Culture* 16, no. 4 (2009): 409–26.

Ahmed, Sara. *The Feminist Killjoy Handbook: The Radical Potential of Getting in the Way*. Seal Press, 2023.

Ahmed, Sara. *Living a Feminist Life*. Duke University Press, 2017.

Ahmed, Sara. "Negotiating Gender Equity Through Decentralised Water Management in Coastal Gujarat: The Case of UTTHAN." In *Flowing Upstream: Empowering Women*

Through Water Management Initiatives in India, edited by Sara Ahmed, 51–92. Foundation Books and the Centre for Environment Education, 2005.

Alcoff, Linda Martín, Michael Hames-Garcia, Satya P. Mohanty, and Paula M. L. Moya, eds. *Identity Politics Reconsidered*. Springer, 2006.

Alexander, M. Jacqui. *Pedagogies of Crossing: Meditations on Feminism, Sexual Politics, Memory, and the Sacred*. Duke University Press, 2005.

Alexander, M. Jacqui, and Chandra Talpade Mohanty. "Cartographies of Knowledge and Power: Transnational Feminism as Radical Praxis." In *Critical Transnational Feminist Practice*, edited by Amanda Lock Swarr and Richa Nagar, 23–46. SUNY Press, 2010.

Alexander, M. Jacqui, and Chandra Talpade Mohanty, eds. *Feminist Genealogies, Colonial Legacies, Democratic Futures*. Routledge, 1997.

Allard, Jenna, and Julie Matthaei. "Introduction." In *Solidarity Economy: Building Alternatives for People and the Planet*, edited by Jenna Allard, Carl Davidson, and Julie Matthaei, 1–18. ChangeMaker, 2008.

Alvarez, Sonia E. "Translating the Global: Effects of Transnational Organizing on Local Feminist Discourses and Practices in Latin America." *Meridians* 1, no. 1 (2000): 29–67.

Annecke, W. J. "Still in the Shadows: Women and Gender Relations in the Electricity Sector in South Africa." In *Electric Capitalism: Recolonising Africa on the Power Grid*, edited by David McDonald, 288–320. HSRC Press, 2008.

Arditti, R. *Searching for Life: The Grandmothers of the Plaza de Mayo and the Disappeared Children of Argentina*. University of California Press, 1999.

Arya, Sunaina, and Aakash Singh Rathore, eds. *Dalit Feminist Theory: A Reader*. Taylor and Francis, 2019.

Ayers, William, and Rick Ayers. "Education Under Fire: Introduction." Special issue, *Monthly Review* 63, no. 3 (2011). https://monthlyreview.org/2011/07/01/education-under-fire-introduction.

Ayers, William, and Rick Ayers, eds. "Education Under Fire: The U.S. Corporate Attack on Teachers, Students, and Schools." Special issue, *Monthly Review* 63, no. 3 (2011).

Ayotte, Kevin J., and Mary E. Husain. "Securing Afghan Women: Neocolonialism, Epistemic Violence, and the Rhetoric of the Veil." *NWSA Journal* 17, no. 3 (2005): 112–33.

Babb, Florence E. "After the Revolution: Neoliberal Policy and Gender in Nicaragua." *Latin American Perspectives* 23, no. 1 (1996): 27–48.

Balanyá, Belén, ed. *Reclaiming Public Water: Achievements, Struggles and Visions from Around the World*. Transnational Institute, 2005.

Bannerji, Himani, Shahrzad Mojab, and Judith Whitehead. "Of Property and Propriety: The Role of Gender and Class in Imperialism and Nationalism: A Decade Later." *Comparative Studies of South Asia, Africa and the Middle East* 30, no. 2 (2010): 262–71.

Barker, Isabelle V. "(Re)Producing American Soldiers in an Age of Empire." *Politics and Gender* 5 (2009): 211–35.

Barsamian, David. *The Checkbook and the Cruise Missile: Conversations with Arundhati Roy, Interviews with David Barsamian*. South End Press, 2004.

Basarudin, Azza, and Khanum Shaikh. "The Contours of Speaking Out: Gender, State Security, and Muslim Women's Empowerment." *Meridians* 19, no. 1 (2020): 107–35.

Basu, Amrita, ed. *Women's Movements in the Global Era: The Power of Local Feminisms*. Westview Press, 2010.

Batliwala, Srilatha, and Amulya K. N. Reddy. "Energy for Women and Women for Energy (Engendering Energy and Empowering Women)." *Energy for Sustainable Development* 7, no. 3 (2003): 33–43.

Bayliss, Kate. *Privatization of Electricity Distribution: Some Economic, Social and Political Perspectives*. Public Services International Research Unit, University of Greenwich, April 2001.

BDS. "A Call to Action from Indigenous and Women of Color Feminists." July 17, 2011. https://bdsmovement.net/news/call-action-indigenous-and-women-color-feminists.

Beall, Jo. "Decentralizing Government and Decentering Gender: Lessons from Local Government Reform in South Africa." *Politics and Society* 33, no. 2 (2005): 253–76.

Beckman, Ericka. "The Eighth Encuentro." *NACLA Report on the Americas* 34, no. 5 (2001): 32–33.

Bekhauf Azaadi Campaign. "Why the Govt's Ordinance Is an Eyewash and a Mockery of the Justice Verma Recommendations." *Kractivist*, February 4, 2013. http://kractivist.wordpress.com/2013/02/04/why-the-govts-ordinance-is-an-eyewash-and-a-mockery-of-the-justice-verma-recommendations/.

Benería, Lourdes. "Structural Adjustment Policies." In *The Elgar Companion to Feminist Economics*, edited by Janice Peterson and Margaret Lewis, 687–95. Elgar, 1999.

Bennett, Vivienne, Sonia Dávila-Poblete, and Nieves Rico, eds. *Opposing Currents: The Politics of Water and Gender in Latin America*. University of Pittsburgh Press, 2005.

Berda, Yael. "Managing Dangerous Populations: Colonial Legacies of Security and Surveillance." *Sociological Forum* 28, no. 3 (2013): 627–30.

Bergeron, Suzanne. "Political Economy Discourses of Globalization and Feminist Politics." *Signs: Journal of Women in Culture and Society* 26, no. 4 (2001): 983–1006.

Bernal Santa-Olaya, Elena Begona, Sharon Bissel, and Ana Cortes. "Effects of Globalization on the Efforts to Decriminalize Abortion in Mexico." *Development* 42, no. 4 (1999): 130–33.

Bhambra, Gurminder K. "'Forget Westphalia. The Modern State Was Born from Colonialism': Why Is Mainstream International Relations Blind to Racism?" *Foreign Policy*, July 3, 2020. https://foreignpolicy.com/2020/07/03/why-is-mainstream-international-relations-ir-blind-to-racism-colonialism/.

Bhan, Mona, and Haley Duschinski. "Introduction. Occupations in Context: The Cultural Logics of Occupation, Settler Violence, and Resistance." Special issue, *Critique of Anthropology* 40, no. 3 (2020): 285–97.

Bhatt, Shakti. "State Terrorism vs. Jihad in Kashmir." *Journal of Contemporary Asia* 33, no. 2 (2003): 215–44.

Bhattacharjee, Anannya. "Private Fists and Public Force: Race, Gender, and Surveillance." In *Policing the National Body: Race, Gender, and Criminalization*, edited by Jael Silliman and Anannya Bhattacharjee. South End Press, 2002.

Bierria, Alisa, Jakeya Caruthers, Brooke Lober, Amanda Priebe, and Andrea J. Ritchie. *Abolition Feminisms*. Haymarket Books, 2022.

Boelens, Rutgerd, and Margreet Zwarteveen. "Prices and Politics in Andean Water Reforms." *Development and Change* 36, no. 4 (2005): 735–58.

Boxer, Marilyn. *When Women Ask the Questions: Creating Women's Studies in America*. Johns Hopkins University Press, 1998.

Boyce Davies, Carole, and Babacar M'bow. "Towards African Diaspora Citizenship: Politicizing an Existing Global Geography." In *Black Geographies and the Politics of Place*, edited by Katherine and Clyde Woods, 14–45. Between the Lines, 2007.

Bradford, Clare. "Representing Islam: Female Subjects in Suzanne Fisher Staples's Novels." *Children's Literature Association Quarterly* 32, no. 1 (2007): 47–62.

Brah, Avtar. *Decolonial Imaginings: Intersectional Conversations and Contestations*. Goldsmiths Press, 2022.

Braidotti, Rosi. "A Critical Cartography of Feminist Post-Postmodernism." *Australian Feminist Studies* 20, no. 47 (2005): 169–80.

Branco, Adelia de Melo, and Vanete Almeida. "Women, Mobilization and the Revitalization of Water Resources: The Case of Northeastern Brazil." Paper presented at the Forum for Water in the Americas in the 21st Century, Mexico City, October 1, 2002.

Brennan, Teresa. *Globalization and Its Terrors*. Routledge, 2003.

Brenner, Johanna. "Transnational Feminism and the Struggle for Global Justice." *New Politics* 9, no. 2 (2003): 78.

Brown, Rebecca. "Unequal Burden: Water Privatization and Women's Human Rights in Tanzania." *Gender and Development* 18, no. 1 (2010): 59–67.

Budlender, Debbie, and Guy Hewitt. *Engendering Budgets: A Practitioners' Guide to Understanding and Implementing Gender-Responsive Budgets*. Commonwealth Secretariat, 2003.

Budlender, Debbie, Martha Melesse, and Celia M. Reyes. "Gender-Responsive Budgeting Through the CBMS Lens." No. 2006–17. PIDS Discussion Paper Series, 2006.

Buhle, Mari Jo. "Introduction." In *The Politics of Women's Studies: Testimony from 30 Founding Mothers*, edited by Florence Howe. Feminist Press, 2000.

Burman, Jenny. "Deportable or Admissible? Black Women and the Space of 'Removal.'" In *Black Geographies and the Politics of Place*, edited by Katherine McKittrick and Clyde Woods, 177–92. Between the Lines, 2007.

Burnham, Linda. "Sexual Domination in Uniform: An American Value." *War Times*, May 19, 2004. http://www.war-times.org.

Butalia, Urvashi, ed. *Speaking Peace: Women's Voices from Kashmir*. Zed Books, 2002.

Çağatay, Nilüfer. "Gender Budgets and Beyond: Feminist Fiscal Policy in the Context of Globalization." *Gender and Development* 11, no. 1 (2003): 15–24.

Campt, Tina, and Deborah A. Thomas. "Gendering Diaspora: Transnational Feminism, Diaspora and Its Hegemonies." *Feminist Review* 90, no. 1 (2008): 1–8.

Castro, José Esteban. "Poverty and Citizenship: Sociological Perspectives on Water Services and Public-Private Participation." *Geoforum* 38, no. 5 (2007): 756–71.

Cecelski, Elizabeth. "Enabling Equitable Access to Rural Electrification: Current Thinking and Major Activities in Energy, Poverty and Gender." Briefing paper, Asia Alternative Energy Unit, January 2000. https://www.energia.org/assets/2015/06/27 -Enabling-Equitable-Access-to-Rural-Electrification2.pdf.

Chen, Chao-Ju. "The Difference That Differences Make: Asian Feminism and the Politics of Difference." *Asian Journal of Women's Studies* 13, no. 3 (2007): 7–36.

Chigudu, Hope. "Deepening Our Understanding of Community-Based Participatory Research: Lessons from Work Around Reproductive Rights in Zimbabwe." *Gender and Development* 15, no. 2 (2007): 259–70.

Chishti, M. "Gender and the Development Battlefield in Afghanistan: Nation Builders Versus Nation Betrayers." *Comparative Studies of South Asia, Africa and the Middle East* 30, no. 2 (2010): 250–61.

Chomsky, N. "U.S. Savage Imperialism." Talk given June 2010. Published in *Z Magazine*, December 2010. http://www.zcommunications.org/zspace/noamchomsky.

Choudry, Aziz. "Transnational Activist Coalition Politics and the De/Colonization of Pedagogies of Mobilization: Learning from Anti-Neoliberal Indigenous Movement Articulations." *International Education* 37, no. 1 (2007): 97–112.

Chronicle of Higher Education. "Diversity in Academe." September 26, 2008, sec. B.

Churchill, Ward, and Winona LaDuke. "Native North America: The Political Economy of Radioactive Colonialism." In *The State of Native America: Genocide, Colonization, and Resistance*, edited by M. Annette Jaimes, 241–66. South End Press, 1992.

Clancy, Joy. "Policies, Projects and the Market Empowering Women? Some Initial Reactions to Developments in the Energy Sector." Working Paper Series: Technology and Development Group, No. 105. Technology and Development Group, University of Twente, 2000.

Clancy, Joy, M. M. Skutsch, and Simon Batchelor. "The Gender-Energy-Poverty Nexus: Finding the Energy to Address Gender Concerns in Development." DFID Project CNTR998521, 2002.

Clark, Roger. "Why All the Counting? Feminist Social Science Research on Children's Literature." *Children's Literature in Education* 33, no. 4 (2002): 285–95.

Cleaver, Frances. "Analyzing Gender Roles in Community Natural Resource Management Negotiation, Life Courses and Social Inclusion." *IDS Bulletin* 31, no. 2 (2000): 60–67.

Cleaver, Frances. "Choice, Complexity, and Change: Gendered Livelihoods and the Management of Water." *Agriculture and Human Values* 15, no. 4 (1998): 293–99.

Comfort, Susan. "Introduction: Invisible Battlegrounds." *Works and Days* 29 (2011): 7–39.

Comfort, Susan, ed. "Invisible Battlegrounds: Feminist Resistance in the Global Age of War and Imperialism." Special issue, *Works and Days* 29 (2011).

Coogan-Gehr, Kelly. "The Politics of Race in US Feminist Scholarship: An Archaeology." *Signs: Journal of Women in Culture and Society* 37, no. 1 (2011): 83–107.

Cooke, Miriam. "Saving Brown Women." *Signs: Journal of Women in Culture and Society* 28, no. 1 (2002): 468–70.

Das, Runa. "Broadening the Security Paradigm: Indian Women, Anti-Nuclear Activism, and Visions of a Sustainable Future." *Women's Studies International Forum* 30, no. 1 (2007): 1–15.

Davies, Bronwyn, and Peter Bansel. "Governmentality and Academic Work: Shaping the Hearts and Minds of Academic Workers." *Journal of Curriculum Theorizing* 26, no. 3 (2010): 5–20.

Davies, Bronwyn, Michael Gottsche, and Peter Bansel. "The Rise and Fall of the Neo-Liberal University." *European Journal of Education* 41, no. 2 (2006): 305–19.

Davis, Angela. "Race and Criminalization: Black Americans and the Punishment Industry." In *The Angela Y. Davis Reader*, edited by Joy James, 61–73. Blackwell, 1998.

Davis, Angela Y. *Violence Against Women and the Ongoing Challenge to Racism*. Kitchen Table Press, 1985.

Davis, Angela Y., Gina Dent, Erica R. Meiners, and Beth E. Richie. *Abolition. Feminism. Now*. Vol. 2. Haymarket Books, 2022.

Davis, Angela Y., and Eduardo Mendieta. *Abolition Democracy: Beyond Empire, Prisons, and Torture*. Seven Stories Press, 2005.

Deer, Sarah. "Federal Indian Law and Violent Crime." In *Color of Violence: The Incite! 6 Anthology*, edited by Incite! Women of Color Against Violence, 32–41. South End Press, 2006.

Delgado, Juana Rosa Vera. "Irrigation Management, the Participatory Approach, and Equity in an Andean Community." In *Opposing Currents: The Politics of Water and Gender in Latin America*, edited by Vivienne Bennett, Sonia Dávila-Poblete, and María Nieves Rico, 109–22. University of Pittsburgh Press, 2005.

de Lima Costa, Claudia. "Being Here and Writing There: Gender and the Politics of Translation in a Brazilian Landscape." *Signs: Journal of Women in Culture and Society* 25, no. 3 (2000): 727–60.

de Lima Costa, Claudia. "Lost (and Found?) in Translation: Feminisms in Hemispheric Dialogue." In *Feminist Theory Reader*, edited by Carole McCann, Seung-kyung Kim, and Emek Ergun, 66–73. Routledge, 2020.

De los Reyes, Paulina, Irene Molina, and Diana Mulinari. *Maktens olika förklädnader: Kön, klass och etnicitet i det postkoloniala Sverige* [The various guises of power: Gender, class, and ethnicity in postcolonial Sweden]. Atlas, 2002.

Desai, Manisha. "Transnational Solidarity: Women's Agency, Structural Adjustment, and Globalization." In *Women's Activism and Globalization: Linking Local Struggles and Transnational Politics*, edited by Nancy Naples and Manisha Desai, 15–33. Routledge, 2004.

DeVault, Marjorie. *Liberating Method: Feminism and Social Research*. Temple University Press, 1999.

Dingo, Rebecca. "Securing the Nation: Neoliberalism's U.S. Family Values in a Transnational Gendered Economy." *Journal of Women's History* 16, no. 3 (2004): 173–86.

Dodson, Lisa, Deborah Piatelli, and Leah Schmalzbauer. "Researching Inequality Through Interpretive Collaborations: Shifting Power and the Unspoken Contract." *Qualitative Inquiry* 13, no. 6 (2007): 821–43.

Duschinski, Haley. "Destiny Effects: Militarization and the Institutionalization of Punitive Punishment in Kashmir Valley." *Anthropological Quarterly* 82, no. 3 (2009): 691–718.

Duschinski, Hayley. "Reproducing Regimes of Impunity: Fake Encounters and the Informalization of Everyday Violence in Kashmir Valley." *Cultural Studies* 24, no. 1 (2010): 110–32.

Dutta, Soma. "Mainstreaming Gender in Energy Planning and Policies." In UNESCAP *Project on Capacity Building for Integration of Energy and Rural Development Planning*. Background paper for Expert Group Meeting. 2003.

Eisenstein, Zillah. *Against Empire: Feminisms, Racism and the West*. Zed Books, 2004.

Eisenstein, Zillah, ed. *Capitalist Patriarchy and the Case for Socialist Feminism*. Monthly Review Press, 1979.

Eisenstein, Zillah. *Sexual Decoys: Gender, Race and War in Imperial Democracy*. Zed Books, 2007.

Eisenstein, Zillah. "Sexual Humiliation, Gender Confusion and the Horrors at Abu Ghraib." *PeaceWomen*, June 4, 2004. http://www.peacewomen.org/news/Iraq/June04/abughraib.html.

Eisenstein, Zillah, and Chandra Talpade Mohanty. "In Support of Occupy Wall Street." *Feminist Wire*, October 14, 2011. http://thefeministwire.com/2011/10/in-support-of-occupy-wall-street/.

Eley, Geoff. "Historicizing the Global, Politicizing Capital: Giving the Present a Name." *History Workshop Journal*, no. 63 (2007): 154–88.

Elson, Diane. "Gender Awareness in Modeling Structural Adjustment." *World Development* 23, no. 11 (1995): 1851–68.

Enloe, Cynthia. *The Curious Feminist: Searching for Women in a New Age of Empire*. University of California Press, 2004.

Enloe, Cynthia. *Globalization and Militarism: Feminists Make the Link*. Rowman and Littlefield, 2007.

Escobar, Arturo. *Territories of Difference: Place, Movements, Life, Redes*. Duke University Press, 2008.

Evans, Linda. "Playing Global Cop: US Militarism and the Prison-Industrial Complex." In *Global Lockdown: Race, Gender, and the Prison-Industrial Complex*, 215–27. Routledge, 2005.

Farris, Sara. *In the Name of Women's Rights: The Rise of Femonationalism*. Duke University Press, 2017.

Federici, Silvia. "War, Globalization, and Reproduction." Archive of Global Protests, January 2001. http://www.nadir.org/nadir/initiativ/agp/free/9-11/federici.htm#a2.

Feigenbaum, Anna. "The Teachable Moment: Feminist Pedagogy and the Neoliberal Classroom." *Review of Education, Pedagogy, and Cultural Studies* 29, no. 4 (2007): 337–49.

Feldman, Jonathan. *Universities in the Business of Repression: The Academic-Military-Industrial Complex in Central America*. South End Press, 1989.

Felski, Rita. "The Doxa of Difference." *Signs* 23, no. 1 (1997): 1–21.

Ferguson, Roderick A. "An Interruption of Our Cowardice." The Racial Imaginary Institute. Accessed May 20, 2024. https://www.theracialimaginary.org/viewing-room/an-interruption-of-our-cowardice.

Fine, Ben, and David Hall. "Terrains of Neoliberalism: Constraints and Opportunities for Alternative Models of Service Delivery." In *Alternatives to Privatization: Public Options for Essential Services in the Global South*, edited by David A. McDonald and Greg Ruiters, 45–70. Routledge, 2012.

Gago, Verónica. *Feminist International: How to Change Everything*. Verso Books, 2020.

"Gender and Human Security Network Manifesto." In *Security Disarmed: Critical Perspectives on Gender, Race, and Militarization*, edited by Sandra Morgen, Barbara Sutton, and Julie Novkov, 70–72. Rutgers University Press, 2008.

Genz, Stéphanie. "Third Way/ve: The Politics of Postfeminism." *Feminist Theory* 7, no. 3 (2006): 333–53.

George, Asha. "Using Accountability to Improve Reproductive Health Care." *Reproductive Health Matters* 11, no. 21 (2003): 161–70.

Gilmore, Ruth Wilson. "Race and Globalization." In *Geographies of Global Change: Remapping the World*, edited by R. J. Johnston, Peter J. Taylor, and Michael J. Watts, 2nd ed., 261–74. Blackwell, 2002.

Giroux, Henry A. "Bare Pedagogy and the Scourge of Neoliberalism: Rethinking Higher Education as a Democratic Public Sphere." *Educational Forum* 74, no. 3 (2010): 184–96. https://doi.org/10.1080/00131725.2010.483897.

Giroux, Henry A. "Campus Protests Are Fighting Militarism and Corporatization at Home and Abroad." *Truthout*, May 9, 2024. https://truthout.org/articles /campus-protests-are-fighting-militarism-and-corporatization-at-home-and -abroad/.

Giroux, Henry A. "Rethinking Neoliberal Fascism, Racist Violence, and the Plague of Inequality." *Communication Teacher* 35, no. 3 (2021): 171–77.

Giroux, Henry A. "Spectacles of Race and Pedagogies of Denial: Anti-Black Racist Pedagogy Under the Reign of Neoliberalism." *Communication Education* 52, no. 3–4 (2003): 191–211.

Golash-Boza, Tanya. "The Parallels Between Mass Incarceration and Mass Deportation: An Intersectional Analysis of State Repression." In "Coloniality of Power and Hegemonic Shifts," special issue, *Journal of World-Systems Research* 22, no. 2 (2016): 484–509.

Gomez, Ana Ella. "A New Definition of Hope." In *Changing the Flow: Water Movements in Latin America*, edited by Beverly Bell, Crossley Pinkstaff, Jeff Conant, Marcela Olivera, and Phillip Terhorst, 13–15. Food and Water Watch, Other Worlds, Reclaiming Public Water, Red VIDA, and Transnational Institute, 2009.

Gordon, Avery F. "Abu Ghraib: Imprisonment and the War on Terror." *Race and Class* 48, no. 1 (2006): 42–59.

Grande, Sandy. "Refusing the University." In *Toward What Justice? Describing Diverse Dreams of Justice in Education*, edited by Eve Tuck and Wayne Yang, 47–65. Routledge, 2018.

Greenberg, Jonathan D. "Generations of Memory: Remembering Partition in India/Pakistan and Israel/Palestine." *Comparative Studies of South Asia, Africa and the Middle East* 25, no. 1 (2005): 89–110.

Gupta, Jyotsna Agnihotri. "Towards Transnational Feminisms: Some Reflections and Concerns in Relation to the Globalization of Reproductive Technologies." *European Journal of Women's Studies* 13, no. 1 (2006): 23–38.

Gutiérrez, Laura, Christina B. Hanhardt, Miranda Joseph, Adela C. Licona, and Sandra K. Soto. "Nativism, Normativity, and Neoliberalism in Arizona: Cenges Inside and Outside the Classroom." *Transformations: The Journal of Inclusive Scholarship and Pedagogy* 21, no. 2 (2011): 123–48.

Hall, David. "Energy Privatization and Reform in East Africa." Public Services International Research Unit, 2007.

Hall, Elaine J., and Marnie Salupo Rodriguez. "The Myth of Postfeminism." *Gender and Society* 17, no. 6 (2003): 878–902.

Harcourt, Wendy. "Building Alliances for Women's Empowerment, Reproductive Rights and Health." *Development* 46, no. 2 (2003): 6–12.

Harcourt, Wendy. "The Global Women's Rights Movement: Power Politics Around the United Nations and the World Social Forum." *UNRISD Civil Society and Social Movements Paper (UNRISD)* 25 (2006): 1–25.

Harcourt, Wendy, and Arturo Escobar, eds. *Women and the Politics of Place*. Kumarian Press, 2005.

Harding, Sandra, and Uma Narayan. *Decentering the Center: Philosophy for a Multicultural, Postcolonial, and Feminist World*. Indiana University Press, 2000.

Harvey, David. *A Brief History of Neoliberalism*. Oxford University Press, 2005.

Hennessy, R. "Gender Adjustments in Forgotten Places: The North-South Encuentros in Mexico." *Works and Days* 29 (2011): 181–202.

Hernández Castillo, R. Aída. "Indigeneity as a Field of Power: Multiculturalism and Indigenous Identities in Political Struggles." In *The SAGE Handbook of Identities*, edited by Chandra Talpade Mohanty and Margaret Wetherell, 379–98. Sage, 2010.

Hernández Castillo, R. Aída. "Indigenous Law and Identity Politics in Mexico: Indigenous Men's and Women's Struggles for a Multicultural Nation." *PoLAR* 25, no. 1 (2002): 90–109.

Holdren, John P., and Kirk R. Smith. "Energy, the Environment, and Health." In *World Energy Assessment: Energy and the Challenge of Sustainability*, edited by José Goldemberg, 61–110. New York: UN Development Programme, 2000.

Hull, Akasha (Gloria T.), Patricia Bell Scott, and Barbara Smith. *All the Women Are White, All the Men Are Black, but Some of Us Are Brave*. Feminist Press, 1982.

Husain, Bonojit. "From Delhi to Djakarta, Protests Against Sexual Violence Across Borders." *Kafila Online*, January 15, 2013. https://kafila.online/2013/01/15/from-delhi-to-djakarta-protests-against-sexual-violence-across-bordersbonojit-husain/.

IFAD. "Gender and Water: Securing Water for Improved Rural Livelihoods: The Multiple-Uses System Approach." IFAD, 2006.

Inside Higher Ed. "Higher Ed's Top 10 Developments of 2023." December 18, 2023. https://www.insidehighered.com/opinion/blogs/higher-ed-gamma/2023/12/18/higher-eds-top-10-developments-2023.

Inter-Agency Task Force on Gender and Water (GWTF). "Gender, Water and Sanitation: A Policy Brief." Accessed December 16, 2024. https://www.un.org/waterforlifedecade/pdf/un_water_policy_brief_2_gender.pdf.

Jad, Islah. "The Demobilization of a Palestinian Women's Movement: From Empowered Active Militants to Powerless and Stateless 'Citizens.'" In *Women's Movements in the Global Era: The Power of Local Feminisms*, edited by Amrita Basu, 343–74. Routledge, 2010.

Jad, Islah. "NGOs: Between Buzzwords and Social Movements." *Development in Practice* 17, no. 4–5 (2007): 622–29.

Jad, Islah. "The Politics of Group Weddings in Palestine: Political and Gender Tensions." *Journal of Middle East Women's Studies* 5, no. 3 (2009): 36–53.

Jayawardena, Kumari. *The White Woman's Other Burden: Western Women and South Asia During British Rule*. Routledge, 1995.

Johnson, Penny. "Displacing Palestine: Palestinian Householding in an Era of Asymmetrical War." *Politics and Gender* 62, no. 2 (2010): 295–304.

Johnson, Penny, and Eileen Kuttab. "Where Have All the Women (and Men) Gone? Reflections on Gender and the Second Palestinian Intifada." *Feminist Review* 69, no. 1 (2001): 21–43.

Kaba, Mariame, and Andrea J. Ritchie. *No More Police: A Case for Abolition*. New Press, 2022.

Kannan, Vani. "The Third World Women's Alliance: History, Geopolitics, Form." PhD diss., Syracuse University, 2018.

Kapoor, Priya. "Shaheen Bagh: Muslim Women Contesting and Theorizing Citizenship and Belonging During COVID-19." *Frontiers*, September 22, 2022. https://www .frontiersin.org/articles/10.3389/fcomm.2022.857350/.

Karim, K. M. Rabiul. "Gendered Social Institutions and the Management of Underground Irrigation Water Resources in a Bangladeshi Village." *Gender, Technology and Development* 10, no. 1 (2006): 13–36.

Katz, Cindi. "On the Grounds of Globalization: A Topography for Feminist Political Engagement." *Signs: Journal of Women in Culture and Society* 26, no. 4 (2001): 1213–34.

Kaul, Nitasha. "India's Obsession with Kashmir: Democracy, Gender, (Anti-)Nationalism." *Feminist Review* 119, no. 1 (2018): 126–43.

Kelly, Tobias. "Documented Lives: Fear and Uncertainties of Law During the Second Palestinian Intifada." *Journal of the Royal Anthropological Institute* 12, no. 1 (2006): 89–107.

Kennedy, Elizabeth Lapovsky, and Agatha Beins, eds. *Women's Studies for the Future: Foundations, Interrogations, Politics*. Rutgers University Press, 2005.

Khan, N. *Islam, Women and Violence in Kashmir: Between India and Pakistan*. Palgrave Macmillan, 2009.

Khosla, Prabha. *Water, Equity and Money: The Need for Gender Responsive Budgeting in Water and Sanitation*. Netherlands Council of Women, 2003.

Klein, Naomi. "Dancing the World into Being: A Conversation with Idle No More's Leanne Simpson." *Yes Magazine*, March 5, 2013. http://www.yesmagazine.org/peace -justice/dancing-the-world-into-being-a-conversation-with-idle-no-more-leanne -simpson.

Kotef, H. "Objects of Security: Gendered Violence and Securitized Humanitarianism in Occupied Gaza." *Comparative Studies of South Asia, Africa and the Middle East* 30, no. 2 (2010): 179–91.

Kotef, Hagar, and Amir Merav. "(En)Gendering Checkpoints: Checkpoint Watch and the Repercussions of Intervention." *Signs: Journal of Women in Culture and Society* 32, no. 4 (2007): 973–96.

Krishnan, Kavita. "Capitalism, Sexual Violence, and Sexism." *Kafila Online*, May 23, 2013. https://kafila.online/2013/05/23/capitalism-sexual-violence-and-sexism-kavita-krishnan.

Kuttab, Eileen. "Empowerment as Resistance: Conceptualizing Palestinian Women's Empowerment." *Development* 53, no. 2 (2010): 247–53.

Kuttab, Eileen. "Palestinian Women's Organizations: Global Cooption and Local Contradiction." *Cultural Dynamics* 20, no. 2 (2008): 99–117.

LaDuke, Winona. *Recovering the Sacred: The Power of Naming and Reclaiming*. Between the Lines, 2005.

Larner, Wendy. "Neo-Liberalism: Policy, Ideology, Governmentality." *Studies in Political Economy* 63, no. 1 (2000): 5–25.

Larner, Wendy. "Theorising 'Difference' in Aotearoa/New Zealand." *Gender, Place and Culture: A Journal of Feminist Geography* 2, no. 2 (1995): 177–90.

Laurie, Nina. "Gender Water Networks: Femininity and Masculinity in Water Politics in Bolivia." *International Journal of Urban and Regional Research* 35, no. 1 (2011): 172–88.

Lawrence, Bonita, and Enakshi Dua. "Decolonizing Antiracism." *Social Justice* 32, no. 4 (102) (2005): 120–43.

Liinason, Mia. "Feminism and the Academy: Exploring the Politics of Institutionalization in Gender Studies in Sweden." PhD diss., Lund University, 2011.

Liinason, Mia. "Institutionalized Knowledge: Notes on the Processes of Inclusion and Exclusion in Gender Studies in Sweden." *NORA: Nordic Journal of Feminist and Gender Research* 18, no. 1 (2010): 38–47.

Liinason, Mia, and Ulla M. Holm. "PhDs, Women's/Gender Studies and Interdisciplinarity." *Nordic Journal of Women's Studies* 14, no. 2 (2006): 115–30.

Lister, Ruth. "Feminist Theory and Practice of Citizenship." Paper presented at the annual conference of the DVPW (German Political Science Association), Mainz, September 2003.

Lowe, Lisa. "Reflections on Race, Class, and Gender in the USA: A Discussion with Angela Y. Davis and Lisa Lowe." In *The Angela Y. Davis Reader*, edited by Joy James, 307–25. Blackwell, 1998.

Luft, Rachel. "Intersectionality and the Risk of Flattening Difference." In *The Intersectional Approach: Transforming the Academy Through Race, Class, and Gender*, edited by Michele Tracy Berger and Kathleen Guidroz, 100–117. University of North Carolina Press, 2009.

Lutz, Catherine. "Making War at Home in the United States: Militarization and the Current Crisis." *American Anthropologist* 104, no. 3 (2002): 723–35.

Lykke, Nina. "Between Particularism, Universalism and Transversalism: Reflections on the Politics of Location of European Feminist Research and Education." *NORA: Nordic Journal of Feminist and Gender Research* 12, no. 2 (2004): 72–82.

Lykke, Nina, Christine Michel, and Maria Puig de la Bellacasa, eds. *Women's Studies: From Institutional Innovation to New Job Qualifications. Report from ATHENA Panel 1a.* University of Southern Denmark, 2001.

Mackey, Robert. "Hungarian Leader Rebuked for Saying Muslim Migrants Must Be Blocked 'to Keep Europe Christian.'" *New York Times*, September 3, 2015. https://www.nytimes.com/2015/09/04/world/europe/hungarian-leader-rebuked-for-saying-muslim-migrants-must-be-blocked-to-keep-europe-christian.html.

Mahmood, Saba. "Feminism, Democracy, and Empire: Islam and the War on Terror." In *Gendering Religion and Politics: Untangling Modernities*, edited by Hanna Herzog and Ann Braude, 193–215. Palgrave Macmillan, 2009.

Malik, Inshah. "Gendered Politics of Funerary Processions: Contesting Indian Sovereignty in Kashmir." *Economic and Political Weekly* 53, no. 47 (2018): 63–67.

Mama, Amina. "Demythologising Gender in Development: Feminist Studies in African Contexts." *IDS Bulletin* 35, no. 4 (2004): 121–24.

Mama, Amina. "Is It Ethical to Study Africa? Preliminary Thoughts on Scholarship and Freedom." *African Studies Review* 50, no. 1 (2007): 1–26.

Mama, Amina. "Rethinking African Universities: Gender and Transformation." *Scholar and Feminist Online* 7, no. 2 (2009). http://sfonline.barnard.edu/africana /mama_01.htm.

Manase, Gift, Jerry Ndamba, and Fungai Makoni. "Mainstreaming Gender in Integrated Water Resources Management: The Case of Zimbabwe." *Physics and Chemistry of the Earth*, pts. A/B/C 28, no. 20–27 (2003): 967–71.

Marchand, Marianne H., and Jane L. Parpart, eds. *Feminism/Postmodernism/Development*. Routledge, 1995.

Marchand, Marianne H., and Anne Sisson Runyan, eds. *Gender and Global Restructuring: Sightings, Sites and Resistances*. Routledge, 2010.

Martines, Juan Pablo. "Keepers of Water." In *Changing the Flow: Water Movements in Latin America*, edited by Beverly Bell, Crossley Pinkstaff, Jeff Conant, Marcela Olivera, and Phillip Terhorst, 27–28. Food and Water Watch, Other Worlds, Reclaiming Public Water, Red VIDA, and Transnational Institute, 2009.

Martinez, Egla. "Vilified and Prohibited Memories: The Making of a Gendered and Racialized National-Transnational Enemy." *Canadian Women's Studies* 27, no. 1 (2009): 23–28.

Matthaei, Julie. *An Economic History of Women in America: Women's Work, the Sexual Division of Labor, and the Development of Capitalism*. Schocken Books, 1982.

McClennen, Sophia A. "Neoliberalism and the Crisis of Intellectual Engagement." *Works and Days* 51 (2008–9): 52–53.

McDonald, David. "Electric Capitalism: Conceptualising Electricity and Capital Accumulation in (South) Africa." In *Electric Capitalism: Recolonising Africa on the Power Grid*, edited by David McDonald, 1–49. HSRC Press, 2009.

McKittrick, Katherine. *Demonic Grounds: Black Women and the Cartographies of Struggle*. University of Minnesota Press, 2006.

McKittrick, Katherine, and Linda Peake. "What Difference Does Difference Make to Geography?" In *Questioning Geography: Fundamental Debates*, edited by Noel Castree, Alisdair Rogers, and Douglas Sherman, 39–54. Blackwell, 2005.

McKittrick, Katherine, and Clyde Woods, eds. *Black Geographies and the Politics of Place*. Between the Lines, 2007.

McLaughlin, Lisa. "Feminism and the Political Economy of Transnational Public Space." *Sociological Review* 52, no. 1 (2004): 156–75.

McRobbie, Angela. "Top Girls? Young Women and the Post-Feminist Sexual Contract." *Cultural Studies* 21, no. 4–5 (2007): 718–37.

Meinzen-Dick, Ruth, and Margreet Zwarteveen. "Gendered Participation in Water Management: Issues and Illustrations from Water Users' Associations in South Asia." *Agriculture and Human Values* 15 (1998): 337–45.

Melo, Mabel. "Alternatives for Another, Possible World." In *Changing the Flow: Water Movements in Latin America*, edited by Beverly Bell, Crossley Pinkstaff, Jeff Conant, Marcela Olivera, and Phillip Terhorst, 29–30. Food and Water Watch, Other Worlds, Reclaiming Public Water, Red VIDA, and Transnational Institute, 2009.

Members of the Feminist Initiative of Cartagena. "In Search of an Alternative Development Paradigm: Feminist Proposals from Latin America." *Gender and Development* 11, no. 1 (2003): 52–58.

Mendoza, Breny. "Transnational Feminisms in Question." *Feminist Theory* 3, no. 3 (2002): 295–314.

Messer-Davidow, Ellen. *Disciplining Feminism: From Social Activism to Academic Discourse*. Duke University Press, 2002.

Mies, Maria. *Patriarchy and Accumulation on a World Scale: Women in the International Division of Labor*. Zed Books, 1984.

Miller, Elizabeth. "An Open Letter to the Editors of Ms. Magazine." RAWA: Revolutionary Association of Women in Afghanistan, April 20, 2002. http://www.rawa.org/tours /elizabeth_miller_letter.htm.

Mindry, Deborah. "Nongovernmental Organizations, 'Grassroots,' and the Politics of Virtue." *Signs: Journal of Women in Culture and Society* 26, no. 4 (2001): 1187–211.

Miraftab, Faranak. "Invited and Invented Spaces of Participation: Neoliberal Citizenship and Feminists' Expanded Notion of Politics." *Wagadu* 1 (2004): 1–7.

Mitchell, Katharyne. "Educating the National Citizen in Neoliberal Times: From the Multicultural Self to the Strategic Cosmopolitan." *Transactions of the Institute of British Geographers* 28, no. 4 (2003): 387–403.

Moallem, Minoo. Review of *Feminist Scholarship and the Internationalization of Women's Studies*, by Estelle Freedman, Uma Narayan, Sandra Harding, Chandra Mohanty, and Adrien Katherine Wing. *Feminist Studies* 32, no. 2 (2006): 332–51.

Moghadam, Valentine M. *Globalizing Women: Transnational Feminist Networks*. Johns Hopkins University Press, 2005.

Mohanty, Chandra Talpade. "Borders and Bridges: Securitized Regimes, Racialized Citizenship, and Insurgent Feminist Praxis." In *Transnational Feminist Politics, Education, Crises and Social Justice: Post Democracy and Post Truth*, edited by Sheila Macrine and Silvia Edling, 23–41. Bloomsbury, 2022.

Mohanty, Chandra Talpade. "Cartographies of Struggle: Third World Women and the Politics of Feminism." In *Third World Women and the Politics of Feminism*, edited by Chandra Talpade Mohanty, Ann Russo, and Lourdes Torres, 43–84. Indiana University Press, 1991.

Mohanty, Chandra Talpade. *Feminism Without Borders: Decolonizing Theory, Practicing Solidarity*. Duke University Press, 2003.

Mohanty, Chandra Talpade. "Imperial Democracies, Militarized Zones, Feminist Engagements." *Economic and Political Weekly* 43, no. 13 (2011): 76–84.

Mohanty, Chandra Talpade. "Privatized Citizenship, Corporate Academies, and Feminist Projects." In *Feminism Without Borders: Decolonizing Theory, Practicing Solidarity*, 169–89. Duke University Press, 2003.

Mohanty, Chandra Talpade. "Towards an Anti-Imperialist Politics: Reflections of a Desi Feminist." *South Asian Popular Culture* 2, no. 1 (2004): 69–73.

Mohanty, Chandra Talpade. "Transnational Feminist Crossings: On Neoliberalism and Radical Critique." *Signs: Journal of Women in Culture and Society* 38, no. 4 (2013): 967–91.

Mohanty, Chandra Talpade. "Under Western Eyes: Feminist Scholarship and Colonial Discourses." *Feminist Review* 30, no. 1 (1988): 61–88.

Mohanty, Chandra Talpade. "'Under Western Eyes' Revisited: Feminist Solidarity Through Anticapitalist Struggles." *Signs: Journal of Women in Culture and Society* 28, no. 2 (2003): 499–535.

Mohanty, Chandra Talpade, Ann Russo, and Lourdes Torres, eds. *Third World Women and the Politics of Feminism*. Indiana University Press, 1991.

Mohanty, Satya P. "Social Justice and Culture: On Identity, Intersectionality, and Epistemic Privilege." In *Handbook on Global Social Justice*, edited by Gary Craig, 418–27. Elgar, 2018.

Mojab, S. "Introduction: Gender and Empire." *Comparative Studies of South Asia, Africa and the Middle East* 30, no. 2 (2010): 220–23.

Molyneux, Maxine. "Mobilization Without Emancipation? Women's Interests, the State, and Revolution in Nicaragua." *Feminist Studies* 11, no. 2 (1985): 227–54.

Molyneux, Maxine, Adrija Dey, Malu A. C. Gatto, and Holly Rowden. "Feminist Activism 25 Years After Beijing." *Gender and Development* 28, no. 2 (2020): 315–36.

Moraga, Cherríe, and Gloria Anzaldúa, eds. *This Bridge Called My Back: Writings by Radical Women of Color*. Persephone Press, 1981.

Moya, Paula, and Michael Hames-Garcia, eds. *Reclaiming Identity: Realist Theory and the Predicament of Postmodernism*. University of California Press, 2000.

Mukhopadhyay, Maitrayee. "Mainstreaming Gender or 'Streaming' Gender Away: Feminists Marooned in the Development Business." *IDS Bulletin* 35, no. 4 (2004): 95–103.

Mulinari, Diana, Suvi Keskinen, Sari Irni, and Salla Tuori. "Introduction: Postcolonialism and the Nordic Models of Welfare and Gender." In *Complying with Colonialism: Gender, Race and Ethnicity in the Nordic Region*, edited by Suvi Keskinen, Salla Tuori, Sari Irni, and Diana Mulinari, 1–16. Routledge, 2016.

Mulinari, Diana, and Nora Räthzel. "Politicizing Biographies: The Forming of Transnational Subjectivities as Insiders Outside." *Feminist Review* 86, no. 1 (2007): 89–112.

Murdock, Donna F. "Neoliberalism, Gender, and Development: Institutionalizing 'Post-Feminism' in Medellín, Colombia." *Women's Studies Quarterly* 31, no. 3/4 (2003): 129–53.

Nagar, Richa. "Footloose Researchers, 'Traveling' Theories, and the Politics of Transnational Feminist Praxis." *Gender, Place and Culture: A Journal of Feminist Geography* 9, no. 2 (2002): 179–86.

Nagar, Richa. "Postscript: NGOs, Global Feminisms and Collaborative Border-Crossings." In *Playing with Fire: Feminist Thought and Activism Through Seven Lives in India*, by Sangtin Writers, 132–56. University of Minnesota Press, 2006.

Nanda, Priya. 2002. "Gender Dimensions of User Fees: Implications for Women's Utilization of Health Care." *Reproductive Health Matters* 10, no. 20 (2002): 127–34.

Naples, Nancy. "Changing the Terms: Community Activism, Globalization, and the Dilemmas of Transnational Feminist Praxis." In *Women's Activism and Globalization: Linking Local Struggles and Transnational Politics*, edited by Nancy A. Naples and Manisha Desai, 3–14. Routledge, 2002.

Narrain, Arvind. "The Verma Committee: Alchemizing Anger to Hope." *Kafila Online*, January 25, 2013. https://kafila.online/2013/01/25/the-verma-committee-alchemizing-anger-to-hope-arvind-narrain/.

National Network for Immigrant and Refugee Rights. "Injustice for All: The Rise of the U.S. Immigration Policing Regime." Produced by HURRICANE, December 2010. http://www.nnir.org.

Nde' North American Newswire. "Indigenous Peoples' Truth and Memory Must Be Explored in Depth and Through a Formal Mechanism." Lipan Apache Women Defense, September 7, 2012. https://lipanapachecommunitydefense.blogspot.com/2012/09/nde-woman-selected-to-participate-in.html.

Nelson, Jill. *Economics for Humans.* University of Chicago Press, 2006.

Nguyen, Mimi Thi. "The Biopower of Beauty: Humanitarian Imperialisms and Global Feminisms in the Age of Terror." *Signs: Journal of Women in Culture and Society* 36, no. 2 (2011): 359–83.

Nordstrom, C. *Shadows of War: Violence, Power, and International Profiteering in the Twenty-First Century.* University of California Press, 2004.

Ochieng, Ruth Ojiambo. "Supporting Women and Girls' Sexual and Reproductive Health and Rights: The Ugandan Experience." *Development* 46, no. 2 (2003): 38–44.

Okin, Susan Moller. "Feminism, Women's Human Rights, and Cultural Differences." *Hypatia* 13, no. 2 (1998): 32–52.

Olivera, Marcela. "A Struggle for Life." In *Changing the Flow: Water Movements in Latin America*, edited by Beverly Bell, Crossley Pinkstaff, Jeff Conant, Marcela Olivera, and Phillip Terhorst, 33–35. Food and Water Watch, Other Worlds, Reclaiming Public Water, Red VIDA, and Transnational Institute, 2009.

O'odham Solidarity Across Borders Collective. "Movement Demands Autonomy: An O'odham Perspective on Border Controls and Immigration." April 27, 2010. http://oodhamsolidarity.blogspot.com/2010/04/movement-demands-autonomy-oodham.html.

O'Reilly, Kathleen. "'Traditional' Women, 'Modern' Water: Linking Gender and Commodification in Rajasthan, India." *Geoforum* 37, no. 6 (2006): 958–72.

Osterweil, Michal. "Place-Based Globalism: Locating Women in the Alternative Globalization Movement." In *Women and the Politics of Place*, edited by Wendy Harcourt and Arturo Escobar, 174–87. Kumarian Press, 2005.

Outlook. "How Shaheen Bagh Became Hub of Anti-CAA Protests in 2019–20." Last updated May 9, 2022. https://www.outlookindia.com/national/shaheen-bagh-demolition-row-how-it-became-hub-of-anti-caa-protests-in-2019-news-195713.

Oza, Rupal. "Contrapuntal Geographies of Threat and Security: The United States, India, and Israel." *Environment and Planning D: Society and Space* 25, no. 1 (2007): 9–32.

Paik, A. Naomi. *Bans, Walls, Raids, Sanctuary: Understanding Immigration for the Twenty-First Century.* University of California Press, 2020.

Paik, Shailaja. "Building Bridges: Articulating Dalit and African American Women's Solidarity." *Women's Studies Quarterly* 42, no. 3/4 (2014): 74–96.

Palestinian Feminist Collective. "Shut Down Colonial Feminism on International Day for the Elimination of Violence Against Women." Accessed November 26, 2024. https://palestinianfeministcollective.org/shut-down-colonial-feminism-2023/.

Panda, Smita Mishra. "Mainstreaming Gender in Water Management: A Critical View." *Gender, Technology and Development* 11, no. 3 (2007): 321–38.

Panda, Smita Mishra. "Women's Role in Local Water Management: Insights from SEWA's Millennium Water Campaign in Gujarat (INDIA)." Paper presented at the Euro-Med Participatory Water Resources Scenarios (EMPOWERS) regional symposium, End-User Ownership and Involvement in Integrated Water Resource Management, Cairo, Egypt, November 2005.

Panitch, Leo, and Sam Gindin. "Global Capitalism and American Empire." *Socialist Register* 40 (2004): 1–42.

Peake, Linda, Karen De Souza, Amanda L. Swarr, and Richa Nagar. "Feminist Academic and Activist Praxis in Service of the Transnational." In *Critical Transnational Feminist*

Praxis, edited by Amanda Lock Swarr and Richa Nagar, 105–23. State University of New York Press, 2010.

Pembina Institute. "Environmental Groups, First Nations Join in Opposition to Omnibus Bill C-45." November 21, 2012. https://www.pembina.org/media-release /environmental-groups-first-nations-join-opposition-omnibus-bill-c-45.

Phillips, Lynne, and Sally Cole. "Feminist Flows, Feminist Fault Lines: Women's Machineries and Women's Movements in Latin America." *Signs: Journal of Women in Culture and Society* 35, no. 1 (2009): 185–211.

Pinto, V. Oliveira. "The Lessons of Candomblé, the Lessons of Life." In *Sing, Whisper, Shout, Pray! Feminist Visions for a Just World,* edited by M. Jacqui Alexander, Lisa Albrecht, Sharon Day, and Mab Segrest, 704–8. EdgeWork Books, 2003.

Pitkin, Kathryn, and Ritha Bedoya. "Women's Multiple Roles in Economic Crisis: Constraints and Adaptation." *Latin American Perspectives* 24, no. 4 (1997): 34–49.

Platt, Kamala. "Women on Wars and Walls: Cultural Poetics from Palestine to South Texas." *Works and Days* 29 (2011): 329–60.

Pradhan, Bina. "Measuring Empowerment: A Methodological Approach." *Development* 46, no. 2 (2003): 51–57.

Prashad, Vijay. *Struggle Makes Us Human: Learning from Movements for Socialism.* Haymarket Books, 2022.

Pratt, Minnie Bruce. "Syracuse Passes Trans Rights Bill." *Workers World,* November 30, 2012. http://www.workers.org/2012/11/30/syracuse-passes-trans-rights-bill.

Puar, Jasbir K., and Amit Rai. "Monster, Terrorist, Fag: The War on Terrorism and the Production of Docile Patriots." *Social Text* 20, no. 3 (2002): 117–48.

Qassoum, M. "Imperial Agendas: 'Civil Society' and Global Manipulation Intifada." *Between the Lines* 3, no. 19 (2003): 6–26.

Radcliffe, Sarah A., Nina Laurie, and Robert Andolina. "The Transnationalization of Gender and Reimagining Andean Indigenous Development." *Signs: Journal of Women in Culture and Society* 29, no. 2 (2004): 387–416.

Randriamaro, Zo. "African Women Challenging Neo-Liberal Economic Orthodoxy: The Conception and Mission of the GERA Program." *Gender and Development* 11, no. 1 (2003): 44–51.

Ransby, Barbara. *Making All Black Lives Matter: Reimagining Freedom in the Twenty-First Century.* University of California Press, 2018.

Rao, Sameer, and Tiye Rose. "LGBTQ Activists of Color Talk Trump and What They're Doing to Create Change" [video]. *Colorlines,* January 25, 2017. https://colorlines.com /article/lgbtq-activists-color-talk-trump-and-what-theyre-doing-create-change -video/.

Raveendran, Rehnamol. "Ayodhya Issue Reflects the Increasing Masculinization of Politics in India." Feminism in India, September 2, 2020. https://feminisminindia.com /2020/09/02/ayodhya-masculinisation-of-indian-politics/#google_vignette.

Reddy, Amulya K. N. "Energy and Social Issues." In *World Energy Assessment: Energy and the Challenge of Sustainability,* edited by José Goldemberg, 39–60. New York: UN Development Programme, 2000.

Rege, Sharmila. *Writing Caste/Writing Gender: Narrating Dalit Women's Testimonios.* Zubaan, 2006.

Resurreccion, Bernadette P., Mary Jane Real, and Panadda Pantana. "Officializing Strategies: Participatory Processes and Gender in Thailand's Water Resources Sector." *Development in Practice* 14, no. 4 (2004): 521–32.

Reyes, Erasto. "The Power That Makes Pitchers Overflow and Rivers Flood Their Banks." In *Changing the Flow: Water Movements in Latin America*, edited by Beverly Bell, Crossley Pinkstaff, Jeff Conant, Marcela Olivera, and Phillip Terhorst, 16–19. Food and Water Watch, Other Worlds, Reclaiming Public Water, Red VIDA, and Transnational Institute, 2009.

Riley, Robin L., Chandra Talpade Mohanty, and Minnie Bruce Pratt, eds. *Feminism and War: Confronting U.S. Imperialism.* Zed Books, 2008.

Roberts, Adrienne. "Privatizing Social Reproduction: The Primitive Accumulation of Water in an Era of Neoliberalism." *Antipode* 40, no. 4 (2008): 535–60.

Rocheleau, Dianne. "Political Landscapes and Ecologies of Zambrana-Chacuey: The Legacy of Mama Tingo." In *Women and the Politics of Place*, edited by Wendy Harcourt and Arturo Escobar, 72–85. Kumarian Press, 2005.

Rodríguez, Dylan. *Forced Passages: Imprisoned Radical Intellectuals and the US Prison Regime.* University of Minnesota Press, 2006.

Roy, Arundhati. *An Ordinary Person's Guide to Empire.* South End Press, 2004.

Rubin, David. "Women's Studies, Neoliberalism, and the Paradox of the Political." In *Women's Studies for the Future*, edited by Elizabeth Lapovsky Kennedy and Agatha Beins, 245–61. Rutgers University Press, 2005.

Safa, Helen Icken. "Women's Social Movements in Latin America." *Gender and Society* 4, no. 3 (1990): 354–69.

Saliba, Nadine. "International Women's Day Statement." *La Voz de Esperanza*, April 2008, 4.

Saliba, Nadine. "Resistance Through Remembering and Speaking Out." *La Voz de Esperanza*, May 2006, 7–10.

Saliba, Therese. "On the Bodies of Third World Women: Cultural Impurity, Prostitution, and Other Nervous Conditions." *College Literature* 22, no. 1 (1995): 131–46.

Sampaio, Anna. "Transnational Feminisms in a New Global Matrix." *International Feminist Journal of Politics* 6, no. 2 (2004): 181–206.

Samson, Melanie. "Producing Privatization: Re-Articulating Race, Gender, Class and Space." *Antipode* 42, no. 2 (2010): 404–32.

Sangtin Writers. *Playing with Fire: Feminist Thought and Activism Through Seven Lives in India.* University of Minnesota Press, 2006.

Sanhati. "AWS Open Letter to Home Minister and Press Statement Following the Police Harassment at National Conference, Wardha, 21–24 January 2011." January 26, 2011. http://sanhati.com/articles/3190/.

Sarkar, Saurav. "Meet the Activist Coalition That Outlawed Caste Discrimination in Seattle." *In These Times*, April 3, 2023. https://inthesetimes.com/article/an-activist-coalition-outlawed-caste-discrimination-in-seattle-heres-how-they-did-it.

Sassen, Saskia. *Globalization and Its Discontents: Essays on the New Mobility of People and Money.* New Press, 1998.

Savera. *HAF Way to Supremacy: How the Hindu American Foundation Rebrands Bigotry as Minority Rights.* Political Research Associates, 2024. https://www.wearesavera.org/resources/reports/.

Schaeffer-Grabiel, Felicity. "Planet-love.com: Cyberbrides in the Americas and the Transnational Routes of US Masculinity." *Signs: Journal of Women in Culture and Society* 31, no. 2 (2006): 331–56.

Seidel, Linda. Review of *Feminism Without Borders: Decolonizing Theory, Practicing Solidarity*, by Chandra Talpade Mohanty. *Feminist Teacher* 15, no. 2 (2005): 163–64.

Sen, Gita. "Gender, Markets and States: A Selective Review and Research Agenda." *World Development* 24, no. 5 (1996): 821–29.

Sen, Gita, and Caren Grown. *Development, Crises, and Alternative Visions.* Monthly Review Press, 1987.

Sengupta, Shuddhabrata. "Water Cannons, Tear Gas, Ordinance: How the State Responds to Protests Against Rape and the Justice Verma Committee." *Kafila Online*, February 3, 2013. https://kafila.online/2013/02/03/water-cannons-tear-gas-ordnance-how-the-state-responds-to-protests-against-rape-and-the-justice-verma-committee/.

Shiva, Vandana. *Earth Democracy: Justice, Sustainability, and Peace.* South End Press, 2005.

Shope, Janet Hinson. "'You Can't Cross a River Without Getting Wet': A Feminist Standpoint on the Dilemmas of Cross-Cultural Research." *Qualitative Inquiry* 12, no. 1 (2006): 163–84.

Sidhwa, Bapsi, and Urvashi Butalia. "Discussion on the Partition of India." *History Workshop Journal* 50 (2000): 230–328.

Silliman, Jael, and Anannya Bhattacharjee, eds. *Policing the National Body: Race, Gender, and Criminalization.* South End Press, 2002.

Simpson, Leanne. "Dancing the World into Being: A Conversation with Idle No More's Leanne Simpson." Interview by Naomie Klein. *Yes*, March 6, 2013. http://www.yesmagazine.org/peace-justice/dancing-the-world-into-being-a-conversation-with-idle-no-more-leanne-simpson.

Singh, Nandita. "Women's Participation in Local Water Governance: Understanding Institutional Contradictions." *Gender, Technology and Development* 10, no. 1 (2006): 61–76.

Skutsch, Margaret M. "Gender Analysis for Energy Projects and Programs." *Energy for Sustainable Development* 9, no. 1 (2005): 37–52.

Smith, Andrea. *Conquest: Sexual Violence and American Indian Genocide.* South End Press, 2005.

Smith, Andrea. "Heteropatriarchy and the Three Pillars of White Supremacy: Rethinking Women of Color Organizing." In *Color of Violence: The Incite! Anthology*, edited by Incite! Women of Color Against Violence, 66–73. South End Press, 2006.

Smith, Andrea. "Indigenous Feminism Without Apology." *New Socialist* 58 (2006): 16–17.

Smith, Anna Marie. "Neoliberalism, Welfare Policy, and Feminist Theories of Social Justice." In "Feminist Theory and Welfare," special issue, *Feminist Theory* 9, no. 2 (2008): 131–44.

Souza, Celina. "Participatory Budgeting in Brazilian Cities: Limits and Possibilities in Building Democratic Institutions." *Environment and Urbanization* 13, no. 1 (2001): 159–84.

Sparr, Pamela, ed. *Mortgaging Women's Lives: Feminist Critiques of Structural Adjustment.* Palgrave Macmillan, 1994.

Spronk, Susan. "Roots of Resistance to Urban Water Privatization in Bolivia: The 'New Working Class,' the Crisis of Neoliberalism, and Public Services." *International Labor and Working-Class History* 71, no. 1 (2007): 8–28.

Srivastava, Sarita. "'You're Calling Me a Racist?': The Moral and Emotional Regulation of Antiracism and Feminism." *Signs: Journal of Women in Culture and Society* 31, no. 1 (2005): 29–62.

Staunæs, Dorthe. "Where Have All the Subjects Gone? Bringing Together the Concepts of Intersectionality and Subjectification." *NORA: Nordic Journal of Women's Studies* 11, no. 2 (2003): 101–10.

Subrahmanian, Ramya. "Making Sense of Gender in Shifting Institutional Contexts: Some Reflections on Gender Mainstreaming." *Feminisms in Development: Contradictions, Contestations and Challenges*, edited by Andrea Cornwall, Elizabeth Harrison, and Ann Whitehead, 113–21. Zed Books, 2007.

Sudbury, Julia, ed. *Global Lockdown: Race, Gender, and the Prison-Industrial Complex.* Routledge, 2005.

Sudbury, Julia. "Introduction: Feminist Critiques, Transnational Landscapes, Abolitionist Visions." In *Global Lockdown: Race, Gender, and the Prison-Industrial Complex*, edited by Julia Sudbury, xi–xxviii. Routledge, 2005.

Sudbury, Julia, and Margo Okazawa-Rey. "Introduction: Activist Scholarship and the Neoliberal University." In *Activist Scholarship: Antiracism, Feminism, and Social Change*, edited by Julia Sudbury and Margo Okazawa-Rey, 1–16. Paradigm, 2009.

Sultana, Farhana. "Community and Participation in Water Resources Management: Gendering and Naturing Development Debates from Bangladesh." *Transactions of the Institute of British Geographers* 34, no. 3 (2009): 346–63.

Sutton, Barbara, Sandra Morgen, and Julie Novkov, eds. *Security Disarmed: Critical Perspectives on Gender, Race, and Militarization.* Rutgers University Press, 2007.

Tambe, Ashwini. "Coda." *Comparative Studies of South Asia, Africa and the Middle East* 30, no. 2 (2010): 218–19.

Támez, Margo García. "Our Way of Life Is Our Resistance: Indigenous Women and Anti-Imperialist Challenges to Militarization Along the U.S.-Mexico Border." *Works and Days* 29, no. 1/2 (2011): 281–318.

Téllez, Michelle. "Community of Struggle: Gender, Violence, and Resistance on the US/Mexico Border." *Gender and Society* 22, no. 5 (2008): 545–67.

Thobani, Sunera. *Exalted Subjects: Studies in the Making of Race and Nation in Canada.* University of Toronto Press, 2007.

Thobani, Sunera. Review of *Feminism Without Borders: Decolonizing Theory, Practicing Solidarity*, by Chandra Talpade Mohanty. *Hypatia* 20, no. 3 (2005): 221–24.

Thornton, Margaret. "Feeling Chilly (Again) in the Legal Academy." *Australian Feminist Law Journal* 18, no. 1 (2003): 145–51.

Ticktin, Miriam. "Building a Feminist Commons in the Time of COVID-19." *Signs: Journal of Women in Culture and Society* 47, no. 1 (2021): 37–46. http://signsjournal.org/covid/ticktin/.

Trawick, Paul. "Against the Privatization of Water: An Indigenous Model for Improving Existing Laws and Successfully Governing the Commons." *World Development* 31, no. 6 (2003): 977–96.

Trevenen, Kathryn. "Stretching 'the Political': Governmentality, Political Society, and Solidarity Across Borders." *Political Theory* 33, no. 3 (2005): 426–31.

Tricontinental. "The Students Will Not Tolerate Hypocrisy: The Eighteenth Newsletter (2024)." May 2, 2024. https://thetricontinental.org/newsletterissue/students-for -palestine/.

Trotz, Alissa. "Red Thread: The Politics of Hope in Guyana." *Race and Class* 49, no. 2 (2007): 71–79.

Tuck, Eve, and K. Wayne Yang, eds. *Toward What Justice? Describing Diverse Dreams of Justice in Education.* Routledge, 2018.

Udas, Pranita B., and Margreet Z. Zwarteveen. "Can Water Professionals Meet Gender Goals? A Case Study of the Department of Irrigation in Nepal." *Gender and Development* 18, no. 1 (2010): 87–97.

UNIFEM. "Gender Responsive Budgeting." *Newsletter*, no. 3, 2009.

Upadhyay, Bhawana. "Gendered Livelihoods and Multiple Water Use in North Gujarat." *Agriculture and Human Values* 22 (2005): 411–20.

Urbina, Ian. "Using Jailed Migrants as a Pool of Cheap Labor." *New York Times*, May 24, 2014. http://www.nytimes.com/2014/05/25/us/using-jailed-migrants-as-a-pool-of -cheap-labor.html.

Urea, Danilo. "Protecting Territory, Protecting Culture." In *Changing the Flow: Water Movements in Latin America*, edited by Beverly Bell, Crossley Pinkstaff, Jeff Conant, Marcela Olivera, and Phillip Terhorst, 7–8. Food and Water Watch, Other Worlds, Reclaiming Public Water, Red VIDA, and Transnational Institute, 2009.

van Koppen, Barbara. "Water Rights, Gender, and Poverty Alleviation: Inclusion and Exclusion of Women and Men Smallholders in Public Irrigation Infrastructure Development." *Agriculture and Human Values* 15 (1998): 361–74.

Vellanki, Vivek. "Breaking the Collective—Notes from Jantar Mantar and Koodankulam." *Kafila Online*, January 11, 2013. https://kafila.online/2013/01/11/15292/.

Vergès, Françoise. *A Decolonial Feminism.* Translated by Ashley J. Bohrer. Pluto Press, 2021.

Villagomez, Elisabeth. "Gender Responsive Budgets: Issues, Good Practices and Policy Options." Paper presented at the Regional Symposium on Mainstreaming Gender into Economic Policies, Geneva, Switzerland, 2004. https://unece.org/fileadmin/ DAM/Gender/documents/gender.2004.grb.pdf.

Walia, Harsha. *Undoing Border Imperialism.* Vol. 6. AK Press, 2014.

Weber, Brenda R. "Teaching Popular Culture Through Gender Studies: Feminist Pedagogy in a Postfeminist and Neoliberal Academy?" *Feminist Teacher* 20, no. 2 (2010): 124–38.

Weigman, Robyn. *Women's Studies on Its Own.* Duke University Press, 2002.

whimsy mimsy BoroGoves. "Freedom Without Fear/Bekhauf Azadi." *Whimsy Mimsy BoroGoves* (blog), February 12, 2013. http://whimsymimsyborogoves.blogspot.com /2013/02/freedom-without-fearbekhauf-azadi.html.

Wieringa, Saskia. "Women's Interests and Empowerment: Gender Planning Reconsidered." *Development and Change* 25, no. 4 (1994): 829–48.

Wilson, Amrit. "India's Anti-Rape Movement: Redefining Solidarity Outside the Colonial Frame." *Open Democracy*, April 8, 2013. http://www.opendemocracy.net/5050/amrit -wilson/indias-anti-rape-movement-redefining-solidarity-outside-colonial-frame.

Wilson, Kalpana, Jennifer Ung, and Navtej Purewal. "Gender, Violence and the Neoliberal State in India." *Feminist Review* 119, no. 1 (2018): 1–6.

Wing, Adrien Katherine, ed. *Global Critical Race Feminism: An International Reader.* New York University Press, 2000.

Wing, Bob. "The Color of Abu Ghraib." *War Times.* Accessed May 17, 2024. https://znetwork.org/znetarticle/the-color-of-abu-ghraib-by-bob-wing/.

Winrock International. "Report on Assessment of Rural Energy Development Program (REDP): Impacts and Its Contribution in Achieving MDGs." Winrock International, Nepal, n.d. http://www.redp.org.np/phase2/pdf/impactsandcontricution.pdf.

Wire Staff. "Ayodhya Ram Temple Inauguration Sets a 'Dangerous Precedent,' Say Diaspora Groups." *The Wire*, January 22, 2024. https://thewire.in/religion/diaspora-groups-ram-temple-consecration-precedent.

Woodly, Deva. "Black Lives Matter and the Democratic Necessity of Social Movements." Humanities New York, November 22, 2017. https://humanitiesny.org/freedom-from-margin-to-center/.

Woodly, Deva R. *Reckoning: Black Lives Matter and the Democratic Necessity of Social Movements.* Oxford University Press, 2022.

World Resources Institute. *Power Politics: Equity and Environment in Electricity Reform.* Edited by Navroz K. Dubash. WRI, 2002.

Wynter, Sylvia. "Breaking the Epistemological Contract on Black America." *Forum NHI* 2, no. 1 (1995): 41–57, 64–70.

Yamahtta-Taylor, Keeanga. *How We Get Free: Black Feminism and the Combahee River Collective.* Haymarket Books, 2018.

Young, Iris Marion. "The Logic of Masculinist Protection: Reflections on the Current Security State." *Signs* 29, no. 1 (2003): 1–25. https://doi.org/10.1086/375708.

Young, Marilyn. "Imperial Language." In *The New American Empire: A 21st-Century Teach-In on U.S. Foreign Policy*, edited by Lloyd C. Gardner and Marilyn B. Young, 32–50. New Press, 2002.

Zitzewitz, Karin. "A Timeline of Events in the Delhi Gang-Rape Case." *Feminist Wire*, February 2, 2013. http://thefeministwire.com/2013/02/a-timeline-of-events-in-the-delhi-gangrape-case/.

Zomers, Adriaan. "The Challenge of Rural Electrification." *Energy for Sustainable Development* 7, no. 1 (2003): 69–76.

Zwarteveen, Margreet Z. "Water: From Basic Need to Commodity: A Discussion on Gender and Water Rights in the Context of Irrigation." *World Development* 25, no. 8 (1997): 1335–49.

Index

Clancy, Joy, 59

class, 55, 89–90, 94, 115, 121, 126, 145, 162, 184, 188, 191, 209; and citizenship, 38, 151; and Dalit feminism, 17–19; and decolonial abolitionist feminism, 16, 30–31; and gender, 48, 49–52, 58, 61–65, 96, 194–95, 197; and higher education, 134, 211; and neoliberalism, 187; and place-based politics, 74–77; and race, 98, 100; and transnational feminist praxis, 85–88, 100–109; and violence against women, 6, 17–18, 92, 111–12; and women's and gender studies, 151–52

classism, 187, 201n2

climate destruction, 7, 120, 209

Clinton, Bill, 145

Coalition of Seattle Indian-Americans (CSIA), 19, 25n34

coalitions, 13, 106

Cochabamba Water Wars, 62–63

COINTELPRO, 146

Cold War, 142

Cole, Sally, 196

collaboration, 5, 21, 25n37, 42, 120, 131, 137n36, 147, 159–60, 162, 194, 196, 211

Colombia, 35, 74, 84

colonialism, 7, 83, 100, 105–6, 166, 178, 180n18, 201n1, 203n34; and border securitization, 133; British, 34, 142, 156n5; Canadian, 114; and capitalism, 4, 12, 14, 30; and citizenship, 23, 125, 207; discursive, 197–98, 204, 204n38; and higher education, 12–13; and imperialism, 31, 142–45, 175–76, 194; Indian, 124; Israeli, 10–13, 18, 122, 124, 126–27, 129, 133–34, 184–85; neo-, 41, 50, 125, 146, 160–61, 169, 174–75, 198; and neoliberalism, 51–53; pre-, 68; and racialized gender, 31–32, 49–50, 168, 188; and security states, 124; settler, 1, 4, 10, 12, 15, 18, 30, 147, 176–77, 211; and transnational feminist praxis, 19, 21–23, 84, 86, 116, 120–21, 161, 193–200, 209; US, 124, 131, 133, 142–45, 152; and white feminism,

98; and women's and gender studies, 167–73. *See also* anticolonialism; decoloniality; imperialism; postcolonialism

color blindness, 190

Columbia University, police raid of protesters, 12, 24n16

Combahee River Collective (CRC), 2–3, 8–9, 13

Committee on Academic Freedom in Africa (CAFA), 165–67

commodification, 88, 135–36, 164, 184, 186, 188, 191; of public services, 22, 48, 54–56, 59, 76–77

common differences, 1, 120–21, 181n33

Common Differences conference (1983), 120–21

Communist Party USA, 43–44

Community Based Monitoring System (CBMS), 71–72

community organizations (COs), 65

community-supported agriculture (CSA), 39

Community Working Group on Health (CWGH), 69

comparative feminist studies, 181n33

complicity, 9, 12–13, 97, 104, 142–43, 145, 152, 154, 167, 174, 191

compulsory heterosexuality, 208

conservatism, 11, 14, 85, 88–89, 107, 134, 147, 151, 189, 212; neo-, 122

Conservative Party (Canada), 113

constitution-free zones, 128–29, 131

Coogan-Gehr, Kelly, 186, 188, 202n23

Cooke, Miriam, 146

Cordova, Teresa, 84, 93, 101, 105, 116n3

CoreCivic. *See* Corrections Corporation of America

Corrections Corporation of America (CoreCivic), 36–37

cosmopolitanism, 186, 189

Costa Rica, 70

Countering Violent Extremism (CVE), 6, 123, 125, 136n9

counterinsurgency, 128

education (*continued*)
24n16, 35; and neoliberalism, 11–13, 97, 143–55, 165, 184, 186–87, 189, 192–93, 196, 201, 211–12; Palestine solidarity suppression in, 11–13; political, 24n16, 68, 162, 165–67; privatization of, 37, 149, 165, 167, 186–87; study abroad programs, 134, 160, 166, 211. *See also* academic feminism; syllabi; women's and gender studies (wGS)

Egypt, 95, 106–7, 115–16

Eisenstein, Zillah, 84–85, 96, 100, 116n3, 124, 143, 147

el Saadawi, Nawal, 84, 115

elsewhere rule, 169–71, 174, 176, 178

Elson, Diane, 77, 79n25

Enloe, Cynthia, 143

Ensler, Eve, 112

environmental justice, 73, 110, 114, 133

environmental racism, 40

epistemic privilege, 3–4, 7, 10, 24n4, 199

Equality Labs, 19, 25n34

Erdoğan, Recep Tayyip, 17, 120

Escobar, Arturo, 73, 193–94

Esperanza Center, 130, 133

essentialism, 3, 23, 98, 185, 201n5

ethnic studies, 150–51, 163, 187, 203n34; attacks on, 133

Eurocentrism, 160, 170–71, 174, 193–95, 203

Europe, 4, 9, 11, 18, 22, 30, 51, 84, 102, 129, 135, 192, 210–11; European colonialism, 130; European Marxism, 32; European refugee crisis, 123–24, 128; and women's and gender studies, 170–71, 195. *See also* *individual countries*

European Enlightenment, 164

European Union (eu), 128, 195

Evans, Linda, 146

faith-based initiatives, 39, 147

Farah, Leila, 97, 104, 116n3

Farris, Sara, 5

fascism, 4, 7, 9, 108, 120, 136, 208–9; neoliberal, 208. *See also* antifascism; authoritarianism; Modi, Narendra; Orbán, Viktor; Trump, Donald

Federal Bureau of Investigation (fbi), 123. *See also* cointelpro

Federation of Agricultural Workers (fetape), 66

Federici, Silvia, 180n11, 213

Feinberg, Leslie, 109

Feldman, Jonathan, 149, 166

femininity, 10, 52, 69, 112, 143

Feminism Without Borders, 180n15, 181n33, 185, 191, 195, 203n34

feminist commons, 213

feminist communities, 9, 17, 21, 85, 120–21, 193–94, 198, 201

feminist genealogies, 84–86

Feminist Genealogies, Colonial Legacies, Democratic Futures, 159–60, 178

Feminist Majority Foundation, 152

feminist participatory action research (fpar), 72

feminist politics, 8, 13, 16, 19, 84, 102, 142, 188, 201; relation to theory, 2

Feminist Review, 192

feminists of color, 4, 5, 8–10, 13–14, 16, 84–85, 89, 91, 98, 120–21

feminist studies, 10, 23, 160, 169, 181n33

feminist theory, 1, 184, 188, 191; hegemonic, 30–31; relation to politics, 2; translation of, 196; transnational, 88, 173, 185; Western, 193, 195

feminization, 49, 78n4

femonationalism, 5–6

Ferguson, Rod, 11

Ferguson uprising (2014, US), 8, 124

Fine, Ben, 50

First Nations, 113–15, 118n27, 176. *See also* Indigenous peoples

first-wave feminism, 171

Floyd, George, 119, 124, 135

Fong, Clara, 5

Ford-Smith, Honor, 84, 96, 100–101, 116n3

Foucault, Michel, 170, 186

Free CeCe movement, 108–9

freedom horizons, 4, 7

Free Feminist University, 212

free-trade policies, 33, 87

French, Joan, 94, 101, 116n3

fundamentalism, 6; religious, 2, 7, 63, 107, 115, 126, 128, 135, 172, 208

Gago, Veronica, 213

García Támez, Eloisa, 131

gay marriage, 110

gay rights, 99

Gaza solidarity activism, criminalization of, 11–13, 24n16

gender and development (GAD) discourse, 188

Gender and Economic Reforms in Africa (GERA), 70

gender binary, 70–71, 104

gender budgeting initiatives (GBIs), 66, 71

gender equality, 59, 195

gender equity, 48, 50, 53–54, 60–78, 194–96, 198

gender fatigue, 107

gender justice, 4, 6–7, 15, 50, 53, 60–62, 67–68, 73–78, 86, 121, 135, 153, 187–88, 189, 190, 194, 200, 214

gender mainstreaming, 53–54, 62, 78

gender neutrality, 59, 67, 70, 153

gender pluralism, 153–54

gender roles, 57, 70

gender studies, 5, 7, 22, 187, 191, 193–95; attacks on, 18; syllabi, 162, 166–74

gender violence, 7, 15, 25n34, 91–92, 110–11, 126. See also domestic violence; sexual violence

General Agreement on Trade in Services (GATS), 91

genocide, 9, 41, 176–77; Israeli in Palestine, 4, 9–14, 17

Germany, 108, 123, 192

Gilmore, Ruth Wilson, 13, 24n10

Gindin, Sam, 143, 156n5

Giroux, Henry, 12, 208

glass ceiling feminism, 120, 209

Global Critical Race Feminism, 185

global economic crisis (2008, 2020), 120, 209

globalism: place-based, 74–75; vs. transnationalism, 208

globalization, 37, 74, 117n8, 134, 159–61, 212; grassroots, 99; and higher education, 149, 180n15; and imperialism, 23, 31, 143–44, 148, 155; and militarism, 31, 35, 143–44, 148; and neoliberalism, 88, 96, 117n8, 175; of poverty, 100; and prisons, 34, 175, 177, 197; and women's and gender studies, 162, 170–74, 180nn18–19. *See also* antiglobalization movement

global land rights movements, 15

global police state, 146

global right, 2, 7, 16–17

global sisterhood, 160, 170, 199

Golash-Boza, Tanya, 124

Gomez, Alan, 137n43

Gómez, Ana Ella, 63

Gordon, Jessica, 113

governmentality, 126, 128–29, 188–89

Gramsci, Antonio, 8

Grande, Sandy, 12

Grassroots Leadership, 37, 132

grassroots organizing, 3–4, 9, 19, 67, 99, 111, 113–14, 165, 167, 179, 194–95, 198

Great Britain, 87, 103, 112–13, 192; British colonialism, 34, 142, 156n5. *See also* United Kingdom

Greece, 124

Grenada, 87

Guatemala, 197, 204n38

Gujarat riots (2002, India), 18

Gupta, Jyotsna Agnihotri, 202n24

Guyana, 90, 104

Guy-Sheftall, Beverly, 100, 107, 116n3

Hall, David, 50, 55

Hames-García, Michael, 3

Hans, Asha, 107, 116n3

Harcourt, Wendy, 52, 62, 73

Harper, Stephen, 91, 114

Secure Fence Act (2006, US), 130–31
securitization, 22, 119–36, 214
security studies, 160
Sedgwick, Eve Kosofsky, 170
Self-Employed Women's Association (SEWA), 64–65, 68, 72
Sen, Gita, 51
Sengupta, Shuddhabrata, 111–12
Serbia, 124
settler colonialism, 1, 12, 15, 18, 147, 176–77, 211; Israeli, 4, 10; US, 130
Severa, 19
SEVIS, 149, 166
sexism, 17, 92, 111, 136, 189. *See also* misogyny; patriarchy
sexuality studies, 11, 170, 173–74; and transnational feminism, 174. *See also* LGBTQ/queer studies
sexual justice, 189
sexual violence, 4, 10, 15, 17–18, 92, 110–12, 128–29, 147, 176, 213; state-approved, 128, 147. *See also* gender violence; violence against women
sex work, 145, 175; labor movements, 34
Shafik, Baroness Minouche, 24n16
Shaheen Bagh protest (2019–20), 214
Shanley, Kate, 176
Sheikh, Khanum, 123
Sidhwa, Bapsi, 122, 136n5
Signs, 192, 202n23
Silicon Valley, 43
Singh, Nandita, 58
Skutsch, Margaret, 58
slavery, 12, 51, 102, 147, 211; and prison-industrial complex, 36
Slovakia, 124
Smith, Andrea, 115, 118n27, 176
Smith, Barbara, 6
socialism, 87, 128, 146, 149, 171
socialist feminism, 2, 17, 31, 105
Social Justice (organization), 175
social reproduction, 49, 52, 54, 110
Sodexo, 37
solidarity economy, 50, 61

Somos Arizona, 133
South Africa, 12, 55–56, 71, 78n4
South African Women's Budget Initiative (WBI), 71
South America, 22, 84. *See also individual countries*
Spanish colonialism, 34
Spronk, Susan, 74
Sri Lanka, 34, 42
Srivastava, Sarita, 144, 152
Standing Rock Sioux, 8
Stanger, Anya, 116n1
state violence, 3, 8–9, 16–17, 19, 124, 126–27, 129–30, 214. *See also* migrant detention; Nakba; prisons
Structural Adjustment Programs (SAPs), 34–35, 52–53, 91, 95, 160, 165, 174. *See also* neoliberalism
Student Nonviolent Coordinating Committee (SNCC), 2
study abroad programs, 134, 160, 166, 211
Sudbury, Julia, 146, 174–75, 187
superexploitation, 43
Sweden, 23, 190, 194, 196, 203nn34–35; Swedish feminism, 195, 200
syllabi, 162, 166–74, 177–78, 180nn17–18
Syracuse, 40, 109
Syracuse University, 180n10
Syria, 123, 210
systemic analysis, 184–85, 191, 194, 196, 200–201, 211

Taliban, 6, 157n26
Támez, Margo, 131
Tanzania, 55, 87
Taylor, Breonna, 119
Téllez, Michelle, 197
terrorism, 12, 14, 98, 121–31, 136n9, 146–47, 150, 210; counter-, 125. *See also* war on terror
terrorism studies, 160
Texas, 36, 121–22, 125, 127–28, 131–33; San Antonio, 130
Thatcher, Margaret, 87